DATE DUE

Demco

Mathematics in Early Years Education

This third edition of the best-selling *Mathematics in Nursery Education* provides an accessible introduction to the teaching of mathematics in the early years. Covering all areas of mathematics learning – number and counting, calculation, pattern, shape, measures and data handling – it summarises the research findings and underlying key concepts and explains how adults can help children to learn through practical experiences, discussion and more direct intervention.

This new edition has been fully updated to incorporate the latest research and thinking in this area and includes:

- why mathematics is important as a way of making sense of the world
- how attitudes to mathematics can influence teaching and learning
- how children learn mathematics
- new material on sorting, matching and handling data
- ideas for observation and questioning to assess children's understanding
- examples of planned activities
- suggestions for language development
- assessment criteria.

This textbook is ideal for those training to be teachers through an undergraduate or PGCE route, those training for Early Years Professional Status and those studying early childhood on foundation or honours degrees, as well as parents looking to explore how their young children learn mathematics. This will be an essential text for any early years practitioner looking to make mathematics interesting, exciting and engaging in their setting.

Ann Montague-Smith was formerly Principal Lecturer in Primary Education at the University of Worcester.

Alison J. Price has worked extensively with 3–7-year-olds in a range of settings and was formerly Principal Lecturer in Primary Teacher Education at Oxford Brookes University.

Mathematics in Early Years Education

Third Edition

Ann Montague-Smith and Alison J. Price

Routledge
Taylor & Francis Group

LONDON AND NEW YORK

First edition published 1997
as *Mathematics in Nursery Education*
by David Fulton Publishers

Second edition published 2007
as *Mathematics in Nursery Education*
by Routledge
2 Park Square, Milton Park, Abingdon, Oxon OX14 4RN

This third edition published 2012

Simultaneously published in the USA and Canada
by Routledge
711 Third Avenue, New York, NY 10017

Routledge is an imprint of the Taylor & Francis Group, an informa business

© 2012 Ann Montague-Smith and Alison J. Price

British Library Cataloguing in Publication Data
A catalogue record for this book is available from the British Library

Library of Congress Cataloging in Publication Data
 Montague-Smith, Ann.
 Mathematics in early years education / Ann Montague-Smith and Alison J. Price. — 3rd ed.
  p. cm.
 Rev. ed. of: Mathematics in nursery education, 1997.
 Includes index.
 1. Mathematics—Study and teaching (Early childhood)—Great Britain. I. Price, Alison
 II. Montague-Smith, Ann, Mathematics in nursery education III. Title.
 QA135.5.M5813 2012
 372.7'049—dc23
 2011044503

ISBN: 978-0-415-67467-6 (hbk)
ISBN: 978-0-415-67469-0 (pbk)
ISBN: 978-0-203-81038-5 (ebk)

Typeset in Bembo
by RefineCatch Limited, Bungay, Suffolk

Printed and bound in Great Britain by
TJ International Ltd, Padstow, Cornwall

Contents

Figures and tables

Figures

Tables

Acknowledgements

My thanks go to the many people who have helped and supported me in the production of this book. To the adults and children at those settings which have allowed me to observe, participate and take photographs, especially The Slade Nursery School and St Nicholas' Primary School in Oxford. To Sharon Evans and other students who have provided examples and evidence of children's understanding and recording, and to Oxford University Press for permission to use images of Numicon.* To my colleagues from Oxford Brookes University who have reviewed drafts and offered helpful suggestions, and to Julie Fisher for her expertise in early years education and her attention to detail.

Special thanks go to my husband Tony who has supported and encouraged me throughout and my colleague Bill Domoney who has always provided a sounding board for ideas.

Finally, I dedicate this book to my grandchildren and all the children of the future; may they enjoy learning mathematics as much as I enjoy teaching it.

Alison J. Price
September 2011

*Numicon, copyright © Oxford University Press, and published by Oxford University Press, www.numicon.com. Numicon materials are reproduced with their permission.

Introduction

In the introduction to the second edition of *Mathematics in Nursery Education*, Ann Montague-Smith wrote 'I find my students still search for books which are detailed about the wealth of research evidence available, current good professional practice and appropriate mathematics concepts and content' (2002: vii). Ten years on, there are still few other books which cover all of these areas comprehensively and I hope that this new edition will continue to satisfy this need.

Changes in provision for preschool children have resulted in a greater range of settings and variety of adults training to work with them. In England, the welcome extension of the early years curriculum to include reception classes, revision of the Foundation Stage curriculum, the Birth to Three Curriculum and a wider variety of training for practitioners in early years settings have greatly expanded early years training, provision and practice. The change in title and revision of content is aimed to address these changes. The term nursery no longer has the relevance it once had and has generally been replaced with early years to reflect the variety of preschool settings. However, 'early years' can refer to different age groups in different contexts and therefore needs some explanation. This book mainly addresses the mathematics learning of children aged 3–5+, although for those working in birth to three settings it describes development of concepts from birth, and it will aid teachers working with six- and seven-year-olds in understanding what many of their children have already learnt and assist in planning for low achieving children. The book is intended for anyone working in early years settings with young children and for those in training to do so. Clarification of specific mathematical vocabulary is provided in a glossary towards the end of the book.

Two new chapters have been added. Chapter 1 sets early years mathematics in a wider context aimed to help practitioners understand what mathematics is, how attitudes to mathematics are important, and the theoretical and practical considerations of how children learn mathematics. The wider range of training for early years practitioners means that these issues are seldom addressed in depth elsewhere in their study. Chapter 7 focuses on sorting, matching and handling data, setting in context activities which have long been carried out in preschool settings.

Ideas of number and counting, and calculation have been more clearly defined in Chapters 2 and 3. Throughout, the book has been brought up to date with recent research and has a greater focus on the reader's understanding of key mathematical concepts in Chapters 2–7, each of which cover:

- what the area of mathematics entails
- the research evidence on how children learn the concepts
- key concepts
- how adults can help children learn these concepts through appropriate experiences
- some examples of planned activities
- suggestions for language development and key questions
- assessment criteria.

Chapter 8 provides an overview of planning and assessment for mathematics.

Specific references to the content of the Foundation Stage Curriculum have been removed to make the book relevant to a wider audience and less susceptible to changes in the curriculum. The book is not about the mathematics children have to learn because 'the powers that be' say so, but the mathematical ideas that children will enjoy exploring as part of making sense of their world.

Finally, I hope that the book fulfils its purpose, namely to encourage adults working with young children to have increased understanding of the mathematics and to become more confident in and enjoy planning, teaching and assessing mathematical learning. I was delighted to be asked to take over the mantle from Ann and hope that readers will feel that I have done it justice.

Alison J. Price

CHAPTER

1

Learning mathematics in early years settings

- What is mathematics?
- Why do people have so many hang-ups about it?
- How do young children learn mathematics?
- What mathematics should they learn?
- How can we best help them?

This chapter sets out to answer some of the questions people ask about mathematics and teaching in the early years and sets the scene for the rest of the book. It is new to this edition since, with the increased focus on training for early years practitioners at foundation degree and early years profession status levels, students may no longer address these issues in a wider study of mathematical learning. The chapter considers what mathematics is, looks at attitudes to learning mathematics from the point of view of both the practitioner and the children they are working with, summarises some of the theoretical perspectives on learning mathematics, considers the range of mathematics young children can learn and draws out the implications for settings.

The chapter is, by nature, theoretical and some readers may wish to skim read it at this stage and come back to it later in their study.

What is mathematics?

One way to view mathematics, like most subjects studied in education, is as a way of looking at and making sense of the world. If we use the example of a tree, we can look at a tree and describe it in words or write poetry about it (language). We can examine it to find out how it grows and produces seeds to create new trees (science). We could explain why it grows in a particular area of the countryside or came to be imported into the country (geography) ... Or we could talk about its shape, measure its size, count how many branches it has, calculate how much it has grown in the past year (mathematics). Mathematics is one way in which we describe and make sense of the world around us – and we do it all the time, even when we are not aware of it. As we will see later in this book, babies start to make sense of the world in mathematical ways from birth: recognising the difference between small numbers of objects and recognising shapes and patterns of familiar objects in the environment around them. No one sets out to teach it to them; it is part of how their brains work. More complex ideas in mathematics, including counting and calculation, build on this initial sense making and are essentially social constructs: created by human beings over time to enable us to make sense of and to control our environment.

We make sense of the world by looking for patterns; we understand people by patterns of behaviour, we make sense of the natural world through patterns of seasons, cycles of growth etc. Most people, if asked what mathematics is, would think first of arithmetic: number and calculation. But this is only part of a much bigger subject and Devlin (2003) defines mathematics as the study of pattern. These patterns may be patterns in number, in algebra, in shape, in spatial position, etc. One of the reasons that many people find mathematics difficult (see below) is that they have not understood that mathematics has pattern.

It is pattern that helps us to understand and to learn mathematics. Let's try a little experiment. Read the following list of letters and think about how you will remember it:

M T E A I S A H M T C

Many of you will have looked to see if there was a pattern to help you and probably did not find one. But how about if it is written as:

M T E A I S
 A H M T C

Perhaps you can now see how the string of letters was produced and could create a rule by which to remember it: from the word 'mathematics' take the odd letters in order and then the even letters. This would be easier to remember than learning the original meaningless string of letters. Even better, you could apply the same rule to another word should you be called to do so. This is, of course, a meaningless task but it makes the point. Understanding the pattern makes the learning easier and also makes that learning adaptable to new situations. Skemp (1971) calls this relational or intelligent learning, rather than instrumental or rote learning.

Once we see mathematics as the study of pattern, rather than as complex, symbolic calculations, it is perhaps easier to see how even young children can look for patterns and start to make sense of the world of number, shape, space and measures.

Mathematics: why do people have so many hang-ups about it?

One student teacher, on hearing that mathematics was a way of making sense of the world, exclaimed, 'So why doesn't it make sense then?!' Her experience of learning mathematics was of a series of unrelated facts that made no sense, which must be rote learnt and reproduced on demand. She is not alone. Many people in our society admit to having negative attitudes to the subject. In England it seems to be acceptable to claim to be poor at mathematics while in other countries people would be ashamed to do so. As the Independent Review of Mathematics Teaching in Early Years Settings and Primary

Schools observes: 'the United Kingdom is still one of the few advanced nations where it is socially acceptable – fashionable, even – to profess an inability to cope with the subject' (Williams 2008: 3).

Mathematics in school is a high stakes subject; everyone is expected to learn it and a good grade at GCSE is required for many careers, including teaching. Perhaps as a result, many people define themselves more by the mathematics which they cannot do than that which they can. Students will often say, 'I am not very good at maths; I was OK until we did "X" and then I totally lost it'. This is not only true of students but of many highly educated adults, including professors in some of our top universities. What 'X' is will vary from one person to the next; however, there does seem to be some commonality: column subtraction, multiplication tables, long division and algebra often being cited. What is interesting is that even people who have studied mathematics to A level and beyond can often identify a sticking point. This way of thinking seems to be distinctive to mathematics. No one when talking about reading, for example, will define their ability in this way: 'I am not very good at reading; I was OK until we did Dickens [or Shakespeare, or whoever] and then I totally lost it.'

We are not born with negative attitudes to mathematics, they are learnt. They may be learnt at home since some parents will have poor attitudes themselves and have low expectations of their children coloured by their own experiences at school: 'you'll not be good at maths, I was always hopeless.' As the Williams review, cited above, continued: 'A parent expressing such sentiments can hardly be conducive to a learning environment at home in which mathematics is seen by children as an essential and rewarding part of their everyday lives' (Williams 2008: 3). Or they may be learnt through experiences at school. Martha, now a secondary school teacher, remembers being in Year 4 at school. At the start of every morning the children each had to complete a workcard with 10 questions on it. When they got them all right they moved on to the next card. She remembers doing the same card over and over again making a different mistake each time. As the pressure increased, her ability to get the right answers decreased. By the end of the academic year she hated maths and saw herself as hopeless at it; many student teachers have shared similar stories.

Buxton (1981) studied adults who admitted to negative mathematical experiences and attitudes and set out to help them understand mathematics and see it differently. The result is a book entitled *Do You Panic about Maths?: Coping with Maths Anxiety*, where he suggests that the state of panic that people feel when asked to do mathematics, especially under pressure, blocks their ability to reason and therefore to work mathematically. Buxton also found a sharp contrast in the way that people think about mathematics and its learning. People who are anxious about mathematics, like the student teacher quoted at the beginning of this section, see it as fixed, uncreative, unrelated to reality, inaccessible, a collection of rules and facts to be remembered, time pressured and mostly about calculation, while those who enjoy mathematics see it as exploratory, creative, accessible, a network of relationships and requiring time for reflection. He observes that it is not easy to exchange one set of beliefs for the other.

Subsequent research into adult attitudes to mathematics, and the affect that attitude has on learning mathematics and on teaching it, has identified that negative attitudes are often developed early in schooling and as a result of poor teaching (Geist 2010;

Ashcroft *et al.* 1998; Leder 1992). It highlights the importance of developing positive attitudes in children, alongside teaching them the necessary facts, skills and concepts. So, the National Statement on Mathematics for Australian Schools states: 'An important aim of mathematics education is to develop in students positive attitudes towards mathematics ... [which] encompasses both liking mathematics and feeling good about one's own capacity to deal with situations in which mathematics is involved' (Australian Education Council 1991: 31, cited in Leder 1992).

How we see ourselves in relation to mathematics, and our attitude to the subject, will affect how we teach it. A teacher in a mixed reception and Year 1 class was observed teaching mathematics over a period of about six months. She was not confident about teaching calculation to young children and repeatedly said to the children, 'don't worry if you don't understand it, it is difficult'. The teacher was trying to reassure the children as she believed that mathematics was too difficult for young children to learn, but the children were receiving two messages: that mathematics is difficult and that it does not matter if you do not understand it, both of which will affect their own attitudes to mathematics. Research shows that female teachers with mathematics anxiety can have more of a negative effect on girls' achievement than on that of boys, perhaps reinforcing stereotypes about boys being better at mathematics (Beilock *et al.* 2010).

So, if we are going to teach children mathematics effectively, we need to address our own attitudes. We do not need to be mathematics geniuses to teach mathematics, in fact often such geniuses are not necessarily the best teachers as they may have found it so easy to learn that they do not understand why the children can't 'just see it'. But we do need to be confident with understanding mathematics at and beyond the level at which the children will be working. Hachey (2009) suggests that in order to break the cycle of mathematics anxiety we must first acknowledge our negative feelings about mathematics and accept that we must be good enough mathematicians since we use mathematics in our everyday life competently in shopping, cooking, crafts etc. We should then re-examine our practice in working with children, offering developmentally appropriate activities and methods. Engaging with the subsequent chapters of this book and reflecting on them as they apply to your setting will build your confidence in understanding the mathematics. And many practitioners have found when they do this, and spend time observing the enjoyment that young children have in engaging with early mathematical learning, that their own attitude to the subject will change.

How do young children learn mathematics?

Theories of learning are many and complex. There does not appear to be a single theory which will explain all forms of learning. Different subject areas may be learnt differently by different people and in different contexts. Even within a single subject such as mathematics, there are facts, skills and concepts about number, shape, space and measures which may have to be learnt in different ways. This may help to explain why some people find some areas of mathematics more difficult than others; people may struggle with calculation but find shape and space easier to learn.

In this section we will briefly consider different theories of learning and discuss what insight they give into how children might learn mathematics and how we should teach it to them. Each of the theories of learning shows us something about the learning situation we are considering; none offers the whole picture but all can contribute to our overall understanding of the complex entity which we call learning.

Behaviourism

Behaviourism asserts that learning involves a predictable change in behaviour as a result of experience and that new learning is transferable for use in new contexts (Schwartz 1978). This would imply that the right activities for the classroom will predict what all children will learn from them. Mathematics teaching has traditionally been seen in terms of 'talk and chalk' transmission of a concept or skill by the teacher, followed by a time for students to practise what they have been taught. This can be related to behaviourism in that:

1 It has been handed down from teacher to pupil, who in turn becomes a teacher, on the grounds that 'if I learnt it like that that it must work for others'; the right activity should predict learning. Where children do not succeed under this model of teaching they are often blamed for not having listened, not concentrating or just not being intelligent enough; it is not the teacher's fault!

2 Repeated practice reinforces a learnt behaviour which can then be used in other contexts.

The approach can work for some areas of mathematics and for some people: for example most people learn to say the counting words in the right order by repeated practice and some people did learn to do long division by this teaching method though many were less successful. So, behaviourism may account for some learning but by no means all. We know that not all children, and especially young children, learn best by being told. However, a positive benefit from the behaviourist debate is that it emphasised that the environment and what teachers do can make a difference (Oates 1994).

Nativism

One of the key arguments in children's learning has been that of nature versus nurture. Are things natural to the child, today we might say are they built into their genes, or are they learnt as a result of the way the child is brought up? Behaviourism came down heavily on the nurture side of the argument – we are a direct result of what we experience. In contrast, nativism comes down heavily on the nature side and argues that some, if not all learning is innate: wired into our brains before birth.

One of the greatest proponents of this theory in early education was Noam Chomsky who argued that human beings can talk while animals cannot due to the presence of a 'language acquisition device' in their brains. Similarly, in mathematics, some have argued for an 'accumulator model' by which children learn to count and understand number (Gallistel and Gelman 1992; Gelman and Meck 1992). Many others disagree, arguing that knowledge of the counting principles is constructed through experience and interaction (Le Corre and Carey 2007). But recent research does seem to show that from birth babies are able to recognise small quantities (subitization, see Chapter 2), shapes and patterns

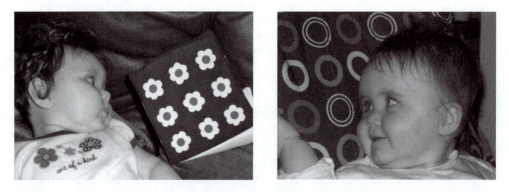

FIGURE 1.1 Babies from birth are interested in number, patterns, regularity and shape

(Figure 1.1), indicating that some very rudimentary mathematical abilities are innate, although later learning can be better explained in other ways.

Neither behaviourism nor nativism acknowledges children as active in their learning: in the first learning is under the control of the environment and in the second it is built into the brain. In contrast the following three theories emphasise an active role to learning and are currently more popular in the context of mathematics education: constructivism, socio-cultural theory and social practice theory.

Constructivism

Constructivist theory draws heavily on the work of Piaget (1966; 1980), who argued that learners construct knowledge for themselves through experience and reflection; knowledge cannot be 'given' to them by someone else. Piaget used the words assimilation and accommodation to describe how learners take in new learning. Learning from each new experience is compared with the learner's existing knowledge and if it agrees with what they already know, it is assimilated, grafted on to their current understanding. When the new learning is in conflict with their existing understanding, accommodation takes place as they change the way they understand that concept. A constructivist approach helps us to understand how children may make sense of the world through concept building and in primary and early years education has resulted in a positive emphasis on the individual learner and on learning through practical activity.

Not all Piagetian theory has been found to be so useful. He also proposed four 'stages of development' (Donaldson 1978) through which children develop in their understanding and abilities:

- the sensori-motor period (0 to 2 years) when children learn mostly through their senses and movement;
- the pre-operational period (2–7 years) when children begin to represent objects with images, drawings and words but are not yet able to reason logically;
- the operational period which is divided into:
    - concrete operations (7–11 years) by which time the child can use logic, but only about actual objects or situations; and

■ formal operations (11 years to adulthood) when reasoning about abstract relationship and concept was possible.

Piaget claimed that teaching in advance of the child's stage of development will be at best unproductive and may be harmful, a claim which resulted in the idea of readiness for learning, waiting until the child was ready to learn reading or number. These stages have since been shown to be too simplistic, based on research which did not allow the children to show what they really understood (Donaldson 1978; Hughes 1986) and are no longer considered helpful in describing how children learn mathematics as will be seen in the following chapters.

Socio-cultural theory

Constructivism has been criticised for not taking account of the role of language, social interaction and social context in learning. Socio-cultural theory draws on the work of Vygotsky who set out to explore 'the relation between human beings and their environment' and 'the relation between the use of tools and the development of speech', and concluded that all understanding is social in origin (Vygotsky 1978: 19). Two key ideas which emerge from his work are particularly relevant here: the zone of proximal development and the role of language in learning.

Zone of proximal development (ZPD)

When solving problems children are able to do some things unaided, which Vygotsky described as their actual developmental level. But with the help of an adult or a more experienced child they are often able to do more: their potential developmental level. The zone of proximal development (ZPD) is described as:

> the distance between the actual developmental level as determined by independent problem solving and the level of potential development as determined through problem solving under adult guidance, or in collaboration with more able peers.
>
> (Vygotsky 1978: 86)

It is within this zone that new learning takes place: what they can do with help one day they will soon learn to do unaided. Others have built on this idea including Wood *et al.* (1976) who use the term scaffolding for the role of the adult in helping a child within their ZPD. They observe that such adult–child interactions are 'a crucial feature of infancy and childhood' (1976: 89). The idea of a ZPD encourages us as practitioners to observe what a child can already do unaided and find ways to scaffold what they will learn next. Coltman *et al.* (2002) describe the role of the adult in scaffolding children's problem solving in shape. However, we should note that in order to scaffold a child's learning the adult must understand both the mathematics and the progression of children's learning so that they know what the next steps might be (Diaz 2008).

The role of language in learning

Vygotsky saw language both as a form of communication and as a tool for thinking. Just as we use physical tools to help us solve practical problems, we use language, spoken or

9

written, as a mental tool to support our intentions and logical reasoning. He observed that children would often give a 'running commentary' on their actions, talking themselves through a task to enable them to carry it out successfully. As they grow older, the running commentary may not be spoken out loud but internalised, leading to more advanced forms of thought and reasoning. Once children master the task, they may no longer need to use language to support it.

Many theorists have adopted an amalgamation of constructivism and socio-cultural theory to form social constructivism (May 2011), although some in the mathematics education community argue that it is not possible to combine them into one single theory (Lerman 1996).

Social practice theory

In the past, and in some countries even today, children have spent their childhood learning how to be an adult in their society. Oates (1994) studied the children of the Gusii tribe in Kenya where, as soon as they are weaned at around two, children are trained to take on adult tasks. By six or seven they are taking on their role in society, for example the girls caring for younger children and helping to cook. For a Gusii child, play is about practising adult behaviour. Children in such societies learn through observing the adults, being given carefully structured subtasks to do and gradually moving to taking over the role.

Social practice theory emerges from such anthropological study: seeing all learning in the context of human life and society. Lave (1988) set out to consider the idea of formal and informal learning through studying how adults learnt mathematics in the workplace, using the example of tailors in Liberia. She concluded that all learning was 'situated' in its social context. She describes groups in terms of 'communities of practice', in which apprentices, newcomers to the group, learn how to become full participants through a process of 'legitimate peripheral participation' (LPP). At the beginning it is OK (legitimate) to take part (participation) on the fringes (peripheral) of a social setting. Many who work in early years settings will recognise LPP as describing how a new child will watch from the edge of a group before, sooner or later, becoming accepted and joining in more fully. LPP means to learn how to be: how to be a child in a preschool group, how to be a tailor, how to be a mathematician ... Through observation, watching how to use the 'tools of the trade', through learning how to communicate using appropriate language and through starting with the simpler tasks and becoming more competent, apprentices became masters.

Social practice theory has two implications for mathematics education in the early years. From the point of view of the learner, it offers the idea of apprenticeship and legitimate peripheral participation: that some things are learnt through observation and gradual participation in the task. This is not only true in the workplace, a child observing his mother baking cakes will, over time, learn to participate in that task and eventually be able to bake one for himself. And it is also true of learning mathematics in the classroom, as can be seen in this example of children learning to count in tens in a mixed reception and Year 1 class with their teacher, Debbie (Price 2003: 4):

DEBBIE: Shall we, er, count with me and we'll go all the way to one hundred and then see if we can keep going. Together 10, 20, 30, ... 100, 110, 120, 130, ... 190, 200 ...

Some children are still counting with the teacher on two hundred, others saying a hundred and twenty, all picked up again at 210. They continued counting to 800.

DEBBIE: I am absolutely amazed. Give yourselves a big clap.

Few of these children could confidently count in 10s to 100, never mind 800, and relied on Debbie to provide the next hundred name, but all were participating as much as they could. Some of the younger children gave up or just mouthed the words but they were all still listening, hearing the count words and feeling part of the group or, in Lave's term, legitimately participating in the activity in which the teacher is the expert and the children the apprentices.

And if we consider social practice theory from the point of view of the experts, their role is to model how to do the task, how to use the tools, how to hand over small parts of the task and how to talk about it. Specific vocabulary and language patterns, both spoken and written, are used and must be learnt over time. So, practitioners must learn to model actions, tools and language that will allow the children access to the underlying mathematical concepts embedded in an activity. The theory also offers ideas for involving children in some activities in which adults use mathematics explicitly, such as cooking, sharing food, shopping and measuring spaces and distances.

These theories of learning have all contributed something to our understanding of learning mathematics and we turn to our next question.

What mathematics should young children learn?

Research shows that children who have a good start in mathematical understanding in the early years make better progress in school mathematics (Aubrey and Godfrey 2003; Aunio and Niemivirta 2010). This does not mean teaching them 'school maths' earlier, in fact there is evidence that such forced teaching has negative effects on their learning. In countries which begin formal schooling later than in the UK (age 6 or 7) children may not know as much at age six but they make faster progress once they reach school (Sharp 1998); however parents and preschools in these counties do a significant amount of informal mathematics with them. From this we can conclude that it is appropriate to teach mathematics in early years settings so long as it is the right mathematics taught in the right way.

Mathematics: content and processes

Mathematics in school can be divided into four main *content* areas and the following list shows how these relate to the early years mathematics as described in the chapters in this book:

- Arithmetic
  - Number and counting: Chapter 2
  - Calculation: Chapter 3
- Algebra
  - Pattern: Chapter 4

- Geometry
  - Shape and space: Chapter 5
  - Measures: Chapter 6
- Data handling/statistics
  - Sorting, matching and handling data: Chapter 7.

The mathematics curriculum for the early years will vary across geographical areas. It may be that the curriculum you are following does not explicitly mention some of these areas of mathematics; however, you will probably find that you are addressing many of these areas anyway and it is helpful to see how they are essentially mathematical and will enable the children better to understand mathematics as they move into more formal schooling. For example, if pattern is not explicitly spelt out in the curriculum, the children will still benefit from looking at patterns in number and will experience patterns in other areas such as art and design, music and movement, and the environment. It is not so much a question of 'what mathematics should the children learn' but of 'what mathematics they will be learning' in early years settings and how we can help them make sense of this.

In addition to the mathematical content outlined above, most mathematics curricula identify mathematical *processes* which also need to be learnt. In the English National Curriculum these are described under the headings of problem solving, communicating and reasoning:

- Problem solving
  - approach problems presented in a variety of forms, in order to identify what they need to do
  - develop flexible approaches to problem solving and look for ways to overcome difficulties
  - make decisions about which operations, problem-solving strategies and mathematical equipment to use when solving problems
  - organise and check their work.
- Communicating
  - use the correct language, symbols and vocabulary associated with number, data, shape, space and measures
  - communicate in spoken, pictorial and written form, at first using informal language and recording, then mathematical language and symbols.
- Reasoning
  - present results in an organised way
  - understand a general statement and investigate whether particular cases match it
  - recognise simple patterns and relationships and make predictions about them
  - explain their methods and reasoning when solving problems.

(summarised from DfEE/QCA 1999)

These targets are for older children but most can be interpreted in terms appropriate for children in the early years as can be seen in the next section in the contexts of problem solving, making connections, language and reasoning, and recording.

How can we best help children learn mathematics?

Problem solving

Problem solving can be seen as 'a major vehicle for learning' (Gifford 2005: 152) and a study of 1–4-year-olds engaged in block play argues that all early mathematics should be seen as logico-mathematical knowledge during problem solving (Kamii *et al.* 2004). In another study, encouraging young children to use mathematics in a range of problem solving activities was found to be more effective than early introduction of symbolic representation of number (Gilmore *et al.* 2007). However, despite its importance, one literature search of early years mathematics research found that:

> Problem-solving was the theme that received the least attention. The lack of literature in this area is a serious concern for early childhood educators. Problem solving has received particular attention in curricula documents over the past two decades … However, only 1.3% of the articles (*n* = 4) within a six-year period addressed young children's ability to problem solve, reason and converse mathematically.
>
> (Fox and Diezmann 2007: 307)

Problem solving can be identified within constructivist, socio-cultural and social practice theory perspectives, as children solve real problems which are exploratory, socially contextualised or embedded in everyday routines. Problem solving in early years settings should mainly arise through such examples, and not through traditional word or symbolic problems such as 'How much is five sweets and two more sweets?' or '5 + 2'. They should be problems which arise within familiar contexts, for meaningful purposes and require some mathematical complexity (Copley 2000). The problem 'how many different way can you share 7 sweets between two people' may have a similar structure to the symbolic problem '5 + 2' but is open ended and requires more mathematical thinking, as well as real world discussions about fairness. Gifford reminds us that the solutions to problems in the real world are not always the same as those in the mathematical world. Children asked to share sweets between a set of teddy bears would take into consideration the size of the bears, giving the smaller ones fewer in case they got sick (2005). When interpreting young children's mathematical problem solving strategies it is important to consider what social-cultural aspects the child might be taking into account and not just to assume they do not understand the mathematics if they do not solve the problem as expected.

Children can be encouraged to develop positive attitudes towards their learning and enjoyment of mathematics and this is particularly important in problem solving activities. 'Problem solving dispositions' have been identified which can be recognised through observation and should be encouraged:

- persevering
- focusing attention on the problem

■ testing hypothesis
■ taking reasonable risks
■ remaining flexible
■ trying alternatives
■ exhibiting self regulation.

(Copley 2000: 31)

Copley emphasises that is important for the adult to allow children sufficient time and opportunity to engage in extended problem solving and sufficient freedom to take risks and try alternative strategies, but also to know when help is needed and offer it sensitively. Solving the problem for them will rob them of the satisfaction that comes from success, and will lower their self-esteem and their willingness to 'have a go' next time.

Clear stages of problem solving have been identified:

1   Understanding the problem
2   Planning how to solve it
3   Carrying out the plan
4   Reviewing the solution

(Polya 1957 cited in Copley 2000)

Some studies have shown that children aged four to five years tend to tackle a problem without having considered the strategies required which will lead to success (Askew and Wiliam 1995), but others show that they are able to plan and reflect when encouraged to do so. One of the roles of the adult is therefore to encourage them to think about what they are going to do when they encounter a problem and consider other ways to do it. Adults may also be involved in discussion and questioning, perhaps asking 'what if?' questions to help the child to seek an improved solution or see a way to overcome a difficulty, or drawing attention to a particular aspect of the problem with 'I wonder' comments.

Children will naturally use a range of problem solving strategies according to their understanding of the task and of the mathematics. These may include:

■ brute force: trying to force a shape into a hole that is too small or the wrong shape
■ trial and error: trying all the options, initially at random but learning to work systematically
■ adaptation: making a change to the problem so that the original solution fits
■ starting again: restarting the task but with more knowledge of what might work
■ analogy: recognising a similarity with a previous task and solution
■ reasoning: often using 'if/then' structures, even when not explicitly used such as '[if] this brick is just too short. [Then] I need to find one about "this" much more'.

They will develop more advanced skills and dispositions through working on practical problems and through reflection on what has been achieved. Children might plan to make a robot from junk materials, deciding how many pieces of junk they will need and what shapes to choose; they might decide to share out some pretend food in the home area and wonder how many pieces they can give to each child; they might be asked to find hidden shapes around the setting and count how many they each collect. All of these experiences are problems to be solved by the young child. Many of the problems which the children attempt to solve are self-initiated, others may be adult initiated. Some problems will be short tasks, ones that can be resolved in moments. Others may be extended tasks which will take a session to solve and perhaps be returned to over the next few days, while the children look for alternative solutions. Some problems may involve just one child; others may involve a group working together to find a solution.

Making connections

As we saw above, many people see mathematics as a series of unrelated facts which have to be remembered, and yet mathematicians see it as an interconnected network of concepts, the study of pattern and relationships. Understanding these relationships makes learning the mathematics much easier to remember, though it may take longer to learn initially (Skemp 1971). An early example of this is the relationship between addition and subtraction so that once the addition facts are learnt, they can be used to solve subtraction problems (see Chapter 3). Some children will find these connections for themselves but many others will not, or will think that it is 'cheating' to use shortcut methods which they have invented. Children in school make better progress when taught by teachers who understand and explain these connections (Askew *et al.* 1997; Price 2001). The English National Curriculum therefore advises that 'Teaching should ensure that appropriate connections are made between the sections on numbers and shape, space and measures' (DfEE/QCA 1999: 16) and pupils should be taught to 'recognise simple patterns and relationships and make predictions about them' (p.19) as a form of reasoning. In order to help the reader understand these relationships more fully, Chapters 2–7 in this book spell out those which are relevant in the early years, with Chapter 4 focusing specifically on pattern in mathematics.

Mathematics arises from experience and interaction with others but is essentially created in the mind with the help of language and images (see for example the discussion of what a number is in Chapter 2). Connections must therefore be made between the elements of mathematical experience. Figure 1.2 is adapted from work by Haylock and Cockburn (1997) and Lesh *et al.* (1987) for use in early years settings. The five elements are explored in more detail below. One or more of the five elements will be present in any learning experience of the concept and a sound understanding requires children to be able to make connections between any one element and any other, for example to be able to talk (spoken language) about the practical mathematics (physical materials), or to draw a picture representing a concept described in a story (real world script).

Physical materials

A wide range of everyday and play materials can be used in learning mathematics as well as more structured mathematical equipment and visual models such as number lines and 100 squares. Each chapter suggests a range of equipment which can be used to develop

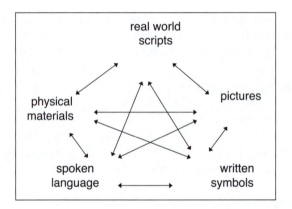

FIGURE 1.2 Relationships between the elements of mathematical experiences

the relevant concepts both in play and in more structured teaching activities. Children will benefit from experiencing the same concept with a wide variety of materials. Materials should be freely available for them to choose in play and problem solving.

Real world scripts

The term 'real world scripts' has been adopted to refer both to mathematics embedded in real world tasks such as cooking and building and also to mathematics which is part of a 'script' in songs, rhymes and stories. A study of children learning the early stages of addition in reception and Year 1 classes identified the role of story in children's understanding and learning (Price 2000a, 2000b). It found that children understood addition more easily if the mathematics was part of a story which related to their real world (including imaginative worlds) rather than being demonstrated in a more abstract way with cubes. Addition is about change and the children could see a reason for numbers changing in the story, for examples some cows going into another field where the grass looked nicer, but there was no reason why the number of cubes should move around. Contrary to constructivist early years practice which emphasised the importance of activity with practical apparatus, children could also understand a concept embedded in a story, even without physical objects with which to model it, an example of the socio-cultural aspect of learning. Story also offers children relevant language with which to talk about the mathematics, and retelling a story allows them to practise using this language in context. Chapters 2–7 identify story contexts and story books which contain mathematical concepts to use in early years settings and for parents to use at home.

Children will invent and use imaginative stories in their play and many of these will have mathematical concepts of number, pattern, shape and space embedded within them. For example, James and Hayley are playing in the sandpit with the dinosaurs and, in this section of the story, exploring ideas of size and position.

JAMES: My triceratops is the biggest [indicating tallest with his hand].
HAYLEY: This one's got a long tail
JAMES: But mine's the biggest of all. He can fight and he's the winner.

James proceeds to fight with the dinosaurs and Hayley's 'dies'.

HAYLEY: I'm going to bury him in the sand, long way down.

JAMES: This one's going to stomp on him, stomp, stomp, on top, now he can't get out.

Spoken language and reasoning

Children will come into preschool with already developing ideas about mathematical concepts but may not have the formal language to describe these (Coltman 2006). One of the key roles of early years mathematics teaching and learning therefore is to enable children to talk about their mathematical experiences, at first using everyday informal language but moving towards using more mathematical language. There are two related ideas here:

- vocabulary: words to describe number, shape, size . . .
- communication: being able to talk about, explain and reason about mathematics.

Chapters 2–7 highlight key vocabulary and language patterns and also include key questions which will encourage discussion with the children. It is important, as discussed in Chapter 8, that practitioners plan for the words which they will use and the way that they will explain mathematical ideas.

In school, reasoning involves children in presenting results in an organised way: understanding a general statement and investigating whether particular cases match it, recognising simple patterns and relationships and make predictions about them and explaining their methods and reasoning when solving problems (DfEE/QCA 1999). How does this apply to preschool children?

Piaget argued that logical *reasoning* was not just difficult for young children but was impossible before the age of about 7. However, research shows that young children can reason in contexts of their own choosing, though they may not yet have sufficient awareness and language to explain their reasoning. Consider these examples of children engaged in mathematics:

- Kalika (3) creates a necklace with red, blue and yellow beads carefully alternating the colours; when asked to describe her necklace she said: 'It's red, blue, yellow. I like it'.
- Eighteen-month-old Thomas tries to force shapes into the holes of a posting box, but at $2\frac{1}{2}$ he is able to turn the block round and try different angles and by 4 can look carefully at the shape and orientate it to fit.
- Four-and-a-half-year-old Amanda throws two dice – 'It's five'; 'That was quick, how did you do that?'; 'I just knowed 2 and 2 was four, because that's just, like on the dices, so it's another one, five'.

All these children are learning to reason: Kalika could recognise and create simple patterns but was not yet able to explain clearly how it was created. Thomas could be seen to be working systematically over time, learning from his mistakes and by $4\frac{1}{2}$ Amanda is able to explain her reasoning about number. Haylock offers seven key processes in mathematical reasoning as they apply in primary school and examples of all of these can be seen in early years settings, as shown in Table 1.1.

TABLE 1.1 Mathematical reasoning

HAYLOCK (2010: 37)	EXAMPLES SEEN IN EARLY YEARS SETTINGS
Generalising: making an observation that is always true	Exploring the shapes box: 'all the triangles have three corners'.
Conjecturing and checking: claiming that something might be true and checking to see if it is so	Playing a track game: 'I'm going to win next' [counts the number of squares to win]. 'Oh no! Cos the dice hasn't got a 7'.
The language of generalisation: being able to express a generalisation as something which is always true	'If you add one on, you always get the next number [on the number line]'.
Hypothesis and inductive reasoning: a generalisation that has not been proven which emerges from experience	'He's bigger [than me] so I think he's 5'.
Counter-examples and special cases: a counter-example shows that a conjecture is not true; some are treated as special cases and ignored (e.g. all prime numbers are odd except 2)	On finding an oval in the shape box: 'this one's not a circle, it's squashed round'.
Explain, convincing, proving and deductive reasoning: being able to explain and convince someone else of your thinking are the first stages of this process	'Counting goes on for ever and ever because you can always add another one on'.
Thinking creatively in mathematics: coming up with unusual solutions and alternative explanations	On trying to find combinations that make five with cubes: 'If I cut this one up, I could have 2½ and 2½'.

In order to encourage reasoning skills, the adult needs to be alert to such examples and recognise them as reasoning, even if the reasoning is flawed; to model reasoning skills for the children, especially the language of reasoning including words like if, then, because and not; and to challenge the children's thinking through questioning, 'Is that always true?', 'How do you know?' and by providing counter-examples such as a 'triangle' with three curved sides instead of straight. Examples of such questions can be found in Chapters 2–7 as they relate to the different areas of mathematics.

Recording mathematics in pictures and symbols

Of the five elements of mathematical experience identified in Figure 1.2, symbols are the most abstract and compact and have traditionally been introduced to children when they reach primary school. However, an interest in emergent writing (Clay 1975; Hall 1987, 1989), children's mark making (DCSF 2008) and in their representation of number (Hughes 1986; Worthington and Carruthers 2006) has resulted in a move to encourage children's mathematical mark making in preschool settings.

The emergent (or developmental) approach to teaching writing encourages children to develop their own writing through being immersed in a literary environment, encouraged in their mark making and watching adults modelling writing, rather than through formal teaching which had often consisted of copying the teacher's own writing. In mathematics Hughes devised a game which involved labelling tins to show how many bricks they contained (Hughes 1986). He showed that children as young as three could begin to record number using a range of pictures or symbols, many of which they could later use to identify a particular tin correctly and still interpret a week later. The coming together of these ideas resulted in exploring the development of an emergent approach to teaching mathematics in preschool and early primary settings (Atkinson 1992; Price 1993) one aspect of which focuses on children's recording.

Worthington and Carruthers have studied young children's mark making in detail. Drawing on Hughes' original classification of children's written numbers, they identify five forms of graphical marks which children may use (Figures 1.3–1.4):

- Dynamic – marks that are lively and suggestive of action, with a freshness and spontaneity
- Pictographic – when children try to represent something they can see in front of them
- Iconic – children sometimes choose to use marks based on one-to-one counting. These are often marks that they have devised, in place of the things they are counting or calculating, and may also resemble tallying
- Written – using letter-like marks or words
- Symbolic – using standard numerals and mathematical symbols (Worthington and Carruthers 2006).

While all such marks will have meaning for the children at the time they are made, children's recording may be functional or non-functional, where functional marks are those which a child can still interpret at a later date (Munn 1997). Over time, more children learn to create functional marks and once they do so they rarely lose this understanding. Some children create function invented symbols, while others do not understand functionality until they have learnt to use formal number symbols.

Worthington and Carruthers emphasise the role of the practitioner in supporting children and suggest that the following four elements 'are essential to support children's mathematical marks:

- an environment that gives children many opportunities to explore mark making
- assessment that is positive and responsive to children's marks and informs the next steps of learning
- adults that model mathematics in meaningful contexts
- adults that understand and can therefore value children's marks (DCSF 2008).

Environments which will support mathematical mark making include: evidence of all areas of mathematics (number, pattern, shapes, measures etc) on walls, notice boards and equipment; mathematically focused displays; resources in role play areas such as calculators, tills, money and prices, stamps, a calendar or diary, telephones, simple telephone directories and address books, clocks, rulers, tape measures, scales; and equipment for mark making

FIGURE 1.3 Pictographic recording: 'Mummy duck (centre) said quack and four came back'

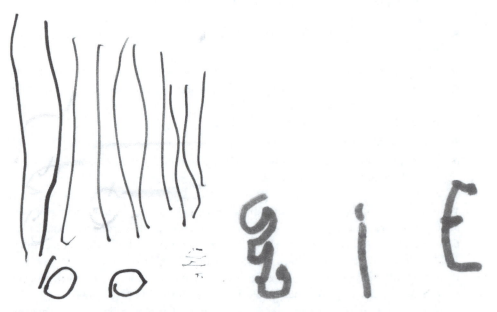

FIGURE 1.4 Iconic and early symbolic recording: 10 ribbons and 3 (the marks 'read' 3, 1, 2)

(paper, pencils, pens, white boards, rulers etc.; see Figure 1.5) in all areas of the setting including the outdoors (Worthington and Carruthers 2006).

The role of the practitioner is to provide stimuli and resources, to model in mathematically rich contexts, to understand and value children's mark making, and to respond in a positive way with attention to how to move the children on (Figure 1.6). Practitioners should understand that such mark making arises spontaneously in play and meaningful contexts, not as an instruction to 'write something down' following more formal instruction, by which time the motivation and depth of mathematical thinking in young children has often passed (DCSF 2008; Carruthers and Worthington 2009).

As the children's understanding of addition and subtraction progresses they can also begin to record calculations. At first they may demonstrate the change in a pictographic way that expresses the change in number, for instance draw a hand taking away some of

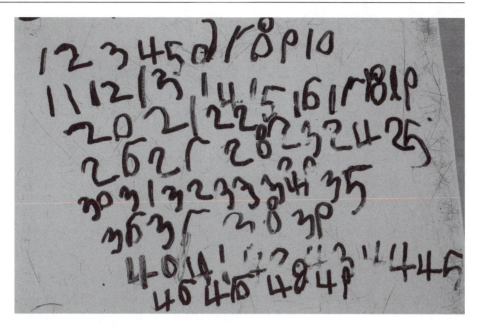

FIGURE 1.5 A whiteboard and pen allowed exploration of numerals

FIGURE 1.6 'Five ducks': this 4-year-old shows a good knowledge of numerals but does not yet know that only the final numeral is needed to record 5

the cubes, or represent them as soldiers and have some of them marching off the page (Hughes 1986; Carruthers and Worthington 2004, 2006). They may invent their own symbols and, if the formal symbols for number operations (+ − =) are modelling by adults, they will begin to use these. One study also found children able to invent their own symbols for fractions (Brizuela 2005).

What next?

Having explored what mathematics is, reflected on attitudes to the subject, discussed how it is learnt, explored what mathematics is relevant for them and how we can enable their learning, we move on to looking at the areas of mathematical learning in detail in the following chapters. These can be read in order, or you may want to focus on a particular aspect of mathematics, while some readers may wish to jump straight to Chapter 8 which picks up in more detail issues of planning, organising and assessment of mathematical learning.

2

Number and counting

Many people when they think of early mathematics will think about simple calculation, for example 3 + 5 = 8, but before children learn to calculate they need to have a good understanding of number. This is therefore the first of two chapters about number, which addresses the underlying concept of number and how children learn to count. Chapter 3 will then look at how children use number and counting to solve problems and develop an understanding of addition, subtraction, multiplication and division.

What is the study of number?

The concept of number is such a basic one that we do not often stop to consider what we mean by it. But on reflection we find that it is an abstract concept. Asked to show someone a ball, you would produce a real ball, not the word 'ball' written on a piece of paper, however if asked to show a number four you would probably think of the numeral '4', the written symbol used to represent the number, as it is impossible to show a number itself. You might offer a number of items but then attention may then be drawn to the items themselves and not to the number of items. This is because number, like colour, is not a physical object but an abstract concept which describes something about collections of objects.

When adults use number words with small children it is usually in the context of small sets of objects; one hat, two shoes, three cups . . . The number word is being used as an adjective to describe something about the set of objects. Gradually the child will recognise what is the same about all the sets of a single number, two cats, two stones, two men etc., and attach the word 'two' to that concept. However, a number does not always refer to a set of things. Numbers can be used in three different ways: cardinal, ordinal and nominal.

Cardinal number is the use of a number to label a set, to say how many. But we also use number to explain the position of something in an order. This is called *ordinal* number and is used, for example, in numbering houses in a road, pages in a book or the position of winners in a race. Sometimes we use the ordinal number words 'first, second, third . . .' but this is only a small part of the concept (Haylock 2010). Traditionally the teaching of early number focused on understanding the cardinal value of sets; the children in many reception classes would study a different number each week with displays and activities focused on the number of the week, say the number three, in order to learn the 'concept of 3'. Connections were not always made between one number and the next

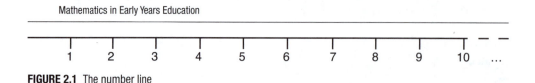

FIGURE 2.1 The number line

(Orton 2005). Ordinal number reminds us that numbers have a sequential relationship; that 'three' is one more than 'two' and one fewer than 'four'. This can be modelled using a number line which at first contains only the counting numbers (Figure 2.1).

As they progress through school children will also learn that there are other numbers which we do not use in counting: zero, fractions, decimals, negative numbers ... which can also be added to the number line. Number is used in an ordinal way in measurement where, for example, thirty and a half centimetres is a point on a measuring line rather than a set of thirty and a half things. Understanding that ordinal number in this sense is crucial to understanding mathematics has led to an increased use of number lines and number tracks in school and preschool settings (a line has points marked as in Figure 2.1, while a track has squares labelled with numerals).

Finally, number is used in a *nominal* way, as a name or label to help us identify something, for example in telephone or bus numbers; the word *nominal* comes from the Latin *nomen* meaning a name. A bus may be labelled number 13 but this does not mean that there is anything 13-ish about it. The number is purely a name which allows us to identify which bus we need. Nominal number is not taught, but practitioners do need to be aware that on occasion children may assume that a number used nominally has some other significance.

So, even a relatively simple number like four may be used to refer to four legs on a chair (cardinal), the fourth house in the road (ordinal) or the number of a bus route. This discussion is complex but it may help us to see that the concept of number is not an easy one, even before children move on to calculating, since 'number development is not a matter of acquiring a single concept' (Sophian 1998: 27). We might begin to wonder how any child can develop ideas of this complexity, and this has been the study for many psychologists over many years; however recent research indicates that babies' brains are sensitive to these concepts, as described below.

How children learn about number – research findings

Piagetian view

Until fairly recently the early years curriculum for number was heavily influenced by Piaget's research (1952), which concluded that young children did not have a logical understanding of number. His famous 'conservation of number' experiment involves showing children two rows of counters with the same number in each and asking whether there are more in one row or the other or whether they are both the same (Figure 2.2).

The researcher then asks the children to watch very carefully and spreads out one row of counters (Figure 2.3) and again asks if there are more in one row or the other or both the same. Adults will know that the number is unchanged (conserved), but young children, up to the age of 6 or 7, will usually think that the spread out row now has more (or sometimes less because there are more spaces). Piaget concluded that until children

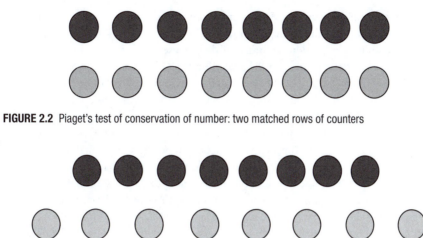

FIGURE 2.2 Piaget's test of conservation of number: two matched rows of counters

FIGURE 2.3 Piaget's test of conservation of number: second row transformed

could conserve number they were unable to carry out meaningful arithmetic (Piaget 1953).

As a result, the mathematics curriculum for preschool children in the 1970s consisted of sorting and matching and attention to one-to-one correspondence in order to teach conservation, rather than focusing on counting and using numbers (Matthews and Matthews 1990).

Challenges to the Piagetian view

Piaget's findings and conclusion were subsequently challenged by researchers who questioned the sense that children are making of Piaget's task and the language used (e.g. Donaldson 1978; Schubauer-Leoni and Perret-Clermont 1997). When the children are asked to pay careful attention to the change they will assume that the transformation is significant, resulting in a different answer; also 'more' can mean numerically more but can also mean longer in some contexts. Researchers found that children could conserve number when the numbers were small and the task was designed in a context which they understood.

Subsequently, research has shown that children have a much greater understanding of number than Piaget gave them credit for and that counting and number activities are valuable in helping the children to develop their understanding (Sophian 1995; Thompson 1997a). However, sorting, matching and one-to-one correspondence are still key ideas used across all areas of the mathematics curriculum, and especially in handling data (see Chapter 7).

Subitization

Psychologists have developed ways of exploring the understanding of babies from birth. They find that babies as young as four or five months are able to tell the differences between different numbers of objects within the range 0–3. The babies do not yet have the ability to count but can quickly recognise how many with small quantities: this is known as subitization, from the Latin *subito* meaning suddenly or quickly. Babies are placed facing a screen and their reactions recorded. If shown a series of pictures of different objects in different orientations but with the same number (say 2) in each, they will soon become habituated to that number (become used to it so as to lose interest). If they are then shown a set of objects with a different number (1 or 3) they will look at the screen for significantly longer (Wynn 1998).

The same part of the brain is used to subitize small quantities as to process symbolic number and so it is an important aspect of number development (Cantlon *et al.* 2006; Le Corre *et al.* 2006). Adults can subitize larger numbers than babies, especially if the arrangement of the objects is ordered, for example the pattern of pips on dominos, dice and playing cards. Young children's subitization skills can be developed through focused activity and the use of structured images (Hannula *et al.* 2007; Gifford 2005). As they learn the early counting words through interaction with others, toddlers will begin to use these words to describe the subitized quantities.

How children learn about counting – research findings

As adults engage with babies and toddlers in counting activities the children will begin to copy counting behaviours. Gelman and Gallistel (1986) describe five principles which are used when counting. These can be divided into two groups: how to count and what to count:

- *How* to count principles:
    - the one-one principle
    - the stable-order principle
    - the cardinal principle
- *What* to count principles:
    - the abstraction principle
    - the order-irrelevance principle.

The one–one principle

The one-to-one (1:1) principle refers to the need to match one and only one counting word to each item in the set to be counted. To do this effectively the items to be counted need to be partitioned (physically or mentally) into two sets, a set of items which have already been given a number word and those yet to be given one.

To understand the one-one principle children will need to:

- Recite the counting words in order (see stable order principle below).
- Coordinate the touch and oral count so that these happen at the same time. Pointing to items as they count is an important aspect of the counting process, as it ensures that each item is considered and touched just once (Gelman and Gallistel 1986).

■ Keep track of which items have and have not been counted, which is easier when the objects are in a straight line. Children find it helpful to move the items as they count in order to keep track and therefore find counting real objects easier than objects in pictures (Potter and Levy 1968).

The stable-order principle

Children must also learn to repeat the counting words in order. Typically young children's counting 'string' will consist of the first few words learnt correctly, a group of correct words but with omissions, then more randomly selected words, with the number of correct words increasing over time (Fuson et al. 1982). Learning to count in English is complex since it involves rote learning of the early counting names which no recognisable pattern until fourteen. In counting beyond twenty, children must recognise the pattern within each decade: 21, 22, 23 . . . and in each new decade name: 30, 40 . . .

Children will often invent their own patterns as in the following example of Liam's counting (5:5):

one, two, three . . . eighteen, nineteen, twenty, twenty-one . . . twenty-nine, twenty-ten, twenty-eleven, twenty-twelve . . . twenty-twenty

At first children may 'chant' numbers, perhaps learnt through number rhymes and stories, and this chant will have little meaning. Gradually, the order of the words takes on meaning and becomes related to items to be counted. Children begin to realise that the order of the counting words is always the same and that in order to count they must reproduce this order: the stable-order principle.

The cardinal principle

Children often learn counting as a process without realising that its purpose is to find out how many in the set. They must learn that the final number in the count does not just label the last item counted but represents how many in total, that is, the cardinal value of the set. So as well as touching and counting one-one, using the counting names in order, they must be able to stop on the last number of the count and recognise that this indicates the total. The cardinal principle is dependent upon the one-one and the stable-order principles and develops later.

While parents engage in many counting acts with their children, many of these are not contexts which required a cardinal value and they emphasise the final count word as significant in only about one-third of cases (Durkin et al. 1986, cited in Sophian 1996). Many children on entering school do not associate counting with finding out 'how many' even though their counting abilities are 'extensive and accurate' (Munn 1997: 16). Adults will often ask children 'how many?' again after they have completed the count in order to ascertain if they have understood the cardinal value of the set. However, if the child sees this as an instruction to count they will recount, whether or not they have understood cardinally. It is therefore important that adults make the purpose as well as the process of counting clear. Suriyakham (2007) recommends the use of gesture at the end of the count, emphasising the final count word with a circular gesture which includes the whole set. Asking children to help a puppet, who is just learning to count and sometimes makes mistakes, can also be used to focus their attention on the purpose for counting and has been found to increase their understanding (Muldoon *et al.* 2007; Thompson 1997b).

One test of cardinal understanding is the 'give-N' task, asking a child to take a small number of items (N) out of a larger collection, for example 'give the doll four of the sweets' (Wynn 1990). Even children who can count when asked 'how many' do not necessarily choose to do so when asked to give-N nor when asked to make a set which matches an existing one, for example 'there are 6 dolls, can you give each doll a toy' (Sophian 1996). These skills are generally developed by the age of four indicating that the child has mastered the cardinal principle.

The abstraction principle

The principles of how to count outlined above can be applied to any counting situation. Children can count any set, whether it is made up of similar objects or unlike objects. In counting a set of similar objects a child might say 'There are four cars'. Here the child is able to name the set as cars. However, where the objects are unlike they will need to find a common property of the set, such as 'There are four things'. Counting can also be applied to things that cannot be seen like sounds, such as drum beats, and to actions, such as jumps or hand claps. The abstraction principle says that anything can be counted, seen or imagined.

As they become more proficient at counting, children will move from counting objects which they can see and touch, or hear, to being able to imagine the items as they say the words. To become efficient at calculation they will need to learn to count forward and backwards starting from any number.

It is also possible to count things where a single item has a value greater than one, such as money. Many young children's counting experience is limited to using single counting objects and most five-year-olds count money, whatever the value of the coin, as 'ones' (Carraher and Schliemann 1990). This limited experience can affect the formation of place-value concepts (hundreds, tens and units) at a later stage, so it is important that children have counting experiences where from the start they will give each item a tag which includes a number name, for example *two* pence, to describe its value. When playing with money in preschool, starting to use the correct money names will be an important step towards this concept.

The order-irrelevance principle

When counting a set of objects it does not matter which number name is assigned to which object, the total number of objects will be the same. Young children did not necessarily appreciate this fact. However, if a puppet is used to mess up the order children are more likely to recognise that the number would to change than if they watch a researcher change the order. Also, children may need to understand the cardinal principle more fully in order to develop the order abstraction principle.

Counting is not just something learnt in preschool. Counting is an essential element in developing calculations skills (Thompson 1997c). Five-year-olds will begin to learn new counting patterns when learning about odd and even numbers, place value (counting in tens and hundreds) and multiplication (multiples of two, five and ten) and these will further develop in primary school (Anghileri 1997).

Young children's understanding of number and counting

Birth to three years of age

Babies appear to be sensitive to quantity from birth. They can distinguish between quantities within the range 0–3, match the number in a small set of objects with the appropriate number of sounds and by six months can notice changes in the number of jumps made by a puppet (Wynn 1998). Toddlers can compare the sizes of small groups of objects: Geist (2001) describes how an 18-month-old child dropped coloured balls over the side of a ball pit. He dropped one ball, then two more over the pit. Then he went to the other side of the pit and dropped two balls. He returned to the first side of the pit and looked again at the grouping of the three balls, then moved back to the second side and dropped another ball over the side. He now had two groups of three balls. He used subitization rather than counting skills to form equal groups and showed an understanding of equality of quantity.

Young children learn the difference between counting and non-counting words at a very early age and so toddlers will start to connect the first few counting words to subitized sets of objects (Fuson *et al.* 1982). They may also copy adults in counting like behaviours and by eighteen months toddlers already understand some of the rules for counting. They prefer to watch counting when the adult uses 1:1 correspondence rather than if they point at the same two objects repeatedly, and prefer the count words in their own language to another (Slaughter *et al.* 2011). Libby enjoyed playing with her ducks and singing 'Five little ducks went swimming one day' with her grandmother. In each verse Granny counted the ducks, touching each as she said the counting words. At 15 months Libby began to copy her, touching each duck in turn. By 18 months she would also make a sound (not yet a recognisable counting word) for each duck, with the final count sound made at a higher pitch.

At about two years of age children will begin to use the language of comparison, such as 'more', 'same' and 'different', to distinguish between quantities (Wagner and Walters 1982). Two-year-olds will start to chant the counting words, though they may not be clearly separated and may not always be in the right order (Sarama and Clements 2009), and they may use them in counting situations. During their third year the number they can subitize and name increases to four. Between $2^1/_2$ and 3 children are more accurate in their counting when checking their own estimations than when asked to count with no obvious purpose (Gelman 2006).

From three to about four years of age

By the age of three, children will be aware that adults use number and counting to solve real world problems, such as 'Have we got out enough plates for all the family?' (Sophian 1987). They subitize and name up to three or four objects and select the correct number of objects in this range from a larger group (Sarama and Clements 2009). They can recite

FIGURE 2.4 Using familiar symbols to record 'five ducks – I'm nearly 5'

the counting words to 5 and then 10, and use 1 to 1 correspondence to assign these to objects, though there may be errors. Even where their counting skills are insufficient to count a larger set they have a sense of size and will choose a bigger number to estimate a larger set (Gelman and Tucker 1975 cited in Gelman and Gallistel 1986).

Usually, during their fourth year, as their subitization and counting skills come together, they will understand that the final count word indicates the cardinal quantity of the set (Griffin and Case 1997). Once this is secure, their understanding of numbers greater than four expands dramatically and they will learn more count words and begin to understand that each number represents one more than the previous one (Wynn 1998; Sarama and Clements 2009). They understand that numerals represent number, recognise numerals of personal significance: ages, house number, the local bus route . . . and may use some of these or their own symbols to record number (Worthington and Carruthers 2006; Figure 2.4).

At about four to five years of age

Once the children have a secure understanding of cardinal number they can use this to compare quantities. They learn to count beyond 10 and by the age of five to recognise the decade structure: 20, 30, 40 . . . (Sophian 1987). They can subitize to five and may recognise structured patterns to ten, for example on dominoes (Sarama and Clements 2009). They recognise numerals to ten and beyond and begin to write these.

By five they can count out up to 10 objects accurately from a larger set, understand that the order objects are counted in does not affect the cardinal value (order-irrelevance principle), learn to count backwards from 10 and begin to learn other counting patterns including multiples of 2, 5 and 10. With experience, they will recognise the numerals to 100 and learn to order these.

Experiences and key concepts in number and counting

So, young children are sensitive to number and will naturally subitize small quantities and by the time they enter preschool many will also have developed some skills in counting. However counting is socially constructed and can only be learnt through interaction with others (Threlfall and Bruce 2005). Many parents and carers will have involved their children in number rhymes and songs and in counting activities and most children will come into preschool already confident in using the counting words especially as they refer to small subitized quantities. However some children may enter preschool without such understanding and those working with the youngest children may need to reinforce these as part of everyday activities.

Key experiences

From the early experience of subitizing and the five principles of counting, there are key experiences which children need in order to become successful at counting. These are opportunities to:

- explore structured representations of numbers to 10 and use these counting words
- recite the number names to 5 (then 10, then 20 and beyond)
- enact movements in time with count words to reinforce 1:1 correspondence
- count items in a set:
  - which can be partitioned (moved)
  - count items which can be touched but not moved (items in a picture) or seen but not touched (items at a distance)
  - count sequences of sounds or actions
- count out a given number of items from a larger group
- recognise the numerals to 10 and beyond and order them
- develop new skills in verbal counting, including:
  - counting on from any small number
  - counting backwards from 10
  - counting in multiples of 2, 5 and 10
- use number and counting for real-world purposes and in problem solving.

This is a long list, but each experience will relate to a range of activities which are part of the normal early years curriculum, and many activities will include more than one aspect of counting.

Explore structured representations of numbers to 10 and use these counting words

A wide range of structured materials can be used to extend children's subitization, initially to five or six and then to ten. These may come from the real world, for example cars with four wheels or five fingers on each hand, from games involving dice, dominoes or playing cards, or from specially structured mathematical materials such as an abacus or Numicon® (Figure 2.5).

As the children become more familiar with each number, different representations of that same number will help them to see it as made up in different ways which will help their future arithmetic skills (Figure 2.6). Cards such as these could be use in snap or matching games.

An abacus which shows the two 5s in each 10 by using different colours (sometimes known as a Slavonic Abacus) helps children to see some of the different ways numbers can be made up (Figure 2.7).

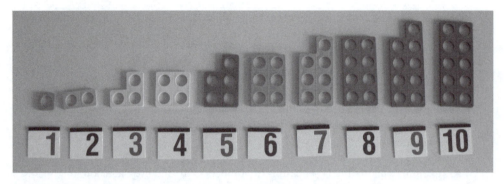

FIGURE 2.5 Numicon tiles 1–10 (Numicon is published by Oxford University Press and Numicon materials are reproduced with their permission)

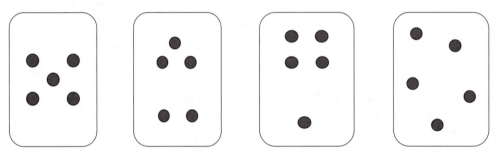

FIGURE 2.6 Different patterns of five suggest different ways it can be made up

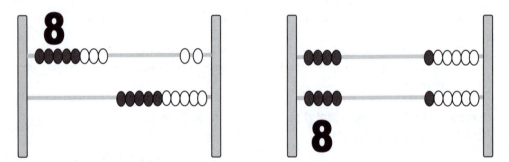

FIGURE 2.7 Different representations of 8 on an abacus, as 5 + 3 and as double 4

Recite the number names to 5 (then 10, then 20 and beyond)

Some children will already be able to recite the number names to ten or more by the time they are three years old. Others will be just beginning to learn these. Singing action number songs and rhymes, stories which involve counting, taking opportunities in the setting to count, such as counting how many children are sitting at the table at snack time, or how many candles are on the birthday cake, will enable children to hear the counting words in order, and to begin to recognise that these have a consistent order. A puppet can be introduced who needs help in counting and sometimes gets the words in the wrong order, misses one word out or says the same word twice. Encouraging the children to correct the puppet will focus their attention on the order of the words.

Enact movements in time with count words to reinforce 1:1 correspondence

Rhythmic counting helps children to focus upon the word pattern of the counting numbers and also reinforces the one-to-one correspondence between word and action. This can be experienced through action number rhymes and songs, and also as a game, where children clap, pat their head or wave their arms in time to the count.

Count items in a set

To develop proficiency in counting, it is not enough just to be able to count objects which can be touched. Using small quantities, children will develop eye coordination with counting in order to count objects which they can see but not touch. They will also begin to understand that anything can be counted, for example sounds that they can hear and also things can be imagined and counted mentally. To this end they benefit from having a wide range of counting experiences, including:

■ *Count items which can be partitioned (moved):* children move items to one side as they are counted so that they have two subsets: those counted and those still to be counted.

■ *Count items which can be touched but not moved (items in a picture) or seen but not touched (items at a distance):* here the children will need to consider how to group the objects visually so that they are sure that they count each one just once. Where the items are at a distance, pointing is still used to keep track.

■ *Count sequences of sounds or actions:* children listen to sounds, perhaps with their eyes shut, and count them. For example they can listen to pennies being dropped into a tin and empty them out to check their answers. This will help them to realise that items to be counted do not have to be things that can be seen or touched and eventually they will accept that anything that can be defined by humans can be counted, including things they imagine. The counting of actions helps children to 'feel' the counting, linking movement with the count.

Count out a given number of items from a larger group (give-N)

Counting out a given number from a larger set involves understanding the target number, keeping it in mind when counting and matching the final number in the count to this number. Incidental experiences of this will occur regularly through the day, such as 'Please put four biscuits on the plate'; 'We need three pencils'. The ability to do this effectively, with numbers greater than those that they can subitize, shows that the child can understand the cardinal principle of counting.

Recognise the numerals to 10 and beyond and order them

At first children will recognise numerals of personal significance, even quite large numbers. With practice they will recognise numerals to ten and beyond and relate these to the numbers they can count. Practitioners may wish to audit their setting for printed

(a)

(b)

FIGURE 2.8 Ordering numbers: a number jigsaw; numbered flowers pegged on a line

numerals on display in a wide variety of contexts, indoors and out, including a number track to 10 or 20 and, when working with four- to five-year-olds, a hundred square. Number track games and jigsaws (Figure 2.8a) can be used; cars and bikes can be labelled with numbers and given a matching numbered 'parking space'. When reading books, attention can be drawn to numerals including page numbers.

Numerals attached to a line with pegs can help children to practise ordering the numbers (Figure 2.8b). 'Spot the problem' games can be used, where a number is removed and the children guess which one. This can be made more difficult if the remaining space is closed up or two (or more) numbers changed round. As they become more proficient all the cards can be removed and the children try to replace them. If the line is set at child height the children will start to play such games with one another.

Larger numbers

Children enjoy large numbers; speculating on thousands, millions and what these mean in particular contexts. All around them, young children will see larger numbers used in everyday life: car number plates, telephone numbers, digital clocks, prices in shop windows, lottery numbers on television and so on. They may play board and card games at home with older brothers and sisters (Bergeron and Herscovics 1990) or handle money and name the coins. So, children have rich opportunities to observe and discuss larger numbers in context, though should not yet be expected to understand how these numbers are made up or their comparative size. Large numbers should be on display in the setting and available in role play situations: shop, cafe, garage, mirroring situations in everyday life.

Developing new skills in verbal counting

Children who are confident in their verbal counting beyond 10 can progress in their counting to:

■ *Counting on from any small number:* in order to be able to develop mental arithmetic skills it is important that children become familiar with counting starting at numbers other than one. One way to practise this is 'quiet counting': identify the number that is to be counted from, then say the words leading up to it very quietly and counting on loudly from that number. Gradually work towards the quiet numbers becoming silent. A game can be played like 'head and shoulders, knees and toes'. The first time through, the children count to 10 and show the correct number of fingers each time. Next time the 'one' is silent and represented only by the finger action, then 'one' and 'two' are silent, and so on. The children will become familiar with hearing and using the counting words starting at higher numbers.

■ *Counting backwards from 10 and then 20:* this is a skill necessary for mental subtraction. Some children will be familiar with this in the countdown for rockets etc. with the familiar 'blast-off' at the end. Setting time limits, such as encouraging everyone to be sitting down on the carpet by the end of the count, is a fun way of letting them hear and join in with backwards counting. Backwards counting can also be done with a number line or track so that the children can see the number before (Figure 2.9).

■ *Counting in multiples of 2, 5 and 10* will help with multiplication and division/sharing. Multiples of two can be started with counting the odd words quietly and the even ones loudly. The number line and later a 100 square can be used to track the multiples (Figure 2.10). Counting in fives and tens can be reinforced using hand actions, with five (or ten) fingers stretched palm out with each count word.

FIGURE 2.9 '6, 5, 4', practising counting backwards from 10 on the number track

Number track:

| 1 | 2 | 3 | 4 | 5 | 6 | 7 | 8 | 9 | 10 | 11 | 12 | 13 | 14 | 15 | 16 | 17 | 18 | 19 | 20 |

100 square:

1	2	3	4	5	6	7	8	9	10
11	12	13	14	15	16	17	18	19	20
21	22	23	24	25	26	27	28	29	30
31	32	33	34	35	36	37	38	39	40
41	42	43	44	45	46	47	48	49	50
51	52	53	54	55	56	57	58	59	60
61	62	63	64	65	66	67	68	69	70
71	72	73	74	75	76	77	78	79	80
81	82	83	84	85	86	87	88	89	90
91	92	93	94	95	96	97	98	99	100

100 square:

1	2	3	4	5	6	7	8	9	10
11	12	13	14	15	16	17	18	19	20
21	22	23	24	25	26	27	28	29	30
31	32	33	34	35	36	37	38	39	40
41	42	43	44	45	46	47	48	49	50
51	52	53	54	55	56	57	58	59	60
61	62	63	64	65	66	67	68	69	70
71	72	73	74	75	76	77	78	79	80
81	82	83	84	85	86	87	88	89	90
91	92	93	94	95	96	97	98	99	100

FIGURE 2.10 Number track and 100 square highlighting multiples of 2, 5 and 10

Many opportunities for counting arise spontaneously from the children's work, but some must be planned through games and group activities, so that all children have a wide range of experience in a variety of contexts. By the age of five, some children may not yet confidently use all the five principles of counting, but they should use the how to count principles in a range of situations and be beginning to understand the abstraction principle even if the order-irrelevance principle is not fully understood.

Use number and counting for real-world purposes and in problem solving

Initially children's counting may be a learnt ritual triggered by the question 'how many?', so they need to be involved in counting tasks which have a clear purpose (Figure 2.11). Games, such as skittles or throwing beanbags into hoops, can encourage counting to record the score, allowing the children to see the significance of the final count word and the importance of counting accurately in order to be fair. Snack time activities can involve counting out the correct number of cups etc. for a group of children. Instructions such as 'only four children can play in the water tray', or 'each pencil pot should have six pencils', with numeral and picture labels where possible, will encourage checking by counting. More challenging questions such as 'Your tower is taller than Ben's but does it have more bricks in it?' (where the bricks are different sizes) could also be used.

Some contexts will use counting in order to create a matching set. When asked to give a biscuit to each child in the group a sharing strategy can be used and there is no need for counting, but if the children are counted in one place and the biscuits collected in another then counting is needed. Story lines can be created, perhaps based on favourite story books, such as trying to entice seven toy kittens out of a basket by placing the correct number of balls of wool for them to play with.

FIGURE 2.11 The boys counted to see how many frogs they managed to flip into the pool; at snack time children estimated how many peas would be in their peapods then counted to check

Concept map

Table 2.1 shows the concepts outlined above in matrix form together with examples of vocabulary which can be developed. Some example activities are included to demonstrate how these concepts might be explored in an early years setting. The map can be used as a basis for planning. Assessment checkpoints and key questions are given to show possible learning outcomes from the activities.

Planning number and counting experiences

The range of counting experiences needed to develop understanding of number and counting will come from both planned activities and incidental adult interventions in children's play. Counting can occur in any play environment and it is the skill of the adult to engage with the children and to extend their number language and their understanding through careful, sensitive commentating, questioning and challenging.

Setting up environments for number and counting

Counting materials

Counting materials may be specific collections of interesting items and trays with mixed collections, or items placed in an environment with the specific purpose of encouraging counting, such as shells and pebbles in the sand tray; carrots and potatoes in the kitchen area; coins and purses in the shop; skittles and balls as part of outdoor play. These should be available for the children to choose for free play as well as items such as beads and laces, farm and animals, garage and cars, and so on. Structured number apparatus should also be provided to encourage subitization including dice, dominoes, playing cards, abacuses and perhaps commercially available materials such as Numicon®.

Books, rhymes and songs

In the book area, counting can be encouraged by ensuring that suitable books are easily accessible, perhaps as part of a special display. These can be used during carpet time, with all the children, or as part of a focused activity with a small group. Counting rhymes and songs, particularly those with actions, help children to practise the number names in order. Some number rhymes count up in ones, such as 'One, two, three, four, five, once I caught a fish alive', and 'Peter taps with one hammer'. Many rhymes count down, for example 'Five currant buns in the baker's shop', 'Ten in the bed' and 'Five little ducks went swimming one day'. Some emphasise counting forward or backwards in twos, such as 'One, two, buckle my shoe' and 'Ten fat sausages, sizzling in a pan'. All of these help children to recognise the counting patterns and to remember the order of the counting names. There are many good quality books and audiotapes of nursery rhymes and songs which include counting rhymes.

The provision of play materials related to number rhymes, songs and stories will encourage children to act out the 'story' and practise counting (Figure 2.12). These may include ducks and a pond; frogs, a log and a pond; currant buns and sausages (made from felt or dough); monkeys and a bed to bounce on; spacemen and a flying saucer . . .

TABLE 2.1 Concept map for number and counting

KEY CONCEPT	VOCABULARY	EXAMPLES OF ACTIVITIES	ASSESSMENT CHECKPOINTS	KEY QUESTIONS
Exploring structured representations of numbers to 10 and use these counting words	How many, number words to 10	A small group of children create a line of dominoes with 1 spot, 2 spots, 3 spots etc. and can name them 1, 2, 3 . . . to 10	• Recognises how many and gives correct word • Recognises numbers can be made in more than one way	• How many? • How do you know? • Why are these the same?
Consistently recite the number names to 5 (then 10, then 20 and beyond)	Number words one to five, then to ten and beyond	Number rhymes and songs; number stories; correcting a miscounting puppet;	• Recites the number names in order to five, ten, beyond ten to . . . • Identifies errors made by puppet and corrects these	• Why do we have to say the number names in the same order? • Which number comes after . . .?
Enact movements in time with count words to reinforce 1:1 correspondence	Number words one to five, then to ten and beyond	Rhythmic counting; counting with finger actions; counting when jumping along a number track	• Coordinates movement with the count • Can match one counting word to one action	• Can we count how many jumps we can do? • Why does sev-en only have one jump?
Count items which can be partitioned (moved)	Number words	Counting: toy farm animals; beads on a lace; pennies in a purse	• Counts each item only once • Coordinates count with the partition	• How many have you counted now? • How many are there still to count? How do you know?
Count items which can be touched but not moved (items in a picture) or seen but not touched (items at a distance)	Number words	Counting spots on dice; people in a photo, pictures on a wall frieze; trees in a field; chimneys on a house	• Counts each item • Counts each item only once	• How many are there? • How do you know you have counted them all?

(Continued)

39

TABLE 2.1 (Continued)

KEY CONCEPT	VOCABULARY	EXAMPLES OF ACTIVITIES	ASSESSMENT CHECKPOINTS	KEY QUESTIONS
Count sequences of sounds or actions	Number words	Counting hand claps; taps on a drum; chiming of a clock; counting jumps, throws of a ball; counting on a game board such as ludo, snakes and ladders	• Counts each sound or move • Counts each sound or move only once	• How many did you count? • Board games — where did you start? How many did you count? Where did you land?
Count out a given number of items from a larger group	Number words	Counting biscuits for snack time; pencils for drawing	• Counts out required number of items	• How many do you need? • How many did you count?
Recognise the numerals to 10 and begin to order them	Number words to 10	Missing number game: adult hides one of the cards from a number track and the children find out which one.	• Recognised numerals to 10 • Can identify missing one by order	• Which is missing? • How did you work it out?
Count on from any small number	Number words	Counting on from a given starting number; counting along a number line from given number; board games	• Can count on from any small number	• Which number comes after 7?; and after 8?
Count backwards from 10	Number words 0–10	Countdown to deadline for being ready, or to a special event (days before holiday starts)	• Can count backwards from 10	• Which number comes before 9?; and before 8?
Count in multiples of 2, 5 and 10	Number words	Activity counting with finger actions: 2s (match fingers in pairs across hands); 5s (one hand); 10s (two hands)	• Knows multiples of 2 to 20; of 5 to 50; of 10 to 100	• Can you count in 2s; 5s; 10s?
Use number and counting for real-world purposes and in problem solving	What could we try next? Count, sort, group, set, match, list	Are there enough?: matching the count of two sets of objects	• Uses counting strategies to solve problems	• How many do you need? • How do you know that? • How do you work it out?

FIGURE 2.12 Using the numbers jigsaw while singing '5 little ducks went swimming one day'

Number frieze and tracks

A wide variety of representations of number quantities and symbols is essential. A number frieze shows the link between the numeral and its cardinal value, for example, 3 and a picture of three frogs. A number track, where the numerals can be placed in order, is a worthwhile resource to emphasise the ordinal nature of number. The numerals can be large, perhaps half the height of the children themselves. If they are made from tactile materials the children can also experience touching and tracing the shapes of the numerals. Such a number track can become part of the children's play: Carruthers (1997) describes how the children developed games which involved the numerals, made personal choices of numerals, such as their age numerals, and made their own, written number lines. Number cards can be pegged onto a 'washing line' allowing the children to order them and play missing number games where someone hides one of the numbers and the others have to find which one is missing.

Other representations of number can be used around the setting. Bikes can be labelled and parking spaces created with matching numbers. Notices can inform the children when there are limits to the number of children allowed to work in a particular area or where children place their name cards on a board to show where they are working (Figure 2.13). They will learn to recognise how many, and check to see if there is a space for them.

Counting display

An interactive number display can be set up on a table or cupboard top to explore counting, with pegs and pegboards, beads and laces, small cubes. Occasionally the children

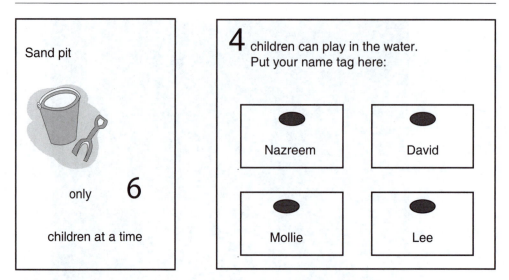

FIGURE 2.13 Notices or name boards by the sand or water play areas encourage children to count, check and interpret data

could choose a 'number of the day' to explore. When celebrating someone's fourth birthday, children could count out four pegs and see how many different patterns of four they can make then perhaps use these patterns to decorate cupcakes with Smarties. They collect as many different things around the setting with a four-ness about them: a car with four wheels, a dolls house chair with four legs, the four page in a number book and make birthday cards with 4 on.

Number games

Number games, such as simple dice and board games, number dominoes and number snap games, can be available as games for the children to choose or as part of a focused activity with an adult. They should all become familiar with counting games using a dice and board, and number-matching games with jigsaws, playing cards, lotto and dominoes. Games which require children to throw a 'six' or another 'magic' number before they start to play can be frustrating at this age, as children want to play the game, not wait for a dice start number.

Adult intervention in children's play

Adults must learn to recognise whether it is appropriate to intervene in children's play, taking account of what the children are doing and why. Interventions must extend the children's thinking, through careful discussion and questioning, encouraging children to use counting language, and helping them to become familiar with new vocabulary. But it should not interfere with the children's play: insisting that children count when they are happily engaged in purposeful play is unlikely to develop positive attitudes to counting. The following are everyday examples of events in settings:

- Ravit and Ghalib are paying a game with frogs but arguing over who has which frogs. The adult suggests that they share them out equally and encourages the children to count to check that they have the same number.

- Tim and Anna decide to build a slide for the dumper trucks with the large blocks. They ask an adult to help them carry the pieces outside. The adult asks how many they think they will need. Tim says three; Anna says more than that! So they agree to count as they carry them out to see how many they do need.

- Susie is sitting quietly, counting out dough cakes for teddy. One, two, five, three. The adult asks how many cakes teddy has. Susie says 'Lots!' They count them together.

Observing and listening to the children will help the adult to identify children's purpose in their play and offer insight into their understanding. In both adult initiated and directed tasks, all adults should be aware of the purpose of the activities and the types of questions which could extend the children's thinking, to enable then to make purposeful interventions. If the focus for a week is number or counting, it may help to have a poster up reminding adults of the specific language and some key questions that could be asked.

Developing problem-solving strategies through counting

Counting is itself a problem-solving strategy used to answer questions. Counting and number tasks should be purposeful in solving problems rather than context free. Children's ability to count is an essential part of their growing understanding of number and they should be encouraged to ask, and be asked, questions in meaningful contexts such as:

- *How many?* Ghopal wanted to nail two pieces of wood together. He asked Mark to pass him some nails. 'How many do you need?' asked Mark.

- *Who has more?* Joanna was working in the outdoor sandpit making sandcastles and decorating them with flags. She made four sandcastles. She counted them, then counted the flags as she put them onto the sandcastles. 'One, two, three, four. That's just right. There's one for each!'

- *Are there enough?* Steven was assisting a parent helper to put out the biscuits for his group for snack time. He said, as he put out the biscuits on a plate, 'Jo is here and Maria and Lisa. That's one, two, three. That's three biscuits.' The parent reminded him that there were four in the group. 'Four, oh silly me. I forgot me! That's one, two, three, four. Four biscuits!'

Adult focused activities

An adult focused activity is one that is planned with specific learning experiences and outcomes in mind, to be taught by an adult (see Chapter 8). The adult could withdraw a specific group of children for a focused activity, or encourage some children to join them in play, for example in the cafe to role play serving, ordering and giving and receiving money. Some focused activities may be carried out in larger groups such as singing number songs at carpet time. Carefully planned focused activities will ensure that over a period of time children experience activities designed to develop the key concepts as outlined above. The following examples of adult focused counting activities show the underlying thinking behind the planning, including the concepts to be developed and the learning outcomes which might be observed. These elements help to ensure that the purpose of the activity is clear to the adults and this may also be shared with the children at the beginning of the session.

Patterns of 5

An activity for a group of up to four children.

- *Purpose:* to encourage subitization of 5 and see how this can be represented in different ways.
- *Materials:* pegboards and pegs, or playdough and buttons.
- *Language:* number words to 5, enough, same.

How to begin

Show the children a representation of 5 on your pegboard which looks like the 5 on dice. Ask the children how many pegs. Discuss and count if necessary. Ask them to count out five pegs each and make their own pattern. Check numbers and help count if necessary. If they make one the same as yours praise them, then ask if they can make a different pattern. Discuss the patterns made. What is the same about them? What is different? This can be adapted with larger numbers up to 10.

Number rhymes and stories

Activities for everyone as part of carpet time, or for a small group.

- *Purpose:* to learn the order of the counting numbers; to begin to recognise that the order of the counting numbers is stable.
- *Materials:* a selection of counting rhymes where the count is ordered forward from one. Puppets or dressing up clothes can be used if the rhymes are to be acted. A story which uses number, for example *When I was One* by Colin and Jacqui Hawkins.
- *Language:* counting number words.

How to begin

Counting rhymes

Choose a favourite counting rhyme where the counting goes forward, such as 'Peter taps with one hammer'. Children sing this, copying the actions in time with the song.

Sing or recite other rhymes where the counting goes forwards, such as 'One, two, buckle my shoe'; 'One elephant went out to play'; 'One, two, three, four, Mary at the cottage door'. Use fingers to represent the numbers.

Rhythmic counting

Encourage the children to repeat a sequence of numbers with you, alternately slapping knees and clapping hands to make a rhythm at the same time:

Say:	one	two	one	two	one	two	one	two	one	two ...
Action:	slap	clap	slap	clap	slap	clap	slap	clap	slap	clap ...

Say:	one	two	three	four	one	two	three	four	one	two ...
Action:	slap	clap	slap	clap	slap	clap	slap	clap	slap	clap ...

Count in threes, slapping knees, clapping hands, hands on heads:

Say:	one	two	three	one	two	three	one	two	three	one ...
Action:	slap	clap	head	slap	clap	head	slap	clap	head	slap ...

Count in fives, this time saying the numbers one to four quietly with quiet clapping, and five loudly with a pat on the head:

Say:	one	two	three	four	five	one	two	three	four	five ...
	quiet	*quiet*	*quiet*	*quiet*	*loud*	*quiet*	*quiet*	*quiet*	*quiet*	*loud* ...
Action:	clap	clap	clap	clap	pat	clap	clap	clap	clap	pat ...

A number story

Read a number story. *When I Was One* by Colin and Jacqui Hawkins (Picture Puffin) counts each birthday. Ask:

- Who has a birthday this week? How old will you be? Let's count to four ...
- Who is nearly five years old? Let's count to five ...
- Who has a brother or sister who is more than five? Let's count to ...

A number track could also be used to extend the activity. Can you find the number four? ...

Washing line game

An activity for a group of five children.

- *Purpose:* to develop the language of ordering.
- *Materials:* washing line, pegs, cards with pictures on from one to five or more items, cards with numerals 1 to 10, or beyond.
- *Language:* number words, one more than, one fewer than, before, after, next, first, last ...

How to begin

Start with the picture cards 1–5. The children each take a picture card. They decide the cardinal value of it. They take turns to peg their card onto the washing line:

- Let's peg the cards on in order. Which one comes first?
- Which card comes after three?
- Which one comes next?

When all the cards are in order, ask the children to collect a particular card:

- Jasmin, can you find the card before three?
- John, can you find the one after four?

When they are confident with picture cards, the activity can be repeated with larger quantities. Where children are beginning to recognise numerals, numeral cards instead of picture cards can be used.

Give a dog a bone

An activity for a group of three children.

- *Purpose:* to practise counting out a number from a larger group and making a matching set.
- *Materials:* a set of about 24 small cards with pictures of a dog and 30 matchsticks (without heads) or pictures to represent bones.
- *Language:* counting numbers, same, more fewer.

How to begin

Ask each child in turn to count out seven dog cards and place them on the table in front of them. Observe whether they know when to stop. When all have 7 cards, ask 'How many dogs do you have? How do you know? If the dogs each want a bone, how many bones will you need?' Ask the children to take enough bones. Observe whether they use counting or 1:1 matching (dog to bone). Ask 'Have you got the same number of dogs and bones? How do you know?'

The game can be adapted to fit favourite stories or topics e.g. mother and baby animals . . .

Involving other adults in the planned activities

Where there are children whose home language is not English, there will be opportunities for helpers to encourage counting in their home language as well as in English. Parents may help with this or adults in the setting who speak the home language.

When the staff meet together to plan, they can be made aware of the range of counting activities available during the sessions and agree on the vocabulary which they will try to encourage. Where other adults have not been involved at the planning stage, it is helpful for them to have a prompt sheet which lists briefly the planned activities and their purpose, with examples of questions which can be used to encourage the children to extend the children's understanding.

Setting up environments for number and counting activities

Table 2.2 shows suggestions for contexts across the setting which could offer opportunities for discussions about number and counting during child initiated learning, or be set up for adult initiated or focused activities.

TABLE 2.2 Number and counting activities across areas of the setting

ENVIRONMENT	CONCEPT/SKILL	CONTEXTS
carpet time	• stable order counting • count how many • show a given number, e.g. of fingers	• counting stories • number action rhymes • acting out a story: dressing up; using puppets; imagination games
daily routines	• count how many • recognising numerals • count out a given quantity	• taking the register • finding the number card for number of dinners required • counting out snacks, drinks • counting out/away, e.g. paintbrushes, scissors • counting how many can work in the sand, water . . .
art and craft areas	• count by touching and partitioning • count pictures • count in 2s	• counting how many, to make a collage: pieces of scrap paper, pasta shells, shiny things . . . • sticking pictures cut from a catalogue; painting a picture: counting how many . . . • making dough models: counting how many . . . models, how many eyes (count in 2s) . . .
table top games and collections	• use subitizing skills to recognise how many • count by touching and partitioning • count physical movements • recognising numerals in order	• recognising quantities: playing number snap, lotto . . . • counting how many: beads on a lace; pegs on a pegboard . . . • counting along a track: board games with dice
sand and water	• count out a given quantity • count how many	• making three, four sandcastles • putting four cups of water in the water wheel
construction	• counting out a given quantity • count how many • making two groups the same	• making a tower with five bricks • counting how many big blocks to make a road • this tower has more; make that one have the same number of bricks

(Continued)

TABLE 2.2 *(Continued)*

ENVIRONMENT	CONCEPT/SKILL	CONTEXTS
role play	• counting out a given quantity • count how many • recognising numerals	• dressing up: role playing, e.g. The Three Bears: chairs, beds, porridge, using telephone • shopping, playing customer/shopkeeper roles: counting out coins, using till and calculator • preparing food in the home area: counting out enough plates for the four guests, using diaries and calendar for making appointments
small world play	• counting out a given quantity • count how many	• doll's house: putting three people in the kitchen; two in the bedroom . . . • road floor plan: counting how many cars on this road; how many lorries . . .
outside play	• counting how many • recognising numerals	• playing skittles: how many did you knock down? Find numeral to record score • counting how many beanbags you can throw into hoop • counting along a number track

Assessment

What to look for

Regular observations of individual children, noting their use of language and how they count, will give useful evidence of what children can do and what they understand, and identify aspects of counting where children lack confidence. The assessment checkpoints and key questions in Table 2.1 can be used to help with assessment. These include both closed questions (how many?) and open questions (how do you know?) which encourage reflection. Observations can be recorded, with evidence of the child's behaviour to support their understanding. Regular observations will show whether a child:

■ knows number names in order to 5, 10, 20, . . .

■ can match counting words and items

■ knows that the last number in the count is the cardinal value of the set

■ counts by touching and partitioning; counts by pointing; counting 'in head', . . .

■ recognises numerals to 10 and beyond and can order them

■ counts on and/or back from any number, counts in steps of 2, 5, 10

■ uses number and counting flexibly in solving problems.

Children respond well to questions such as 'How many do you have?' 'Have I got the same number?' especially where they have been encouraged to use the mathematical vocabulary that they hear the adults using. Gradually they begin to respond in sentences and this should be encouraged. Initially young children tend not to respond to reflective questions such as 'How do you know that one has six?', but with practice, and if adults model the sort of answers they might give, they learn to answer such questions.

Errors in number and counting

Children's understanding and use of number and counting will develop considerably between the ages of three and five. Most counting errors are due to immature concept development and so will indicate the kinds of experiences children will need to develop their understanding. Misconceptions and difficulties which children encounter with counting include:

- errors related to stable order principle:
    - counting words limited to first two or three and use of 'many' for greater quantities
    - counting words not yet stable: sometimes repeated, missed out or used in a different order
    - consistent errors made in counting string e.g. always missing out 14
    - making generalisation errors when counting larger numbers e.g. eighteen, nineteen, tenteen.
- errors related to one-to-one principle:
    - not able to coordinate touch and count: touching item to be counted more than once or not at all; reciting counting words faster than can touch
    - not recognising that number words with two syllables, e.g. sev-en, or number words with more than one word, e.g. twenty-two, are still single labels and so assigning these to more than one item.
- errors related to cardinal principle:
    - not understanding that final count word applies to the whole set
    - not stopping at target number when counting out.

For all these errors, children will benefit from more experience of counting, using a range of different contexts. All adults in the setting should be made aware of which children are experiencing difficulties, what types of errors they make and which experiences will help the children to improve their counting skills when counting opportunities arise in play. Focused activities can also be planned to give further, specific experience of counting.

In English, children need to learn ten discrete number names, then order them, in order to be able to count from one to ten. Once children begin to count beyond ten, our English number names are confusing. We say eleven, twelve, thirteen ... There is no discernable pattern of naming the numbers here, nor of helping the children to understand what these numbers mean. This makes counting more difficult than in some other languages, which use a system with structured counting numbers after ten: *ten-one, ten-two* ...; then *two-ten, two-ten-one* ... Children will benefit from having many opportunities to say number names in order so that the words become secure.

Joseph was six years old and had just learnt to count beyond twenty. He was in a class of children who were a year younger than him, in order to provide him with further early literacy and mathematical experiences. He announced one morning, 'I can do it!' and was asked to count for all of the children to hear. All went well at first: *eighteen, nineteen, twenty, twenty-one, twenty-two* ... And then *twenty-eight, twenty-nine, twenty-ten, twenty-eleven* ... Joseph had learnt that the number patterns repeat. What he still had not figured out was how the number names changed with the new decade.

Working in partnership with parents and carers

For partnership between home and setting to develop effectively, many parents will welcome opportunities to work with their children at home, reinforcing and extending the experiences which their children have had during the day. To support the partnership, some nurseries have set up lending libraries of books, toys and games which parents organise for themselves.

Activities for number and counting at home

These activities do not require any special equipment, as they make use of everyday items in the home.

Number and counting everyday things at home

- the cans of baked beans to go into the cupboard; the carrots into the rack; the apples into the fruit dish
- all the red cars; all the play people; the bricks as they go away; the stairs on the way to bed
- enough plates for everyone for dinner; biscuits for each child; fish fingers onto the plates; enough for everyone to have a sweet
- noticing and using numerals (number symbols) on the TV remote, telephone, calendar ...

Number and counting on the way to setting

- the houses along the street; the cars that go past; the trees in the garden; the windows in that house; the chimneys on the roof
- noticing the numerals on houses, cars, road signs; identifying which bus to catch by the number.

Number and counting when out shopping

- coins for paying for goods; all the pennies; the postage stamps for the letters; how many cakes for tea; enough oranges for everyone to have one
- noticing prices and comparing costs and quantities.

Number and counting games which can be played at home

These can be game packs for lending to parents, or homes may already have some. Again, they do not require sophisticated equipment, relying upon playing cards, boards, dice and dominoes. Special children's picture cards can be purchased from toy shops. If using

FIGURE 2.14 Domino match

standard playing cards you may want to take out the larger numbers and picture cards, starting with just 1–5 then 1–10.

- *Card games:*
    - *Snap:* matching for number.
    - *Pelmanism:* cards are placed face down either in rows or in a random arrangement, and two are turned over each time; when matching quantities are found, the player keeps that pair and the winner has the most pairs of matching cards.
- *Lotto:* picture lotto, where the items in the pictures can be counted, gives good experience of pointing and counting pictures.
- *Dominoes:* children match the ends of dominoes for 'sameness' (Figure 2.14).
- *Board games with a dice:* snakes and ladders, ludo and other simple track games can be played where children match the number on the dice with physically counting along the board's track.

Story books, songs and rhymes

Number rhymes and songs are widely available in books and recordings, and you may well know some from your own childhood. Story books have been specially written with a focus on number and counting including *Grey Rabbit's 1, 2, 3* – Alan Baker, *One Bear at Bedtime* – Mick Inkpen, *Anno's Counting Book* – Mitsumasa Anno, as well as a number of traditional stories such as The Three Billy Goats Gruff and The Three Little Pigs. In addition to this, almost all stories offer the opportunity to practise counting when discussing the illustrations.

3

Calculating and problem solving with number

The mathematics of calculation

As discussed in Chapter 2, understandings of number and of counting are essential for the development of calculation strategies (Thompson 1997c) and children need to understand the relationship between numbers before working on more structured calculation. These relationships include comparison, ordering and partitioning and are important concepts which will help their subsequent understanding of calculation and place value (tens and units).

Comparison

As children learn to count they will begin to compare sets of objects. The children may subitize the sets, line up objects to compare them or count them to determine which has more. Through these experiences they will develop an understanding of equivalence and non-equivalence. Comparative language can be explored when making comparisons between sets in the context of play such as a lot, few, too many, more, fewer. Adults can take opportunities to extend the children's understanding of number language:

> Farm animals: Let's put a lot of sheep in this field.
> Will you put a few cows with the sheep?
> Are there more cows or more sheep?
> How do you know?
> Dolls house: Shall we put more chairs into the doll's house kitchen?
> Will you help me to put the dolls on the chairs?
> Are there enough chairs for all the dolls? How can we tell?

Children are sensitive to comparisons of number in situations that matter to them: 'he's got more than me, it's not fair' is frequently heard by parents and early years practitioners. When comparing sets, adults tend to draw attention to the larger one 'There are more cups than plates on the table,' rather than 'There are fewer plates than cups'; so it is important that early years practitioners remember to use the 'few' and 'fewer' forms. Grammatically 'fewer' should be used when describing things that can be counted (cardinal number) while 'less' refers to things that are measured; however, many children, and some adults, will use 'less' in both contexts. Language such as 'a few more' and 'a lot less' can be very confusing to young children because of the use of 'few' with 'more' and 'a lot' with 'less'. Where such language is used, care must be taken to ensure that the children understand what is meant within the context. Once the children can compare sets, questions such as 'How many more?' and 'How do you know?' will extend their thinking.

Ordering

Making sense of ordinal, as well as cardinal number, is essential to developing understanding of number relationships, including the number operations of addition and subtraction. It is important that children see each number in the series as not just bigger than the previous one, but as 'one more' than the next counting number; similarly to see the smaller number as 'one less' than the previous counting number (Carpenter *et al.* 2003). Staircase towers and the number line can be used to discuss these relationships (Figure 3.1).

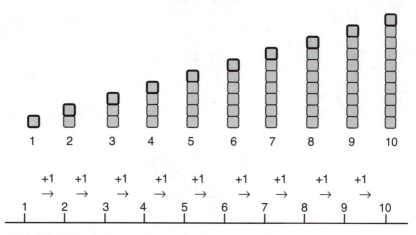

FIGURE 3.1 Using staircase towers and a number line to emphasise 'one more'; 'one fewer'

Partitioning

One of the aspects of subitizing discussed in Chapter 2 was to be able to recognise different representations of that number. This leads to the concept of partitioning, where a number can be broken down into two or more smaller numbers. So 6, for example, can be partitioned into 1 and 5; 2 and 4; 3 and 3; 1 and 2 and 3; 2 and 2 and 2; ... This understanding can lead easily to simple addition and subtraction: if 6 can be made up of 2 and 4, then 2 add 4 is equal to 6, and if 6 can be partitioned into 3 and 3, then 6 take away 3 is equal to 3. Partitioning can also be an interesting way of exploring patterns in number (Figure 3.2, and see Chapter 4).

So, partitioning offers opportunities to discuss the changes involved in addition and subtraction, as the objects are partitioned and described in terms of taking away some from the whole, then recombined, added together again (Figure 3.3). At this stage the formal words, and especially the symbols, are not important.

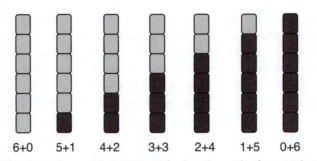

6+0   5+1   4+2   3+3   2+4   1+5   0+6

FIGURE 3.2 Exploring two colour partitioning patterns for 6: as the number for one colour increases the other decreases

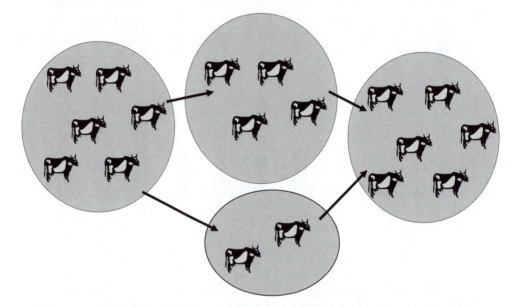

FIGURE 3.3 Partitioning and recombining can be described in terms of subtraction and addition: six cows in a field; two went into a different field leaving four (6 − 2 = 4); they came back together so there are six cows again (4 + 2 = 6)

As well as helping children to understand addition and subtraction, early work on partitioning has been found to help understanding of the structure of place value, being able to partition larger numbers into tens and units (Fischer 1990).

Early concepts of calculation

Young children are able to carry out simple calculations in context (Hughes 1986), however, they are not yet ready to do pages of 'sums', number calculations with symbols which are far removed from any concrete or real world context.

Some years ago children in a reception class were observed doing mathematics. They had sheets on which were written 'sums' such as 3 + 5 = □. Hayley was asked to explain what she was doing. She answered, 'well, you look at the first number, 3, and put three dots on it, then you look at the next number, 5, and put those dots on it and then you count how many dots . . . 1, 2, 3, 4, 5, 6, 7, 8 and you put that in the box'. Asked what she would do if she did not know how to write the number Hayley answered 'you use the numbers (number track) like this to see what it looks like', demonstrating counting to eight along the track. This produced:

$$\underset{3}{\overset{\cdots}{}} \quad + \quad \underset{5}{\overset{\cdots\cdots}{}} \quad = \quad \boxed{8}$$

Her sheet was almost complete by this time and mostly correct, although some of the other children were also following the procedure and producing incorrect answers due to counting errors. Hayley was able to copy the procedure that her teacher had recommended, but did she understand addition? On further questioning she could not explain why she was doing this work, what the + sign indicated or read the sentence back. She was able to count, recognise some numerals and follow the procedure but did not seem to have much understanding of addition.

Contrast this with another classroom where two children choose to play a game in which they take turns to throw a die and take that number of one sort of animal from a pile. They throw again and take that number of another sort of animal. They find out how many they have altogether and the child with the most animals wins a counter: five counters wins the game. Jane has thrown 5 and then 3. She uses her fingers to help calculate the total. Amanda had thrown a 6 on her first go and is about to throw again; 'I need to get more than two' she observes. These children are not worrying about symbols and procedures but are engaged in addition in an enjoyable and meaningful context. As they become more confident with calculation they can be encouraged to record their answers in their own way and eventually introduced to formal recording of calculations. Studies have shown that children who explore solving calculation problems in real life and play contexts, and develop their own strategies for calculation, do better at formal arithmetic later on (Carpenter *et al.* 1998).

Addition and subtraction structures

Problems solved by the use of addition and subtraction may differ not only in their contexts but also in their structure. Researchers have identified many different structures (Haylock 2010) but the following four are those which are common in early years setting.

The simplest structure of addition involves combining two sets and is easily modelled using physical apparatus: in the partitioning example above recombining four cows and two cows gave six cows. This structure is referred to as *aggregation* – bringing together or combining. But addition is also used to solve problems that are about growth: the bean plant was 6 cm tall and has grown another 4 cm. This structure is known as *augmentation* – increasing. As addition becomes a more abstract concept we do addition calculations without being concerned about the underlying structure of the problem, but in the early stages children may seem confused as to why we are using adding to solve a growth problem when they cannot see any separate things to bring together. Augmentation can be modelled using a number line or track (Figure 3.4).

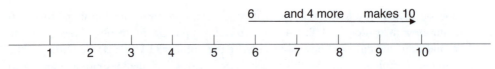

FIGURE 3.4 Modelling addition by increase on a number line

Subtraction also has a range of structures, two of which are important in the early years (Figure 3.5). Many people will think of subtraction as '*take away*' and this is its simplest structure, which again can be modelled with physical apparatus some of which are taken away from the set. In the partitioning example above two cows were taken away into a different field leaving four cows. But subtraction is also used to find the *difference* when comparing two numbers or sets of objects. If Jane has six sweets and her younger brother has only two, we use subtraction to work out how many more Jane has. In this case nothing is actually taken away, the two sets are compared and the extras counted.

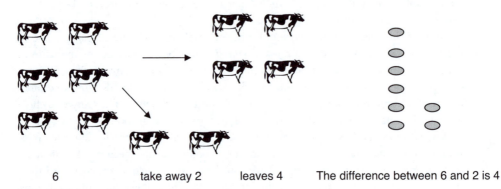

| 6 | take away 2 | leaves 4 | The difference between 6 and 2 is 4 |

FIGURE 3.5 Subtraction as take away and as difference

Division, fractions and multiplication structures

Division, fractions and multiplication are rarely mentioned specifically in Early Years Curricula; however, everyday activities will involve the use of these concepts: for example, sharing out pieces of fruit at snack time and making sure everyone has a fair share. Just as addition and subtraction have more than one structure, so do division, fractions and multiplication.

Division

Sharing involves breaking up a set into a number of equal groups; so $6 \div 2$ is to share six equally into two groups, each one containing three objects (Figure 3.6). Children sharing items between bowls in the home area will compare whether the bowls have fair shares (particularly if they are sharing out things to eat!) and they will find that sometimes quantities cannot be shared fairly, because there is a remainder. However, it is worth noting that in the real world sharing is often done unequally. A family of four sharing eight sausages for dinner may not have two each but the parents have more than the children. Children may therefore share unequally at times, not because they do not

6 **shared**   between 2   6 is three **groups of 2**

FIGURE 3.6 Division: 6 ÷ 2 as sharing and as grouping

understand equal sharing but because there is some social reason for it to be unequal (Gifford 2005).

Division by *grouping*, or repeated subtraction, involves making (or repeatedly subtracting) groups of a particular size from a set and finding out how many groups there are. So, 6 ÷ 2 could also be seen as making groups of two (Figure 3.6). In the early years this structure is less common than sharing though there may be situations when items are put into equal groups, such as pairing up the wellington boots or getting into groups of three to play a game. In singing number rhymes which count back in twos, e.g. 'Ten fat sausages sizzling in a pan', children experience repeated subtraction.

Fractions

In primary school children will be encouraged to look at fractions in two different ways: as fractions of a whole and fractions of a set. *Fractions of a whole* are used when one object, for example a cake or pizza, is divided up into pieces. Mathematically the pieces must be of equal size. *Fractions of a set* refer to the situation when a set of objects are shared equally; if twelve sweets are shared equally between two children they will each receive a half of the total (Figure 3.7). Sharing demonstrates the link between fractions and division: half of a set of eight is the same as 8 divided by 2.

In-depth study of fractions would be inappropriate at preschool, but children will use the concept in social contexts. The language of fractions may occur naturally especially in measuring contexts such as half a cup of water, cutting a piece of string or folding a cloth in half and then into quarters and in sharing situations with sets of objects, you've shared the cars and got half each. Children may not understand that halves must be the same size and will probably want the 'biggest half'!

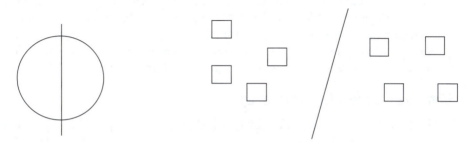

FIGURE 3.7 Fractions: half of a whole circle and half of a set of eight

Multiplication

The simplest structure of multiplication encountered in the early years is that of repeated addition. Multiplication is a more difficult concept to introduce as there are fewer situations where it naturally occurs in early years settings. Also multiplying may mean that the number rapidly increases beyond the children's counting range and has little meaning for them. Gelman and Gallistel (1986) saw multiplication as a development from counting, when repeatedly counting large numbers of objects becomes difficult to control – not a situation which arises naturally for a three- or four-year-old. But Nunes and Bryant (1996) argue that multiplication should not just be seen as in that way, children should be taught to see it as a one-to-many relationship: each one car has four wheels; each table can seat six children ... They admit that this multiplicative reasoning is complex so not something we expect to teach in the early years, but it does indicate some of the contexts in which we might think about multiplication. For older children who are confident in counting, learning multiplication in steps of twos, fives and tens can be explored starting from real world contexts, such as how many wellingtons we need for four children (1 child: 2 wellingtons) or the value of our 5p coins (1 coin: 5 pence).

Young children's understanding of addition and subtraction

Birth to three years of age

Very small babies are aware of changes in number. Babies of about five months were shown one or two dolls which were then hidden behind a screen and watched while a further doll was added $(1 + 1)$ or one taken away $(2 - 1)$. Sometimes a doll was also added or taken away through a hidden trap door. When the screen was lowered they looked longer if the result was not as they expected (Wynn 1992, 1998). The babies cannot of course do addition and subtraction but they have some expectation of the size of the results. At nine months a similar experiment using shapes on a screen shows that even with numbers beyond their subitization range, they expect an increase when they see more added and a decrease when some are removed (McCrink and Wynn 2004, 2009). By the end of their first year, they have a concept of 'more' with small numbers (Strauss and Curtis 1984) and can recognise order in sets of increasing size: one object, followed by two, followed by three ... (Brannon 2002).

By the age of two toddlers can construct equivalent sets of objects, for example putting one bone for each toy dog though this may be spatial matching rather than attention to number (Sarama and Clements 2009). Through their developing counting skills, young children begin to see how number quantities can be changed (Baroody 1987). Given a set of two objects in context they can respond to a request to make three by adding one more, or make one by removing one (Sarama and Clements 2009).

From three to about four years of age

At three children can compare small sets: in a game where they are shown two plates of objects and told that the one with more is the winner, they can tell which of the two plates has more (Gelman and Gallistel 1986). However, even at four if they are shown two

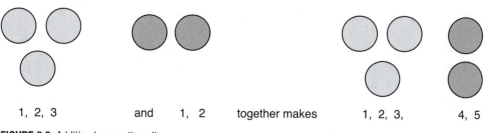

1, 2, 3   and   1, 2   together makes   1, 2, 3,   4, 5

FIGURE 3.8 Addition by counting all

equal sets and told that one set has six counters they may still count to see how many the other set has (Sarama and Clements 2009).

Children as young as three can add and subtract in context with small numbers (Hughes 1986). Young children will begin to solve addition problems by 'counting all': they will count out the first set, count out the second set, combine the two and count the total number (Baroody 1987; Figure 3.8). By four they may also know some number facts: one and one, two and one, two take away one, . . .

Children's initial understanding of subtraction is usually 'take away' through experiences such as eating some of their sweets and finding how many are left, sharing one of their cars or dolls with a friend in play or losing one of their shoes. It is worth noting that, while they will have had experience of the concept, for some children the words 'take away' will apply more to the Chinese restaurant than to mathematics. They will also compare small sets of objects and discuss which has more or fewer, but they will need encouragement to find out how many more.

At about four to five years of age

As they become more confident with the cardinal principle of counting (Chapter 2) children may realise that they do not need to count the first set again, but can use a 'counting on' strategy (Figure 3.9).

Some children as young as four or five will invent counting on and counting back strategies for themselves (Hughes 1986), though often this is limited to contexts in which the first set can be subitized and the number to be added on is small (Price 2000b). This is more common in children from families in higher socio-economic groups (Hughes 1986; Aubrey 1997).

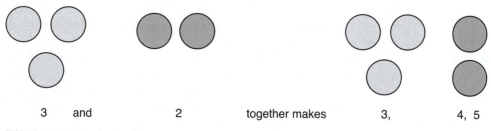

3   and   2   together makes   3,   4, 5

FIGURE 3.9 Addition by counting on

Counting on is complex, requiring the children to use three sub-skills:

- being able to say the count words beginning at any number
- shifting from seeing the final count word of the first set as cardinal to it being a new counting number
- beginning the count of the second set with the next count word (Secada *et al.* 1983).

At some point children will no longer need to use objects and rely instead on verbal counting procedures (Baroody 2000). Counting on mentally requires a fourth sub-skill as children need to keep track of how many they are counting on, often by using their fingers, while saying a different set of counting words: when adding 4 + 3 they need to say and think '4; 5 (is one more); 6 (is two more); 7 (is three more)'. As counting on is dependent on knowing the number words in order, children who can count on with numbers up to ten may not be able to do so confidently with larger numbers.

There is a wide variation and little pattern in the development of individual children's strategies (Siegler 1987) so that while some children start to count on in preschool, most do not understand this strategy and use it with confidence until they are about six years old (Baroody 2000; Sarama and Clements 2009; Fuson and Willis 1988). Explicit teaching of counting on strategies may not help: Weiland (2007) observes that children do not understand counting on if it is taught as a procedure to follow rather than emerging from a good understanding of ordinal counting. Once they have understood counting on, some children may choose to start counting on from the largest number, even if it is not presented first, as this requires fewer steps: adding 3 + 7 as 7, 8, 9, 10. This strategy is possible because addition is *commutative*, numbers can be added together in any order, though young children may use this strategy intuitively and not recognise it as a rule until they are older.

Counting back to solve subtraction problems is also complex, requiring

- knowing the count words backwards from any number
- saying the reverse count words in order
- at the same time keeping track of how many steps back have been taken.

Just as they may use addition by counting on, some four- or five-year-olds may begin to use counting backwards to subtract when working with sets they can subitize and small numbers to take away (Hughes 1986; Gelman and Gallistel 1986). However, children often find counting back more difficult than counting on. While the same words are used in counting on as are used in counting all, just shortened by not saying the first set of count words, the words used when counting back are considerably different from those used when taking away (Fuson 1984). Also the two simultaneous counts are working in opposite directions, for example when counting back 3 from 6 the child must think: 6, one fewer is 5, two fewer is 4, three fewer is 3.

By five children may know a wider range of number facts especially within those numbers which are easily subitized on dice patterns (Baroody 1985, 1989): they will learn combinations that make up to 5, then 7, then 10 and doubles to 10 then 20 (Sarama and Clements 2009). They will begin to build on their number facts to solve problems. Amanda (4½), playing the dice game above had scored 2 and 3:

AMANDA: It's five (instantly).

ADULT: That was quick, how did you do that?

AMANDA: I just knowed 2 and 2 was four, because that's just, like on the dices, so it's another one, five.

Amanda has a mental picture of the four dots on a die as two lots of two and uses her knowledge of double two to solve this new problem.

Young children's understanding of multiplication division and fractions

From three to about five years of age

Three-year-olds share using the dealing method of: 'one for you and one for me'. They seldom count to check that the shares are equal. Other children may just partition items giving one part to a friend and keeping one part for themselves, without any consideration of whether they each have the same quantity (Geist 2001; Pepper and Hunting 1998). Through sharing activities the language of fractions may be used; for example, in sharing out playing cards or dominoes, so that each player has 'half'.

Children encountering problems involving fractions of a whole, sharing a cake or a piece of ribbon etc., will often share unequally and talk about the bigger or smaller 'half' (Brizuela 2005). When asked to share a piece of string equally, four-year-old children cut two roughly equal pieces from a larger length, leaving the remainder. Most three- to five-year-old children engaged in practical sharing tasks were seen to share equally between two, and even between three and four, but when fraction language such as 'half', 'quarter', 'third', was used, hardly any of the children responded correctly (Hunting and Sharpley 1988).

So children can be encouraged to put items in groups, to consider what is fair when sharing out items, to use language of 'half' and 'quarter' and to count forwards and backwards in twos, and later in fives and tens. These experiences will help develop initial concepts of multiplication division and fractions, which they will meet more formally in their early years in school.

Experiences and key concepts in calculation

The number concepts considered in this chapter should be considered as building upon the counting experiences detailed in Chapter 2. The key concepts can be summarised as:

- Comparison, ordering and partitioning:
  - Compare sets and discuss relative sizes.
  - Explore the relationship between sequential numbers: know that each counting number is one more than the previous and one less than the number that follows.
  - Partition a set of objects and recombine them.
- Addition and subtraction:
  - Develop strategies such as finger counting and mental imagery, for addition and subtraction of small quantities.

- Begin to relate addition to combining two groups of objects and subtraction to 'taking away'.
- Use language of addition and subtraction such as and, more, altogether, add, take away.
- Begin to solve addition by counting on and subtraction by counting back.
- Division, fractions and multiplication:
  - Explore sharing an object or set equally.
  - Use language of division, fractions and multiplication, such as share, fair, same, part, half, lots of.
  - Explore and discuss situations that involve dividing a set into equal groups such as putting four pencils into each pencil pot.
  - Explore and discuss situations that involve calculation in one-to-many relationships such as how many wheels there are on a set of cars.

Where possible, each of these experiences arises out of the everyday experiences and play of the children in a setting and out of their developing competence with counting. Specially planned role play activities and stories may also offer contexts in which changes in number can be expressed in terms of calculation. Many of these experiences will also be in the context of problem solving and may offer opportunities for the children's own recording, as discussed in Chapter 1.

These experiences are for the whole range of early years children who may be in a wide range of settings, including some nearly six-year-olds who are about to move into primary school and some may not be appropriate in settings with only 3–4-year-olds.

Making connections

Connections are an essential element of mathematics and it is important that number operations are not learnt in isolation but that connections are made between them (Askew and Wiliam 1995). We showed earlier how the process of partitioning and recombining can make early links between addition and subtraction which are *inverse* operations; they reverse the effect of each other. Understanding this means that children do not need to learn a set of subtraction facts since if $4 + 5 = 9$, then $9 - 4 = 5$. Children as young as four will use this understanding, though they may not understand it fully for some years. We have seen already seen how division can be seen as repeated subtraction, multiplication as repeated addition, and how division and factions are related. Multiplication and division are also the inverse of each other as children will find in primary school.

Children may be exploring more than one of these concepts at any time. Where possible, therefore, connections should be made between different number operations rather than treating them as separate concepts.

Compare sets and discuss relative sizes

In many areas of the setting there will be opportunity to discuss the relative sizes of sets of objects. The children may compare how many toys they each have (Figure 3.10), how many bricks they have used in building their towers, observing that this is not necessarily

FIGURE 3.10 Comparing sets: having shared out the frogs, the boys check to see that they have the same number

the tallest, or finding who has collected the most items on the nature trail. The children will naturally discuss and compare their ages and personal numbers such as how many brothers and sisters they have or how many of the latest toys, games or books. Where the sets are different sizes children's understanding can be extended to finding the difference between the two (subtraction as difference), or working out how many more would need to be added to make them the same.

Explore the relationship between sequential numbers

The children need to learn that each counting number is one more than the previous and one less than the number that follows. As indicated above, this could be done on a focused activity with sequential towers of bricks, or using a number line to 'model' discussions about how old a child is, how old they were last year and will be next year, or how many snack items they will have if they are given another, or eat one. The language of 'one more' and 'one fewer' can be used when discussing nursery rhymes such as 'An elephant went out to play' or 'Five little monkeys bouncing on the bed'.

Partition a set of objects and recombine them

There will be occasions in the children's play when objects are partitioned and recombined, for example toys will be shared and then put back together for storage, but attention will rarely be given to the numbers involved. For this reason focused activities may be needed to bring out the mathematics and use mathematical language to talk about what it happening using, for example, small world activities such as farm animals in fields or enacting stories with finger puppets. Children could be asked how many

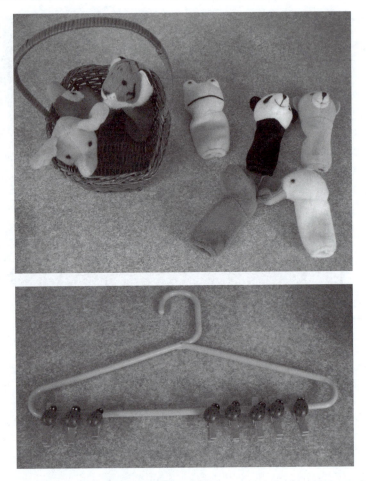

FIGURE 3.11 Partitioning: two activities partitioning eight

different towers they can build with six bricks in each using two different colours of brick and look at the number of each colour, or play with clothes pegs on a line or hanger (Figure 3.11). Where possible such activities should be embedded in a story context or set up as a game.

Working on these concepts in context will develop early calculation concepts. Children will begin to use addition and subtraction to describe number situations, particularly in response to sensitive adult intervention.

Begin to relate addition to combining two groups of objects and subtraction to 'taking away'

Through their experience of partitioning and comparing, children will already have developing concepts of combining and taking away. Adults working with the children will need to model using the language in context so that the children begin to explain what the concepts mean. For example, counting all the red bricks, then the blue bricks,

FIGURE 3.12 'There was five ladybirds (centre) and only one left so four flew away'

then counting all of them leads to an understanding of 'there are three blue bricks and two red ones. There are five bricks altogether.' Similarly, with subtraction as 'taking away' children can use materials to model this. 'I have five sheep. I'll give you two. Now I have three left.' This will encourage the children's own explanations:

- Tara says: There are two dolls in the bed and two in the cot. They can sit on the chairs. (Child points to four chairs at the table.)
- Sam makes patterns on a pegboard, using four pegs. 'What if each pattern had two colours?' Sam changes one of them, using one red and three blue. He explains 'Three and one is four. I can do this one too. Look.' He changes it to two green and two red.
- Matt says 'There was five ladybirds and only one left so four flew away' (Figure 3.12).

Develop strategies such as finger counting and mental imagery

As they become more proficient children will be able to solve simple calculation problems mentally, sometimes using fingers to support them, in contexts where there are no physical objects. They can be encouraged to use mental imagery, for example through games in which they have to visualise objects hidden under a cloth and calculate how many if one is added or taken away. At carpet time 'imagine' games can be played which help develop cardinal images of number and calculation such as: 'close your eyes and imagine two of your favourite biscuits on a plate in front of you. Now I am going to give you another biscuit. Can you see it there on the plate? How many biscuits have you got now? Hold up the same number of fingers to show me. Now you can eat two of your biscuits. Have you got any left? …' Working together with children in this way offers the opportunity for adults to model how these calculations would be written (2 + 1 = 3).

Playing with a number line or floor number track helps children to develop an ordinal image of number as children can jump or step along the track, and look at how far they have moved. 'Let's start on three. Now jump along to five. How many jumps did you make? How many jumps back to three?'

TABLE 3.1 Language of addition, subtraction and equals

+	–	=
add	subtract	equals
and	take away	is the same as
altogether	minus	is equal to
plus	difference between	makes
total	less	leaves
more	remove	is equivalent to
sum	fewer . . .	. . .
combine . . .		

Use language of addition and subtraction

Throughout these activities, the children will be hearing and beginning to use the language of addition and subtraction such as and, more, altogether, add, take away. It is worth noting here that, while symbols are very concentrated representations of a concept, we use a range of spoken words to describe how the numbers are related (Table 3.1).

Some of these words only make sense in some contexts. 'Makes' is a construction word which can be used in place of equals when adding but not subtracting, whereas 'leaves' indicates something has been left after taking away and does not make sense in an adding sentence. When working with young children we do not want to confuse them by using all of these words at the same time so settings may want to give some thought as to which words they will most often use. A poster on the wall can remind adults during unplanned interventions, and inform parents. As a rule, the terms that are most used in everyday language such as 'and, altogether, take away, is the same as, makes or leaves' make a good starting point, but do not be afraid to use more mathematical words once the children become more familiar with the concept. Children are used to objects and people having more than one name and a child who can cope with dinosaur and Tyrannosaurus rex should be able to cope with subtract and equals.

Begin to solve addition by counting on and subtraction by counting back

We saw earlier how young children may count on or back with small numbers where they can keep a mental track of the cardinal value. They will not use these strategies with larger numbers until they have mastered all the sub-skills:

1 Being able to say the count words forwards and backwards, beginning at any number
2 Shifting from seeing the final count word of the first set as cardinal to it being a new counting number
3 Beginning the count of the second set with the next (or previous) count word and

4 Keep track of how many they are counting on or back while saying a different set of counting words.

These indicate the sorts of experiences children will need prior to learning counting on and back. Chapter 2 addressed the importance of learning more complex counting. Drawing attention to the cardinal value of a set and then adding one more, reinforcing that the next total is the next counting word, as described above will help the development of sub-skills 2 and 3, while the fourth will develop as the children become more proficient at using their fingers or mental image to represent number. Games can be designed which use both symbols and representations of sets of objects, for example adding games using two dice, one with dots and the other with numerals. These may encourage recognising the cardinal value of the numeral and then adding on to it. However, many young children will solve this by representing the numeral set on their fingers and then counting all, an indication that counting on is, as yet, a step too far for them.

Explore sharing an object or set equally

Sharing activities will normally occur as part of a social event, such as sharing out food and drinks at snack time, or during play. The sharing at this stage will probably involve cutting up a whole item such as a cake or sharing a set of items one at a time around the group, repeated until all have been given out. Where children have their snack in a small group, the adult can discuss the sharing out with them, using language such as fair, enough, the same, one left over. Fraction language can be introduced whilst children are, for example, cutting up dough, sharing out dominoes to play a game, or folding a cloth:

That's a big cake! Will you give me half?
How many pieces are there now? Are they the same size? Is that fair?
How many bricks are there?
Tom would like half of them.
How many have you? How many has Tom?
You have half each.

Use language of division, fractions and multiplication

While there is no requirement explicitly to teach concepts of division, fractions and multiplication, it is important to consider the language patterns used around these concepts and use the correct terms appropriately in context (Table 3.2).

Explore and discuss situations that involve dividing a set into equal groups

There may be some activities in the setting where objects are put into equal groups. These might include planting three seeds in each flowerpot, putting the same number of pencils into each pencil pot, storing toys four to a box . . . The attention here should be to making the groups of equal size, appealing to the children's sense of fairness. For settings which have an organised PE session, a grouping game can be played. The children move freely

TABLE 3.2 Language of division, fractions and multiplication

÷	FRACTIONS	X
divide	divide	lots (or sets) of
equal share	share	double
fair share	equal part	times
group	half	triple . . .
	quarter	
	third . . .	

around the room until the leader calls out a small number and the children have to get into groups of that number. If you have a large die, this can be thrown to generate the number. Getting into groups of one can sometimes cause confusion. Groups of any other number will highlight that there are sometimes remainders.

Explore and discuss situations that involve calculation in one-to-many relationships

The one-to-many aspect of multiplication can be seen as the inverse (opposite) or the grouping aspect of division which we have just considered. Here we start with a number of groups, pots or boxes and work out how many children, seeds, pencils or toys there are in total. Multiplication questions such as 'if there are four wheels on each car and five cars, how many wheels?', or 'if we need two slices of bread for each sandwich and want to make six sandwiches, how many slices of bread do we need?' could be used. While the calculation as multiplication will be beyond many of the children (though some may be confident with double numbers up to six), finding ways to solve these problems will engage them with the concept.

Concept map

Table 3.3 shows the concepts outlined above in matrix form, together with examples of vocabulary which can be developed along with example activities which demonstrate how these concepts might be explored with the children. The map can be used as a basis for planning and assessment checkpoints and key questions are given to show possible learning outcomes.

Planning number experiences

The range of experiences for developing understanding of number will come from both planned activities and incidental interventions from adults in children's play. Experience of comparing, ordering and partitioning, using number operations and solving problems using number can occur in any early years play environment and it is the role of the adult to engage with the children and to help them to extend their language of number and their understanding through careful, sensitive commentating, questioning and challenging.

TABLE 3.3 Concept map for calculating and problem solving with number

KEY CONCEPT	VOCABULARY	EXAMPLES OF ACTIVITIES	ASSESSMENT CHECKPOINTS	KEY QUESTIONS
Compare sets and discuss relative sizes Calculate difference between two sets	Number words to 5 then to 10, more, fewer, same, fewest, most	'Grab a handful' – the children take a handful of small bricks or toys (of suitable size to create manageable numbers) and compare their grab	• Compares small numbers of objects visually or by counting • Uses comparative language • Can calculate difference	• Who has more/ fewer? • Who has most/ fewest? • How do you know? • How many more?
Explore the relationship between sequential numbers	Counting numbers	Counting how many and one more; beads on lace; food on a plate	• Knows how many for one more/fewer	• How many are there? (add/ subtract one) Now how many are there?
Partition a set of objects and recombine them	Apart, altogether, some, all	Make different necklaces with ten beads on each using only two colours	• Can count each colour separately • Finds total	• How many of each colour? • How many altogether?
Develop strategies such as finger counting, mental imagery, for addition and subtraction of small quantities	Counting numbers; next; before, more, fewer, add, take away, left	Hiding pennies in a money box/play people in the bus; put in two more/take two away; how many now	• Adds and subtracts small unseen quantities with reasonable accuracy	• I put three pennies in the money box, and now two more. How many are there? How do you know? • Five people on the bus. Two get off. How many are left? How do you know?
Begin to relate addition to combining two groups of objects, and subtraction to 'taking away'	Counting numbers, add, take away, leave, and, makes	Combining groups to find the total of: farm animals; cars; play people; threaded beads . . . Taking away from groups of things: crockery and cutlery in the home area; bricks . . .	• Adds and subtracts using materials with reasonable accuracy	• How many cars have you each got? How many altogether? • You have six bricks. If I took three how many would you have? How did you work it out?

(Continued)

TABLE 3.3 (Continued)

KEY CONCEPT	VOCABULARY	EXAMPLES OF ACTIVITIES	ASSESSMENT CHECKPOINTS	KEY QUESTIONS
Use language of addition and subtraction	And, altogether, add, take away, fewer, less, more	Activities above for partitioning, addition and subtraction	• Can use appropriate language for addition, subtraction and equals	• Is there a different way we could say it?
Begin to solve addition by counting on and subtraction by counting back	Count on, count back, add take away	Card and dice games with mixture of numerals and pictures of sets	• Counts on from the first number • Counts back to subtract	• Do you need to count those again? How many have you got here? • What would one less be?
Explore sharing an object or set equally and use vocabulary of division and fractions	Counting numbers; same, more, fewer, different, nearly, share, fair, same, different, nearly, half	Sharing at snack time; sharing out playing cards, dominoes, fairly; putting the same number of dolls into each pram; two play people into each room in the house; cutting paper/clay into two equal pieces; comparing size and shapes of bricks in block play: half the length, half a circle	• Shares a quantity into equal groups or cuts a whole into two similar (equal) pieces • Recognises when a sharing is unfair • Describes result as a share, half, same, etc.	• Share these between us; how many do you have? How many do I have? Is that fair? • How could we make this one cake between us? How much do we get?
Explore and discuss situations that involve dividing a set into equal groups	Equal, same, how many groups	Putting two pieces of fruit on each plate, five toy animals each for a game, by grouping	• Can put items into groups • Can say how many groups there are	• Is each plate/ group equal? • How many plates/ groups?

Explore and discuss situations that involve calculation in one-to-many relationships	Each, altogether, lots of e.g. 6 lots of 2	Work out how many slices of bread are needed for six sandwiches; How many fingers do we each have? How many altogether in our group of five?	• Understands that 2 or 10 need to be added each time • Finds ways to calculate	• How many would we need/have if we had another person?
Use developing understanding of calculation to solve practical problems	Counting numbers; add, take away, difference, share, What could we try next? How did you work it out?	Finding the same number in different contexts; totalling how many beads there are; working out the cost of buying items in the shop	• Uses number-based strategies to solve problems	• How many do you think there are? • How do you know that? • How did you work it out? • What could we try next?

Setting up environments for calculating and problem solving with number activities

Provide items for counting and sharing; materials which can be cut up, broken down or built up, such as dough; construction and block play, beads and laces; all can be used to encourage understanding of number concepts.

Recording

As discussed in Chapter 1, encourage recording by providing paper and pencils, white boards and pens, calculators etc. in the role play areas, such as the home area, cafe, shop and hospital. Children will enjoy writing shopping lists, recording how much money they spend or keeping a tally of how many drinks they serve. They may draw pictures or use tallies, rather than write numerals and calculations as their record. The calculator will be familiar to children as they will have seen it in use at home and in shops and they will include its use in their play. As they become more familiar with the symbols they will want to explore its potential as a tool to help solve problems. Numeral apparatus – such as magnetic, wooden or plastic numerals – can also be available for children to use for recording.

Number games

Games which involve any sort of score or throwing of dice can be adapted so that two numbers are added together (Figure 3.13). Card games can be played which involve turning over two cards, shown as numerals or dots according to the stage

FIGURE 3.13 Addition: rolling two balls down the chute into numbered crates and calculating who gets the highest score

of the children's learning, and finding two which add up to a given total instead of two which match. Games such as dominoes can be adapted so that instead of matching the tiles, the next tile should be one more than the free end. You may want to explain that they need to cycling back to 0 to follow a 6 as there is no 7, or let them problem solve for themselves.

Books, rhymes and songs

Books which include pictures with an increase or decrease of items on each page can be used. Look out too for books which involve other elements of calculation such as sharing e.g. *The Doorbell Rang* by Pat Hutchins. Many number action rhymes count up or down and can be discussed in terms of adding one or taking one away.

Number operations

Children will be problem solving with numbers in many areas of the setting, working out how many more bricks are needed to make the two towers of the bridge equal heights, how many cups are needed if there are two children and three dolls at the tea party, sharing toys out for games . . . Look out for additional resources which may encourage this, for example providing dough food in the home area, which can offer more experiences of sharing, addition and subtraction. Similarly, children can be encouraged to use their number skills through adult focused activities such as cooking.

The children may surprise you, like three-year-old Grace who was able to use calculation to solve a real problem. Following a walk round town, children were asked to draw something they had liked looking at. Grace sat quietly for a while then drew some sky. She drew five houses, created by drawing the dots for squares and triangles and joining them to make lines. The practitioner asked what she had liked the best:

GRACE: I liked the row of houses, but I need to draw four more.
ADULT: Wow, that is fantastic! Why do you need four more?
GRACE: There was nine and I have five and I need to do four more.

She was offered another sheet of paper and drew some more sky and four more houses. When finished she asked for some sticky tape to join the two sheets of paper, then showed the adult saying 'There, now I have nine houses like on the walk' (Figure 3.14).

Number track or line

A number line or number track can be used to focus the children's attention on one more and one fewer as they move along the line. Two children could choose a number each to stand by and the others work out how many steps between them (subtraction as difference). Similarly board games which use numbered tracks can be used.

Adult intervention in children's play

One of the key roles of the adult is to recognise when it is appropriate to intervene in children's play. The intervention needs to extend the children's understanding, through

FIGURE 3.14 'There, now I have nine houses like on the walk'

careful commentating, discussion and questioning, encouraging children to use the mathematical language that they have developed so far and helping them to become familiar with new concepts and related vocabulary. The intervention must be supportive of what the children are doing and not interfere in their play. The following are everyday examples of events:

- James and Abigail are building towers with two different coloured bricks. The adult comments 'I can see that James has got three red bricks and three blue bricks, that's six altogether.' James ($3\frac{1}{2}$) does not respond but looks at the bricks and is hearing the language of addition.
- Ying Sum put three dolls into the aeroplane. She said 'One more, now there are four!' The nursery nurse asked 'And one more? Now how many?' 'Five!'
- Jamie and Peter, who had been working quietly at building trucks using a construction kit, had started to argue about how many wheels each child had. An adult intervened:

'Can you share the wheels between you?' Peter replied 'No. Jamie got four and I only got three. That's not fair.' The adult suggested that there should be another wheel in the box. They looked. Jamie said 'That's it. Now we can have the same, four each.'

■ On the table in front of the four children was a plate of orange segments. The adult asked 'Are there enough for us all to have one? How can we find out?' Emma suggested 'One each; one for you and one for you ... and there's one left over. We've all got two.'

Problem-solving strategies for number

Within children's play there will be opportunities for the adult to ask questions which help the children to use their number skills in order to solve problems. Questions that encourage problem-solving skills (Clarke and Atkinson 1996) to develop include:

■ What if there was one more/fewer?
■ How many more is that?
■ How can we give everyone the same?

Other questions can encourage evaluation of the project, such as:

■ Can you find another way?
■ I don't know if that would work. Let's find out.
■ (To another child in the group) What do you think?

Adult focused activities

The following activities show a range of experiences that can be achieved through carefully planned focused activities for number. Such planning will enable the key concepts as outlined above to begin to develop.

Farm animals

An activity for a group of up to six children.

■ *Purpose:* To count out given quantities, matching the numeral to the count; to compare quantities and use appropriate number language.
■ *Materials:* sets of farm animals with at least as many different animals as children in group.
■ *Language:* number words, number, count, more, the same, nearly the same, match. . .

How to begin

Place the animals on the table and ask the children to sort them into groups. Discuss their sorting and why they have chosen these groupings.

Ask the children to choose a group and ask questions such as:

- How many animals are there in your set?
- Which group has more than yours?
- Which group has the same number as yours?

Ask the children to take turns to count out a given quantity. Let the others watch and check, which will give them experience of counting without touching:

- Beth, please put three sheep in the field.
- Let's count them together: one, two, three. Yes, three sheep.
- Now, Kerry, will you put four cows in the cowshed?
- David, how many sheepdogs shall we put with the sheep?

Children can ask each other questions using numbers and number language, and try new vocabulary.

Here comes the bus

An activity for a small or large group.

- *Purpose:* to practise addition and subtraction.
- *Materials:* a poster-sized picture or drawing of a bus and ten children's faces with Blu-tack on back.
- *Language:* all together, more, fewer, add, take away.

How to begin

This activity is based on a rhyme:

> Here comes the bus, it soon will stop
> Hurry up children in you hop
> Three inside and four on top
> How many altogether?

Each time it is said a different pair of numbers can be used. When playing this with young children (3–4 years) use a bus picture and model the sum sticking the children's faces on the windows. After a while just having the picture of the bus will enable the children to imagine the faces and eventually they can do without the bus altogether. Numbers bonds (combinations) that make the same total each time may be used, for example 1 + 6, 2 + 5 and 3 + 4.

Once the children are familiar with the rhyme, a story can be developed about more children getting on or off, or some of the children running up and down stairs in order to change the numbers rather than repeating the rhyme each time.

Flip-its

An activity for a group of any size (use a bigger flip-it with whole class).

- ■ *Purpose:* to understand partitioning and number combinations to 10.
- ■ *Materials:* A flip-it as described below.
- ■ *Language:* number words, how many.

How to begin

You will need to make a flip-it in advance. This consists of a set of cards about 7 cm square, some plain and others with identical pictures drawn or stuck on, laid out in a pattern and stuck together between two layers of sticky backed plastic with a slight space between the cards so that it can fold on the seams (Figure 3.15). You may want to choose pictures which relate to a favourite story or activity, but keep the pictures identical or the children will be distracted by which pictures they can see rather than how many. This size is suitable for a small group, for a bigger group use bigger cards and pictures.

Show the children the flip-it and ask how many bears they can see. Once they have established that they can see ten, fold over the left hand column towards you and ask:

- ■ How many can you see now?
- ■ How many do you think I can see?

Turn the flip-it round so they can check their answers. Repeat with other combinations. Once the children get better at this activity, you may use a number sentence, for example,

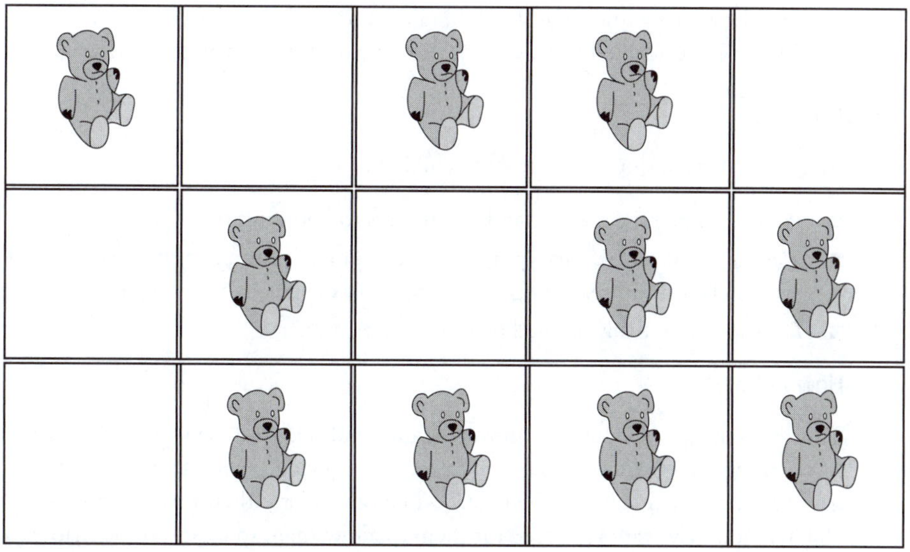

FIGURE 3.15 Flip-it for number combinations to 10

'yes, because nine and one makes ten'; or you may choose to focus on subtraction and say 'yes, because ten take away nine leaves one'. This may provide an opportunity with some children to model how we write the number sentence.

Flip-its can be made with fewer than 10 pictures to practise other number bonds; just make sure that it can be folded to make all the required combinations. The children enjoy playing with these and 'testing' their friends.

Hide the rabbits

An activity for a group of four children.

- *Purpose:* to encourage mental imagery in solving addition and subtraction.
- *Materials:* up to ten toy rabbits (or any other suitable toys); a cloth or box to hide the rabbits in.
- *Language:* how many, more, fewer, add, take away.

How to begin

Introduce the children to the rabbits and allow them to play with them for a while if they are a new resource. Explain that rabbits live in burrows underground and this will be represented by the cloth or box.

Invite one of the children to choose two rabbits, show them to the others and hide them. Ask 'how many rabbits are hiding?' Add another rabbit and ask how many again. How do you know? Watch children to see how they are solving the addition: they may be using their fingers to represent the rabbits, pointing to the cloth and imagining where the rabbits might be, 'seeing' them mentally or just knowing two and one are three. Continue the game adding or subtracting a few at a time according to the children's level of understanding. Once they understand the task the children like to be involved in choosing how many to change and taking turns to make the change.

This could be adapted to fit with any story which is popular in the setting.

First to four

An activity for a group of about three children.

- *Purpose:* to practise adding (and extend this to counting-on).
- *Materials:* two dotted dice (plus one with numerals for extension), paper and pencils or whiteboards for recording, counters, cubes or stickers for winners.
- *Language:* how many altogether, most.

How to begin

The children take it in turns to throw the dice and calculate their total. They may do this by counting the dots, using their fingers or just knowing the number combinations. They have to record or remember their total while others have their turn; with some younger children you may want to record for them to allow them to focus on the mathematics.

When everyone has had a turn the person with the highest total wins a point (counter, sticker etc.). The first to gain four points wins the game.

When the children are competent playing with dotted dice you may wish to replace one of them with a numeral die. Observe how the children deal with this: some may be encouraged to count on from the value of the numeral, others may represent the numeral on their fingers or imagine the dots and still use a count all strategy.

Baking

An activity for four children.

- *Purpose:* to use the language of division and fractions.
- *Materials:* ingredients for making cakes; scales, bowls, spoons, bun tins.
- *Language:* share, fair, the same, more, less, fewer, number words . . .

How to begin

Make the cake mixture as usual. When it is ready to be divided into the bun tins ask:

- How many bun tins do you think we can fill?
- Will there be enough for us all to have a cake?
- How many do you think we can each have?

The children share the cake mixture out, and then discuss what they have done.

- Does each cake have the same amount of mix? Is that fair?
- How many cakes will there be?
- How many people can have cakes?
- If we share them out how many can we have each?

As the children answer the questions, there will be opportunities to observe the strategies they use to count and to share.

When the cakes are cooked and cool, they can be decorated. Children can decide how many sweets will be placed on each cake. When it is time to eat the cakes discussion can include:

- Choose a cake each.
- Jack, how many sweets are there on your cake?
- Who has more sweets on their cake than Jack?
- If you eat two cakes how many sweets will you eat?

Again, this activity could be adapted and related to a story, for example biscuits could be made and discussed in relation to *The Doorbell Rang* by Pat Hutchins (1986).

Involving other adults in the planned activities

Where number experiences have been planned, through either adult initiated or adult focused activities, all adults should be aware of the questions that can be asked to encourage the children to use number language. During the planning sessions, the adults agree on the range of language that might be appropriate and include it on their planning sheet for the week. Number language should be used consistently and correctly. When referring to a cardinal number of countable objects, use few or fewer, not less, which refers to a measurement, such as 'There is less water in this cup', though less can also be used when discussing ordinal numbers in a number line. Opportunities for children to record numbers during the week will occur incidentally. Adults can encourage children to record and to read back their recording, whether pictures, tallies or symbols have been used.

Setting up environments for calculating and problem solving with number

Table 3.4 shows suggestions for contexts across the setting which could offer opportunities for discussions about calculation during child initiated learning, or be set up for adult initiated or focused activities.

Assessment

What to look for

Regular observations of children's use of number will identify their current knowledge and skills and indicate the experiences they need to develop further. Use the assessment checkpoints and key questions in Table 3.3. Observations, with evidence of the child's behaviour to support their understanding, can be recorded.

Observations will show whether children can:

- recognise that a quantity is larger/smaller than another
- combine two sets and say how many
- take away a quantity and say how much is left
- calculate how many more/fewer one set is than another
- begin to use counting on or counting back to solve addition and subtraction
- make fair shares and equal groups
- use appropriate mathematical language for addition, subtraction multiplication, division and fractions
- record changes in number (calculations) using a recognisable system (pictures, tallies, symbols).

Children respond well to questions such as 'There are some blue and red bricks here. Can you share them out with me? Can you find another way?' especially where they have been encouraged to use the mathematical vocabulary that they hear the adults using. Gradually they begin to respond in sentences and this should be encouraged.

Three- and four-year-olds find it more difficult to answer questions which ask 'How do you know?' such as 'How do you know that the answer is ten?', or 'How did you work it out', and tend not to respond. However, with practice, and with examples of how they might answer given by adults, they do begin to answer the 'How do you know?' type of question in a satisfactory way.

TABLE 3.4 Calculating and problem solving with number activities across areas of the setting

ENVIRONMENT	CONCEPT/SKILL	CONTEXT
carpet time	• grouping • comparing, and calculating difference	• children get into pairs or threes for activities or discussion • discussions about family size, ages . . .
daily routines	• addition and subtraction; comparison • making fair shares	• registration: how many children here today, how many absent? Is that more or fewer than yesterday? • snack time: sharing out orange segments; does everyone have the same amount?
art and craft areas	• making fair shares • using fraction language	• sharing out some sequins for collage: does everyone have the same amount? • playdough: sharing the lump of dough equally, cutting the cakes in half
table top games and collections	• board games with numbered tracks, dice • number cards and dominoes	• how many more will you need to win? What dice numbers would add up to this? • when matching numbers, discussing double numbers (6 and 6); adapting games to include calculation rather than just matching
construction	• counting one more/fewer • comparing and calculating difference	• block play: how many? and one more/fewer? • building matching towers for a bridge, train tracks
role play	• adding and subtracting • using fraction language	• home area: two dolls and teddy in the cot: how many altogether? Teddy out of cot: now how many? • sharing out the food: half each
small world play	• comparing and partitioning • adding and subtracting small quantities	• putting some cars on the road and others by the petrol pumps; which has more?; how many altogether? • marina: how many sailboats? and one more/fewer?
outside play	• counting on and back • addition, recording	• number track games • playing skittles: how many have you knocked down? Adding scores over two or more games and keeping a record • scoring throwing beanbags into numbered hoops
pets	• making fair shares	• feeding the rabbits: put the lettuce in the bowls; give them the same amount

Possible errors in calculating and problem solving with number

Counting underpins calculation and therefore the possible counting errors listed in Chapter 2 will also apply to the concepts and skills discussed in this chapter. When counting on a number track or line children may count the number they are already on before moving on.

When sharing objects or sets of items children may make unequal shares when dividing sets of objects or not share out all of the items or object: sharing out some of the fruit or cutting a part of a cake for each person but leaving the rest. This sort of sharing is common in the real world where parents may be given more food than children or the cake may be kept for another day. In mathematical situations emphasis need to be put on sharing equally and sharing out all the resource.

Another source of error arises from the concept of zero which can be confusing as 'nothing' cannot be counted. Children will benefit from discussing what 'nothing' means in different contexts.

Working in partnership with parents and carers

There are many number-based activities which may already be used at home. Where the purpose of an activity is clear to parents and carers they will be encouraged to use carefully selected number vocabulary, as well as to become more aware of opportunities which involve number in normal, everyday life.

Activities at home for developing understanding of number

These activities do not require any special equipment, as they make use of everyday items in and around the home.

Using numbers

- *Addition and subtraction:* at breakfast counting how many slices of toast each person eats, how many in total, how many have been eaten.
- *Division and fractions:* sharing out sweets equally; counting to check; cutting a small cake, or breaking a bar of chocolate, in half to share.

Shopping

- *Addition and subtraction:* involve children in discussions about money and change.
- *Multiplication:* how many plums will we need if we each eat two?

Number games

- *Picture cards:* finding cards which total three, four or five.
- *Dominoes:* playing fives, where the two touching numbers total five.
- *Board games and larger numbers:* snakes and ladders, with numerals to 100.

Story books

- *Cockatoos*: Quentin Blake: there are ten cockatoos; some are hiding, how many are still missing?
- *Kipper's Toybox*: Mick Inkpen: the number of toys keeps changing as the mice take and return them.
- *The Doorbell Rang*: Pat Hutchins: sharing cookies

and many more.

Pattern

Pattern is an essential aspect of mathematics; indeed some have argued that mathematics is all about the study of pattern (Orton 2005; Devlin 2003). Recognising that a sequence of objects makes a pattern, explaining why, being able to copy, extend and create a new pattern are early steps towards an understanding of spatial patterns and number patterns, and an appreciation of the power of algebra. The study of algebra can be exciting as the proposals for the Mathematics National Curriculum recognised (DES 1988):

> Mathematics is not only taught because it is useful. It should also be a source of delight and wonder, offering pupils intellectual excitement, for example, in the discovery of relationships, the pursuit of rigour and the achievement of elegant solutions.

Talking about patterns also encourages children to develop reasoning skills.

Pattern is also an essential aspect of everyday life. Our brains look for patterns in order to make sense of the world. Pattern is all around us in the natural world and in the built environment, and we experience patterns through sound and touch as well as visually.

What is pattern?

Young children will sometimes describe a picture as a 'pretty pattern' emphasising its colour and attractiveness, but in order to be a mathematical pattern it must have some element of repetition or symmetry. Pattern can be described as a systematic arrangement of numbers or shapes which follows a given rule. Three main types of pattern can be identified: repeating, growing and symmetrical pattern.

Repeating patterns

Simple *repeating* patterns are made up of repeated sequences of shapes with each sequence in the same order. The repeat may be in a straight line (linear), or repeated below the original, or even, in more complex patterns, diagonally below (Figure 4.1).

Growing patterns

Growing patterns of shapes or numbers have a similar relationship between one element and the next but the shape or number increases (or decreases) in size (Figure 4.2).

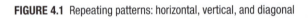

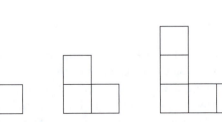

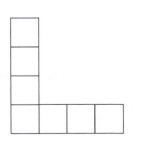

FIGURE 4.1 Repeating patterns: horizontal, vertical, and diagonal

FIGURE 4.2 A growing pattern (which relates to the odd numbers 1, 3, 5, 7 . . .)

Symmetrical patterns

Symmetry is used in creating patterns by reflection and by rotation, and can be found in nature and in the built environment (Figure 4.3). Reflective symmetry is mainly addressed in Chapter 5 in shape and space. Rotational symmetry produces cyclic repeating patterns which are addressed later in this chapter.

FIGURE 4.3 Reflective symmetry (top) and rotational symmetry (bottom) in nature and the built environment

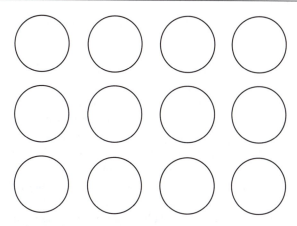

FIGURE 4.4 An array showing three rows of 4 and four columns of 3

Pattern permeates the mathematics curriculum so that, although this chapter focuses on pattern making, there will be aspects of pattern in other areas including:

- recognising (subitizing) numbers on dominos and dice by their pattern (Chapter 2)
- structured apparatus such as Numicon® which emphasise number patterns including odd and even numbers
- the repeating pattern of units in counting beyond ten, emphasised in a 100 square (Chapter 2)
- one more on the number line being the next counting word (Chapter 3)
- seeing patterns in addition facts e.g. 10 + 0; 9 + 1; 8 + 2 ... and the relationship between doubles (e.g. 5 + 5) and near doubles (e.g. 5 + 6) (Chapter 3)
- patterns in arrays (see Figure 4.4) which can be seen as a repeating pattern of three rows of 4 or four columns of 3 and which aids understanding of multiplication (Chapter 3)
- patterns in shape and tessellation (Chapter 5).

How children develop understanding about pattern: research findings

Piaget and Inhelder's (1967) study of children's learning about pattern concluded that, while they recognise pattern from an early age, to make sense of pattern they need to develop ideas of 'next to', 'before', 'after' and 'betweenness', that is, that in a sequence of three, the middle one is between the first and the last. Since these ideas are not explicitly recognised until children are about five, their findings appear to question whether it is appropriate to include pattern work for preschool children.

However, more recent research concludes that recognition of pattern is innate in young children (Sarama and Clements 2009). It is possible to identify a general line of development in pattern understanding for young children, though some researchers have found differences between individuals, across socio-economic groups and across ethnic groups (Garrick et al. 1999; Sarama and Clements 2009; Warren and Miller 2010). The following should therefore be seen as a possible developmental structure but may not fit every child.

Babies

Young babies begin to recognise patterns very early in their life. At first, they recognise spatial succession; for example, when they observe two separate items ranged one before the other. They will see items which are fixed in order, such as the rungs of their cot, or the arrangement of furniture in their bedroom. They will recognise patterns in fabrics and wallpaper and patterns in sounds in familiar rhymes, songs and music. They will also recognise habitual movements, such as the door opening followed by their mother entering the room, and then being fed. As we have seen in Chapter 2 even young babies are able to subitize small numbers of objects or pictures, presumably by patterning and are beginning to recognise patterns related to counting.

Two to three years of age

At this age children will recognise and use reflective symmetry, for example in building with blocks they may put one tower on each side of the castle, but are unable to reverse the more complex order of items, such as reversing red, blue, green, yellow beads to yellow, green, blue, red. At this age, children can be described as pre-explicit patterners: detecting and using pattern in their play and everyday life instinctively but not having the awareness to produce patterns to order (Sarama and Clements 2009). So Piaget and Inhelder (1967) found that children struggle to reproduce a sequence of items in a particular order; they may choose beads which correspond to those already threaded, but cannot copy the threaded sequence.

Three to five years of age

Between three and four years of age, children can recognise and may begin to talk about simple patterns (Sarama and Clements 2009). They create patterns in their play but do not often describe what they are doing (Garrick et al. 1999). They experiment with the basic elements of pattern including colour, position and shape producing combinations and repetitions. Experimenting with position they may begin with random positioning of elements then creating lines, initially horizontal but extending these to vertical and diagonal lines. When using pegboards they begin to use the centre, the corners and the midpoints to create symmetrical patterns. At the same time, their mastery of colour organisation develops so they may:

- make chains with attention to groups of colour but not numbers e.g. 3 green beads, 5 red, 4 yellow
- form chains with equal groupings 3 green, 3 red, 3 yellow
- alternate two or more colours but with different numbers e.g. 3 red, 5 yellow, 2 red, 6 yellow
- alternate colours with similar group sizes e.g. 3 red, 3 yellow, 3 red, 3 yellow.

Garrick *et al.* (1999) found that watching adults making patterns did not significantly affect children's understanding but working in groups and discussing their work with their peers did seem to encourage development. They recommend that settings offer a large range of pattern making materials (beads, pegboards, tiles, shapes etc.) and encourage children to share and discuss their creations together and that adults observe, encourage and talk about patterns created.

By three, children are beginning to be able to copy objects in an order (Piaget and Inhelder 1967). For example, they might peg clothes on a washing line to match the order of the clothes already there, or thread some more beads to match the order of those already threaded. Piaget observed that children would not always reproduce the same order: for example, when copying a bead sequence of red, blue, green, yellow, their order might be green, yellow, red, blue. They are beginning to get some proximities right (the closeness), but not all of them, especially if one colour or shape is repeated within the sequence e.g. red, green, green, blue.

Three- to five-year-old children find enactive patterns easier than pictorial patterns (Rustigan 1976, cited in Threlfall 2005) and Althouse describes how, when making body movement patterns, most four-year-olds could talk through a three-word body sequence, such as touching head–eyes–shoulders, head–eyes–shoulders . . .; and some five-year-olds could teach others five- and six-word body sequences. She noted that when children 'understood "what comes next" in relationship to "what came before" they had no difficulty understanding and making patterns' (1994).

At four years of age, children can complete simple patterns (e.g. ABABAB) with missing elements, and understand order if they can keep a constant check on it. For linear sequences a copy directly under the original enables them to make constant comparisons to copy the sequence (Figure 4.5). Between the ages of four and five they can learn to extend a simple pattern started by someone else and to copy a pattern without needing the original in close proximity. By five they begin to extend more complex patterns including those with a repeated element, e.g. ABBCABBC, but Garrick *et al.* found that

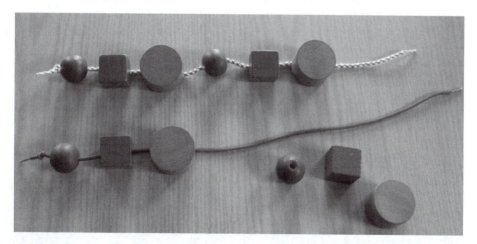

FIGURE 4.5 The original threaded lace is placed above the one to be made so that children can make a direct comparison as they work

even the 4–5-year-old children in their study found it difficult to describe and explain how the patterns were created (1999).

Children can be helped to see the pattern by 'reading' it out loud: 'red, blue, green, red, blue, green, red ...' As they bring together their everyday experience of pattern and the language associated with it they can begin to make sense of more abstract pattern tasks. However, Threlfall (2005) argues that children do not really understand the pattern until they can express the unit of repeat, e.g. by saying 'each time it is red, then blue, then green' rather than just chanting the pattern; being able to identify the element of repeat in this way does not develop until the children are about six years old (Sarama and Clements 2009).

Making patterns and key concepts

To understand pattern, children must be able to identify the similarities and differences between objects as well as their order – that is, what came before, what comes after. The attributes which vary may include:

- *Colour.* Observations of strings of beads with alternating colours will encourage children to note the order of the colours. When children are painting, they can make striped designs, for example, red then blue then green. When children have undertaken a mini-beast hunt they may well have found striped caterpillars, or on a visit to the zoo they may see a zebra with alternating stripes of black and white. These experiences offer opportunities to discuss what is seen and describe the order of colours, which helps children to understand regular, repeating patterns.
- *Shape.* When making a string of beads, children can be encouraged to look at the shapes of beads. In sand play, they might use two different containers to make sandcastles, and alternate these. When building with blocks or other construction kits, children can make repeating patterns with the blocks, noting which shapes they use and checking that the order is consistent (Figure 4.6). Children will often repeat a particular construction, perhaps making a pattern with the blocks, and that when the routine is well established they will collect the blocks needed to make their construction before they begin (Gura 1992). This suggests that they are using order and repetition to build their pattern. Similarly, observing patterns in the built environment, for example in fences, railings and in wire netting, where the order of shapes gives rise to the pattern, will help children to see how elements are ordered.

FIGURE 4.6 Repeating pattern made with different shaped blocks

- *Size.* A role play of the story of The Three Bears encourages children to compare size, and to order by size. They can make dough shapes of the bears, and order these by size, or use structured apparatus like Compare Bears®. Again, it is the use of language which will help children to recognise the order. When making dough shapes, children can make repeats of longer; shorter, longer, shorter . . . worms and describe their position within the order. When using percussion instruments, children can be encouraged to make repeated orders of loud and soft sounds and listen to each other's pattern.

- *Texture.* Some textured velvety fabrics or textured wallpapers have distinct patterns made by alternating raised and flat areas (Figure 4.7). When using pieces of fabric, perhaps to wrap dolls, children can be encouraged to observe the fabric and talk about what they can see and feel, noting the alternating contrasting sections.

FIGURE 4.7 Textures and patterns are all around the setting

- *Position*. Children's own movements can become an ordered pattern, such as 'Stretch up high; crouch down low; stretch up high; crouch down low'. They can experience making these ordered movements, perhaps in time to the pattern of sounds created with percussion instruments, and observe each other. When using pegboards or colouring squared paper they may focus on the centre, the corners and the midpoints on each side indicating their understanding of position.

- *Quantity*. Ordering quantity may occur during children's play. They might make a tower of four bricks followed by one of three bricks, then one of four bricks and so on. Here there are opportunities for comparing quantities, that three is one fewer than four, and of identifying that three follows four, follows three. Similarly, in movement, children can make two jumps and a step, two jumps and a step, and so on. By observing one another they can see and describe the movements and compare the quantities.

Sometimes children will use a combination of the above in order to make a sequence or pattern. Catherine (five years) and Rebecca (four years seven months) were threading beads to make dolls' necklaces:

CATHERINE: Now the red then the blue. Over and over.
REBECCA: Mine's different. Pink and silver. Pretty!
CATHERINE: Look. Red and round, blue and long!

Catherine had realised that she was sorting the beads by more than just colour in order to make a consistent pattern.

Through discussion with one another and with adults, they will learn to use mathematical language of pattern, such as same, different, before, after, next, copy, repeat ... although their ability to create pattern precedes their ability to explain it. The development of ideas about the attributes of objects (colour, shape, etc.) and their similarities and differences, is complementary to developing understanding about numbers and their value, and shapes and their properties. Understanding about pattern involves recognising rules, such as repeating bands of colours on wallpaper where red stripes always follow white ones.

The research quoted above indicated that different children develop differently in relation to pattern, possibly due to different preschool experiences. This section focuses on how children's understanding of pattern concepts can be enhanced by an appropriate early years curriculum. The development of pattern concepts is considered under the following headings, but these should not be considered to be sequential stages:

- recognising pattern in the environment
- talking about an order
- making line and symmetrical patterns
- creating a sequence
- copying and extending a sequence
- recognising and creating a growing pattern
- recognising and creating cyclic patterns
- problem solving with pattern.

Many activities through which children explore concepts of pattern lend themselves to more than one aspect of pattern. The children's own explorations of sequence and pattern will take them into art, music and movement experiences as well as more mathematical ones of shape and number patterns. The concepts associated with order, sequence and pattern are valid in all these areas.

Recognising pattern in the environment

From birth babies will start to recognise patterns in their environment: at four weeks Lotte loved to stare at the black and white stripes formed by the old beams on the living room ceiling and was attracted by clothing with strong stripes or patterns. Babies experience patterns of the day: feed, change, play, sleep . . . As they grow older, children will encounter pattern at home and in almost every area of a well-resourced early years setting, including posters and book illustrations; wallpaper, wrapping paper and fabrics in the home corner and for collage; in nature and the built environment out of doors; in story, rhymes and songs. Drawing attention to these and describing them will help the children to recognise a range of patterns (Figure 4.8).

Talking about an order

Children will experience order in many different contexts: putting dolls onto chairs in order of size; threading beads red, blue, red, blue, or making a printing pattern using alternately a sponge and a cork. Through discussion with an adult, children will begin to describe the order within their pattern. Asking questions such as 'what came first?' and 'what comes next?' will encourage children to note the order of items in a sequence and extend this to their pattern. Children may find it difficult to describe what comes next

FIGURE 4.8 Pattern in the built environment (a pattern walk through Broseley, Shropshire)

when there is a repeat within the pattern e.g. red, blue, green, green; red, blue, green, green; perhaps focusing on red following green without seeing the repeated green.

Making line and symmetrical patterns

In Chapter 5, painting, drawing, printing and sewing as means of exploring lines are considered in a 'shape' context. At first, children will explore lines in a free form way, producing 'scribbles' with crayons (Figure 4.9) or when finger painting, covering the paper without taking account of repeatable actions in their drawing: later they will begin to note the regularity in line patterns.

- *Free form designs and patterns.* Children enjoy using finger paints to make their own designs. They can use sponges to make prints, and feathers, toothbrushes, combs, . . . in order to make random designs on paper. They can be encouraged to describe the design they have made, to hear and use language such as straight, round, curved. When using items such as combs, the print effect will have a sequence of lines in parallel to each other. Scrapers with teeth (the type which come with tubs of tile adhesive) can be used to make swirling, parallel lines. These can also be used to make line patterns in wet sand.
- *Printing with objects.* When children first start making prints with potatoes, cotton reels, foam shapes, leaves . . . the prints may be placed at random on the paper. They can be

FIGURE 4.9 Exploring making lines with crayon on big paper (3-year-old)

FIGURE 4.10 Paint and marbles can be used to produce interesting line patterns

encouraged to print in a straight line, placing one foam-shape print after the other. If two colours are used, then they can make repeats of colour in a straight line.

- *Line patterns* (Figure 4.10). Using pencils, crayons or paint, children can produce straight lines, thick and thin, zigzags, loops, or curves. As they make their repeats they should be encouraged to note the repeated movements which they make. Observing another making these patterns will help them to associate the repeated movements with the pattern. Similarly, such patterns can be made in dry or wet sand using spades, sticks or pencils of different widths so that they can compare their patterns. Alternatively, children can spread finger paint and make line patterns in it. Where children have access to computer drawing software, they can make interesting effects with repeated lines.

- *Direction.* Line patterns which change direction, such as those which can be made on sewing cards, encourage children to recognise the in-and-out, up-and-down patterns. Similarly, computer drawing software will allow them to explore the movements where there is a change of direction.

Tomas and Fiona (both aged four years) worked with an adult, making marble prints, running marbles around a tray with splodges of paint in the bottom, then taking an impression of the design onto a sheet of clean paper. They were totally engrossed in what

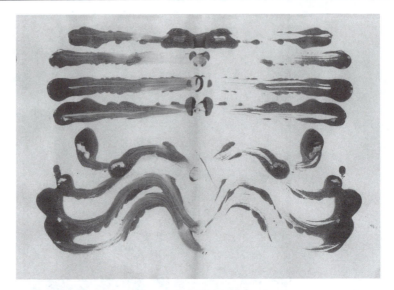

FIGURE 4.11 Blot and fold patterns can produce interesting line effects which show the effect of reflections

they were doing and did not speak as they worked. When they had finished their prints, the adult asked what they could see.

TOMAS: Lots of lines. Look. Long ones.

FIONA: Lots of colours. Look, red and blue and green.

ADULT: When they're dry, shall we mount these to go on the pattern display?

■ *Patterns showing reflective symmetry.* These can be made when playing with building blocks, in using pegboards, experimenting with shapes and making blot and fold pictures (Figure 4.11). Computer software packages are also available which will enable the children to explore symmetrical patterns.

Creating a sequence

Children will create their own sequence, of movement, music, threaded necklace, structures or collage (Figure 4.12). Creating a sequence which is pleasing to the child will involve discussions of likes and dislikes, favourite colours and shapes. Where children work cooperatively, sharing materials, they can be encouraged to compare what they have created, looking for similarities and differences.

During a movement session, the reception class children were asked to copy a simple dance sequence of stretch up tall, curl up small, jump up and stand still. The teacher noted that some produced the movement sequence without error, but that the younger children, who were just four years old, did not seem to remember the sequence and repeated the stretch and curl, or the jump and stand still. She asked some of the children who found this difficult to work with a partner and copy their movements whilst she

FIGURE 4.12 Creating a collage sequence on edging paper

spoke the movements in sequence. Quickly all the children produced the sequence of movements, in order.

When working with manipulative materials children may at first focus on only one element of repeat, for example producing a chain of alternating colours without attention to the number of beads of each colour, or having a consistent number of beads each time but without repeating the colour. With experience and discussion about these elements they will begin to create more complex patterns.

Copying and extending a sequence

Copying a sequence helps children to recognise the order in which the elements of the sequence are placed. Children find copying other people's patterns difficult and so they should have experience of much free play and discussion before they get to this stage. To make an accurate copy they will need to recognise what comes first, what comes next and what is last. Where the sequence is repeated, they will, through careful questioning and discussion with an adult, come to realise that the elements of the sequence are always repeated in the same order, such as making a line of toy vehicles which repeats red bus, blue car, yellow lorry, red bus . . .

- *Making a direct copy.* In most early years classes children will be found copying sequences, of movements, music, words and rhymes, bead patterns and so on. These are activities well within the grasp of most four-year-olds. Through careful observation, and with

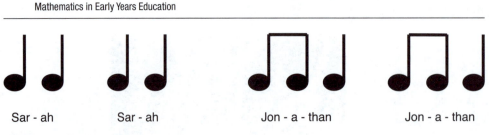

Sar - ah   Sar - ah   Jon - a - than   Jon - a - than

FIGURE 4.13 Clapping patterns

the original sequence directly in front of them, children will copy a simple pegboard sequence, or make a tower of bricks which matches the one their friend has made. In their block play children will repeat, day after day, a particular structure, making the structure from memory demonstrating that making copies is well within their capabilities when they are motivated. Children will copy a simple clapping rhythm, perhaps to represent their name (Figure 4.13).

■ *Extending the sequence.* In learning to copy a simple sequence, children may well copy it over and over again, forming a repeating pattern. This can be seen where children thread beads to make a necklace and copy their original design, such as blue, green, blue, green ... until the necklace is long enough. Similar repeats can be observed in other activities, such as repeating a sequence of taps on a drum or on some chime bars. Davies (1995) describes how a three-year-old developed her own game, moving under a clothes rail which had bottom and top rails and uprights. She repeated her movements, saying 'under and over' again and again, copying her own sequence of movements and words.

■ *Recognising and creating a growing pattern.* This can be a simple staircase pattern, made with rods or bricks, or a pattern where one item grows with each repeat (Figure 4.14). Such patterns are less common in the environment and will need some discussion to show how they differ from repeating patterns. Patterns found in number are often growing patterns.

Recognising and creating cyclic patterns

A cyclic pattern is a repeating pattern which joins to make a seamless, continuous pattern which has rotational symmetry (Figure 4.15). For example, a threaded bead pattern, with red, green, blue, red, green, blue, when looped to make a necklace, will continue the sequence, in order, and without a break.

Cyclic patterns can be made from craft materials, such as making decorated paper bangles or crowns, or by sitting toys around a table, where the toys alternate doll, teddy,

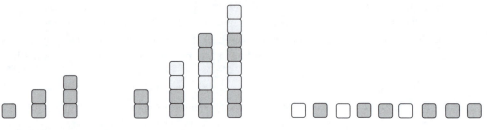

FIGURE 4.14 Growing patterns (1,2,3. . .; 2,4,6,8. . .; 1,1,1,2,1,3. . .)

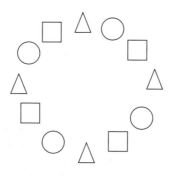

FIGURE 4.15 Cyclic patterns are closed repeating patterns

doll, teddy ... Time patterns are often cyclic, night following day, the order of meals, or the life cycle of plants and mini-beasts, though it should be noted that one day is not exactly the same as the next, nor is the plant or mini-beast identical in each cycle.

- *Making cyclic patterns with apparatus.* Making a pattern which repeats in a cycle can be quite difficult, as children need to ensure that the repeats of the sequence will fit into the space available for the cycle. For example, if a child puts out five chairs around a table and chooses teddies and dolls to sit in an alternating ABAB pattern, then it is not possible to finish the cycle as two toys of the same type will sit next to each other. Discussion with children will help them to identify where their pattern is 'wrong'. Their solution may be to put an additional chair at the table between the two toys which are the same. Children will often complete a cyclic pattern by adding more items until the space closes even if the pattern is incomplete.
- *Recognising aspects of time which are cyclic.* This is another aspect of cyclic pattern which children may wish to explore. For example, they will begin to recognise that there are regular repeating aspects of their lives, such as night follows day follows night follows day ... There will be regular routines, such as the order of events with perhaps story time following snack time and going to the toilet then washing their hands. Those children with younger siblings may recognise the regular order of events with the baby, such as feeding, changing the nappy, baby sleeping ... For all of these, discussion is key, as it helps children to recognise the order of events and that they repeat in a regular pattern. Children may recognise the repeating nature of the days of the week, or of the analogue clock, with its rotating hour and minute hands.

Problem solving

Possibilities for problem solving with pattern will arise as part of children's everyday activities. For example, where new curtains are to be made for the home area, children could decide to decorate them with a printed pattern. They can be encouraged to develop their problem-solving skills by:

- describing the pattern they wish to make
- choosing the materials for printing, refining their choice as they work

- carrying out their plan, with adult intervention to discuss how closely their plan fits their original planning, and the reasons for changes made
- reviewing the finished pattern, describing its features, and checking that the sequences repeat
- using appropriately the language of pattern in their discussions.

The need to solve problems will arise during children's chosen activities. When decorating a paper hat to make a pattern around the crown, children can be encouraged to consider how they will ensure that the pattern is continuous around the crown. This can be quite difficult to ensure as it will involve deciding how many pattern repeats will fit and spacing the pieces around the crown. The adult's role is crucial, ensuring that sensitive questioning and suggestions extend the learning opportunities and encourage children to set and solve problems for themselves.

Children can also be offered patterns with missing elements and be challenged to fix them, or some part covered and asked what is missing.

Concept map

Table 4.1 shows the concepts outlined above in matrix form together with examples of vocabulary which can be developed. Example activities are shown so that the map can be used as a basis for planning. Assessment checkpoints and key questions are given to show possible learning outcomes from the activities.

Planning pattern experiences

It is important for all adults working in early years settings to be aware of possibilities for developing children's understanding of pattern and to have appropriate subject knowledge and understanding of the concepts and vocabulary associated with pattern. At first it is important to be able to identify elements of pattern making in the children's play and comment on these to develop their language of pattern. Drawing attention to patterns made by other children may encourage some children to try for themselves. A child threading beads to make a bangle can be encouraged to make a repeating pattern of colour or shape, or a combination of both, or perhaps to make a growing pattern of bricks, using one, then two, then three, in a row. The adult's role in identifying possibilities and intervening in the child's play in a sensitive manner is most important, as this can produce opportunities to introduce and extend children's understanding of the concepts and vocabulary associated with pattern. Many of the experiences that children will have will come from their own choice, such as working with the blocks, threading beads, printing and using pegboards. All of these experiences offer opportunities for children's awareness of pattern concepts and language to be enhanced.

Adult focused activities

Planned activities for developing pattern concepts will often include opportunities to develop several concepts, rather than just concentrating upon one aspect. The following activities demonstrate both planning for a range of concepts, and activities which concentrate upon just one concept.

TABLE 4.1 Concept map for pattern

KEY CONCEPT	VOCABULARY	EXAMPLES OF ACTIVITIES	ASSESSMENT CHECKPOINTS	KEY QUESTIONS
Recognise pattern in the environment	Pattern, lines, stripes, spots etc.	Going on a pattern hunt around the setting or outdoor area	• Identifies items with some element of pattern • Begins to talk about elements of pattern	• What do you like about this pattern? • Can you find another pattern with stripes?
Talk about an order	Before, after, follows, next to, start, finish, between	Using beads and laces, pegs and boards, mosaic tiles, construction kits describing an order by position	• Identifies positions within the order e.g. before, and uses vocabulary of order appropriately	• What comes next/before/after? How do you know? • Can you make a new pattern using these . . .?
Make line patterns	Lines, loops, straight, thin, thick, zigzags, curves, out, in, up, down . . .	Printing, drawing, painting, imprinting in sand; making patterns and designs and describing the pattern	• Describes the line shape • Uses a range of lines to make patterns and designs	• Which shapes have you used? • Can you make a different pattern using these lines?
Make symmetrical patterns	Matching, balance	Building with blocks, paint, pegboards	• Uses elements of symmetry	• Why did you put this one here?
Create a sequence	Start, finish, middle, between, next, before . . .	Sewing cards and laces, printing, imprints in plasticine, pegboards, imprints in sand; deciding the order and describing position	• Uses imagination to make a sequence • Describes the order	• Can you make a different pattern using the same pieces? • How is it different? • What will come next/between . . .?
Copy and extend a sequence	Copy, same, different, start, finish, repeat, again . . .	Copying a pattern sequence of threaded beads, bricks in a tower, movements, rhythms; describing the sequence; checking the copy is the same	• Copies a sequence accurately • Identifies any differences	• Are these patterns the same? • (Of a sequence with one piece different): is this the same? What is different? Can you make these the same? How did you do that?

(Continued)

99

TABLE 4.1 *(Continued)*

KEY CONCEPT	VOCABULARY	EXAMPLES OF ACTIVITIES	ASSESSMENT CHECKPOINTS	KEY QUESTIONS
Recognise and create a growing pattern	Growing, increasing	Building a staircase with bricks; modelling even numbers	• Identifies how the elements increase • Describes what the next element would look like	• What is different here? • What would come next?
Recognise and create cyclic patterns	Before, after, next, between . . .	Making decorated crowns, bracelets, putting toys in a circle; describing the repeating pattern, e.g. ABAB; talking about time patterns: day/night, order of events of the day . . .	• Describes a cyclic pattern • Finishes a cyclic pattern keeping repeats correct • Uses vocabulary of position and cyclic time	• What comes next? • Can you finish the pattern? • Tell me about you day: what did you do next? . . . and next?
Use developing understanding of pattern to solve practical problems	Pattern, puzzle, what could we try next? How did you work it out?	Plan the pattern, choose materials, carry out the task and review it Identify and fix missing elements of a sequence	• Makes patterns and describes them • Can identify what is missing and complete pattern	• What other patterns could you make? • How did you work it out? • What is missing? How do you know?

Pattern basket

An activity for a group of four children.

- *Purpose:* to focus on aspects of pattern and encourage discussion.
- *Materials:* a basket containing pieces of ribbon, fabric or paper with a variety of pattern and some plain.
- *Language:* patterned, plain, same, different, spots, stripes, lines etc.

How to begin

The children will need time to play and explore the materials before you begin to intervene.

Ask the children to find a piece of material with a pattern on it. Ask them why they chose their material. What makes it a pattern? Can they find another piece with a similar pattern? Choose two pieces of material and compare them using appropriate language. Ask the children to compare theirs with one of yours.

This could be extended to sorting the materials for stripes, spots, flower patterns etc.

Pattern hunt

An activity for a group of about four children.

- *Purpose:* to focus on aspects of pattern and encourage discussion.
- *Materials:* outdoor environment; a camera.
- *Language:* patterned, plain, same, different, spots, stripes, lines etc.

How to begin

Talk to the children about what pattern is and whether they can remember any different sorts of pattern. If possible link this to previous pattern making activities.

Explain that you are going to go outside and they are going to be pattern detectives. Their job is to find things outside with pattern on them. When they find something they are to call the others over and you will take a picture of it for a display.

When something is found, talk about what makes it a pattern and ask if there are any other patterns like it, e.g. can you find another pattern with zigzags on.

Older children (4–5) could be given a sheet with small pictures of patterns (stripes, spots, zigzags, etc.) and have to find and draw something they find with a similar pattern.

Line patterns

An activity for four children.

- *Purpose:* to make and describe line patterns.
- *Materials:* examples of line patterns from wallpaper or fabric samples, paint, paper, brushes of different thicknesses, pieces of stiff card, feathers, old toothbrushes, comb ...
- *Language:* straight, line, thick, thin, loop, curve, zigzag, in, out, up, down ...

How to begin

Show the children some examples of line patterns, and encourage them to use appropriate vocabulary to describe what they see. Ask them to find specific examples of line pattern such as thick straight line, thin curved line, wavy, zigzag and to describe the pattern.

- It's a zigzag. It goes back and forward over and over.
- It's wavy, just like the sea.
- This one is curly.

Ask the children to make a design on their paper, using different sorts of line patterns. They may choose from the painting implements; alternatively, they might use their fingers to make the patterns. When the designs are finished, ask:

- What shape is this? Can you find me another one like it?
- Which lines have curves?
- Which lines have straight pieces?

The children can experiment with various thicknesses of paintbrushes to explore the different line patterns they can make. They may also enjoy making line patterns outside with large brushes and water.

Patterns in the sand

An activity for three or four children.

- *Purpose:* to create patterns.
- *Materials:* sand, sand tools, such as rakes, moulds, buckets, pebbles, feathers, shells, flags ...
- *Language:* start, finish, middle, next, before, copy, same, different ...

How to begin

Ask the children to choose from the tools to help them to make their own repeating pattern in the sand. When they have finished, ask them to describe their pattern:

- Mine has lines, then a pebble, then lines, then a pebble.
- I've got two shells, then a sandcastle.
- First there's a shell, then a pebble, then a feather. I put a line all the way along. Then it's the same.

Ask the children to change their pattern. Look to see if they remember to change the repeat.

Instead of using the large sand tray, these patterns can be made in shallow plastic trays so that children make individual patterns. These can be put on show as part of a pattern display.

People patterns

An activity for everyone during carpet time.

- *Purpose:* to create a linear or growing pattern.
- *Materials:* the children, dressing-up clothes such as hats and scarves.
- *Language:* start, finish, next, more, between, copy ...

How to begin

The children will need to sit in a straight line so that they all observe the activity from the same viewpoint.

Ask one child to put on a hat and another to put on a scarf. They stand in a line in front of the others. The other children say the sequence that they see: hat, scarf.

Ask another child to come out, give him a hat to wear and to stand in line, then the next child to put on a scarf and stand in line. Ask the children still sitting what comes next, a hat or a scarf.

This can be repeated until everyone is in the line, wearing either a hat or a scarf. The children can take turns in saying what they are wearing, along the line, so that they will hear the repeating pattern of the words 'hat, scarf, hat, scarf ...'

Ask everyone to sit down, then choose four children to stand in a line, choosing their own order, such as: hat, hat, scarf, scarf. Ask those still sitting down what they think should come next, and next, and so on, building the repeats of the pattern until everyone is in line. Again, ask the children to say in turn what they are wearing, so that all hear the pattern.

Ask some of the children to stand in your chosen order, such as: sit, stand, sit ... Continue the pattern, making a deliberate mistake. Ask the children as each child joins the line:

- Is this right? What comes next?

Check that they identify the mistake and can tell why it is wrong.

This activity can be repeated with children standing or sitting in different positions, such as:

- hands up, hands up, hands down, hands up, hands up, hands down ...
- legs astride, kneel, sit, legs astride, kneel, sit ...

The pattern repeats can become more complex if this is appropriate and can include growing and shrinking patterns, such as:

- stand, sit, stand, stand, sit, stand, stand, stand, sit ...
- child standing in a hoop, two children in hoop, three children in hoop, four children in hoop, three children in hoop, two children in hoop, one child in hoop.

Note that it is important not to use personal characteristics for this activity. Children may be sensitive about their height, weight, hair colour, wearing glasses or particular clothes etc. People patterns can also be made with small world toys (Figure 4.16).

FIGURE 4.16 People patterns: Hands up, hands down, hands up, hands down . . .

Movement patterns

An activity for everyone during a movement session.

- *Purpose:* to copy and create a movement sequence.
- *Materials:* the children.
- *Language:* first, next, begin, start, finish . . .

How to begin

The children line up one behind the other, with, if possible, adults in the line to help. Explain that the game is a follow my leader one, and that they copy the actions of the leader (an adult). The actions must be a repeated sequence of three or four movements, such as step, step, step, jump. The children follow the leader around the room, repeating the actions. It is helpful if the leader chants the actions so that the children hear and see the sequence.

When the children have learnt the pattern, individuals can demonstrate to others and they can say the repeating sequence.

Now give other simple movement sequences for the children to copy on their own, such as:

- hands up, hands down, crouch down, hands up, hands down, crouch down . . .
- step, step, clap, clap, step, step, clap, clap . . .

This can be extended by individuals making up their own simple sequence for others to copy.

Musical patterns

An activity for everyone during carpet time.

- *Purpose:* to copy and continue a pattern.
- *Materials:* percussion instruments.
- *Language:* start, finish, copy, same, different . . .

How to begin

Choose a familiar song that the children enjoy singing. Decide upon a simple, repetitive rhythm to accompany the song and while the children sing the song clap or tap the rhythm on a percussion instrument. Now ask the children to clap the rhythm as they sing. Ask:

- How does the rhythm start?
- Who can clap it for me?
- Does this sound right? (and clap it, making a mistake)

When they are confident at this, choose some children to use percussion instruments instead of clapping.

Musical tunes

An activity for four children.

- *Purpose:* to create a repeating pattern.
- *Materials:* chime bars which play some notes from the pentatonic scale, items to record the music, such as coloured cubes, coloured crayons, paper, cassette recorder.
- *Language:* start, finish, copy, same, different . . .

The pentatonic scale (Figure 4.17) is very useful as in whatever order the notes of the scale are played it always produces a pleasant sound.

How to begin

Start with just two chime bars each. The children create a simple sound sequence which they copy to make a simple repeating pattern. When they are confident with this, they can use another chime bar to make their musical pattern more complex. Record their patterns using the cassette recorder and play this back. Ask:

- How might you change your pattern?
- What comes first now?

When they are satisfied with their pattern, record it again and play it back.

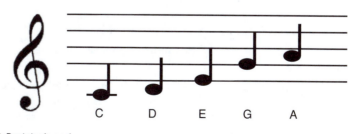

FIGURE 4.17 Pentatonic scale

Encourage the children to explore ways of recording their repeating pattern. They could use coloured cubes to represent the order of the chime bar notes, or make coloured marks on paper. When they have recorded, ask them to play their pattern using their invented musical notation. Then play back the original from the taped version. Ask:

■ Are they the same?

■ What have you changed?

When they are satisfied with their musical pattern and their recording, the taped version and the cube or coloured crayon recording can be placed on the music table for others to enjoy.

Patterns can also be made with mixtures of percussion instruments.

Growing and shrinking number patterns from songs

An activity for everyone during carpet time.

■ *Purpose:* to make shrinking patterns.

■ *Materials:* number rhymes which count forwards such as 'Peter taps with one hammer'; 'This old man'; 'One elephant went out to play' or which count backwards, such as 'Five little buns in the baker's shop'; 'Ten fat sausages'; 'Ten in the bed'.

■ *Language:* count back, how many, start, finish, number names in order forwards and backwards . . .

How to begin

Decide whether to use songs which count forwards or count backwards. Sing the song with the children and ask at the end of the first verse 'How many more. . .?' or 'How many fewer. . .?'

Many children find songs with actions help them to remember the number patterns, for example putting up or down the required number of fingers. Other songs involve one more child standing in front each time, such as in 'One elephant went out to play'.

These rhymes can be used to encourage children to recognise the growing or shrinking pattern of the numbers and to relate these to 'how many'.

Pegboard patterns

An activity for a group of four children.

■ *Purpose:* to copy a sequence and describe its order.

■ *Materials:* pegs and boards, with a simple colour sequence of pegs at the top of each board.

■ *Language:* copy, same, different, start, finish, before, after, follow, next, between. . .

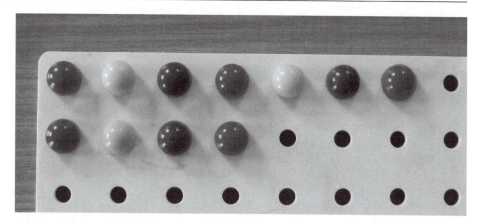

FIGURE 4.18 Pegboard sequence

How to begin

Each child has a board with the same colour sequence of pegs at the top.
   The children describe the position of the pegs in the sequence:

- The red peg is before the blue peg.
- The green peg is after the blue peg.
- The first peg is red.
- It finishes with the green peg.

When they have described the positions of the pegs, they copy the pattern on the next line of the pegboard (Figure 4.18).
   Choose one child's pegboard and ask them all to shut their eyes. Alter the position of one of the pegs in the original sequence and ask the children to open their eyes. Ask:

- What has changed?
- Which peg is first now?
- How do we make Sally's pattern the same as this one?
- Which peg is between the blue and the green?

The children can choose three or four pegs and make their own order. Ask them to describe the position of the pegs.

Number patterns

An activity for a group of four children.

- *Purpose:* to recognise pattern relationships in number.

- *Materials:* Two sets of number cards to 20.
- *Language:* number names, next, before, steps of.

How to begin

Show a series of numbers e.g. 1, 3, 5, 7, 9 and ask:

- What do you notice about these numbers?
- What do you think would come next?

(If this is the first time you have focused on number patterns you may wish to start with 1, 2, 3, 4, 5 . . .)

Discuss the pattern produced and the step between each element (+2). What comes next? And then? . . .

Give the set of cards to each pair of children and ask them to invent a pattern. Discuss each pattern in turn, asking the opposite pair to talk about the pattern.

100 square patterns

An activity for a group of any size.

- *Purpose:* to recognise pattern relationships in the 100 square.
- *Materials:* large 100 square, perhaps on interactive whiteboard.
- *Language:* number names, next, before, steps of.

How to begin

Ask children:

- What do you notice about these numbers?
- Can you see any patterns?

1	2	3	4	5	6	7	8	9	10
11	12	13	14	15	16	17	18	19	20
21	22	23	24	25	26	27	28	29	30
31	32	33	34	35	36	37	38	39	40
41	42	43	44	45	46	47	48	49	50
51	52	53	54	55	56	57	58	59	60
61	62	63	64	65	66	67	68	69	70
71	72	73	74	75	76	77	78	79	80
81	82	83	84	85	86	87	88	89	90
91	92	93	94	95	96	97	98	99	100

1	2	3	4	5	6	7	8	9	10
11	12	13	14	15	16	17	18	19	20
21	22	23	24	25	26	27	28	29	30
31	32	33	34	35	36	37	38	39	40
41	42	43	44	45	46	47	48	49	50
51	52	53	54	55	56	57	58	59	60
61	62	63	64	65	66	67	68	69	70
71	72	73	74	75	76	77	78	79	80
81	82	83	84	85	86	87	88	89	90
91	92	93	94	95	96	97	98	99	100

FIGURE 4.19 100 square highlighting multiples of 2 and 11

Discuss as many patterns as possible, for example: all the numbers with 2 on the end, numbers with the same digits, multiples of 11 (Figure 4.19).

Laminated 100 squares and pens would allow the children to explore these patterns further for themselves.

Involving adult helpers in the planned activities

Pattern, in its broadest sense, occurs all around us and there will be many incidental opportunities to discuss pattern with children. A child wearing a new jumper, with a Fair Isle or jacquard pattern, can be encouraged to describe the pattern, noting the pattern repeats, the colours and the shapes. Language associated with pattern concepts is also language used in everyday life. This language should be used correctly and in appropriate contexts. The language to be developed can be included on the weekly planning sheet and during planning sessions. Work with patterns will produce some attractive results which the children will appreciate being displayed for others to see. Where there is space, a 'pattern table' can be set up, with examples of patterns which children have made.

Where there are adults from other cultures in the setting, they can be encouraged to show examples of patterns from their cultures and traditions and help children to make their own representations. For example, children will admire a beautiful sari, with a border repeat pattern; they will enjoy looking at examples of Islamic patterns. Similarly, special events, such as a child's birthday, can offer opportunities to explore and create patterns, such as making a repeating pattern on a cake, making the same design on each biscuit, or making and decorating with a repeating pattern a piñata for a birthday party.

Festivals are opportunities for adults in the setting to bring to bear the specialised knowledge of how these are celebrated. The following are just a few of the festivals from religions other than Christianity that might be considered.

- *Divali:* a Hindu festival, which means 'row of lights'. Clay lamps are used to provide light, and these can be made from clay or dough. Women make chalk patterns called rangoli outside their houses.
- *Raksha Bandhan:* a Hindu festival, which means 'protection' and is for brothers and sisters. Girls make their brothers a bangle, usually red-coloured, called a rakhi and the brothers give their sisters a present.
- *Eid:* an Islamic festival, which marks the end of the month of fasting, Ramadan. People give Eid cards, which can be decorated with Islamic patterns.

For special interests, it may be possible to invite people in from the community, perhaps to show the children a craft which involves the use of pattern. These might include spinning and weaving, knitting or crochet work.

Setting up environments for pattern activities

Table 4.2 shows suggestions for contexts across the setting which could offer opportunities for discussions about pattern during child initiated learning, or be set up for adult initiated or focused activities.

TABLE 4.2 Pattern activities across areas of the setting

ENVIRONMENT	CONCEPT/SKILL	CONTEXT
Carpet time	• copy a sequence • copy a pattern • create a sequence or pattern	• singing songs with repeats • playing clapping games • composing rhythms and tunes and recording them for playback
Art and craft areas	• create line patterns • create a sequence • create a reflective pattern • copy a sequence • describe sequence or pattern • create a more complex pattern	• making sequences and patterns by: painting, printing, drawing, cutting and sticking • starting sequences for others to copy/continue • making border for a display or special book
Table top games and collections	• create a sequence • copy a sequence • create line patterns • create a pattern • describe sequence or pattern	• using collections to make sequences and patterns: pegs and pegboards, beads and laces, buttons, sorting toys, mosaic tiles, Fuzzy Felt, magnetic tiles . . .
Sand play	• create sequence or pattern • describe sequence or pattern	• making ABAB patterns of sandcastles in damp sand • using sticks, rakes, combs, shells, feathers, imprints, to make line patterns and sequences
Construction	• copy a sequence • create line patterns • create a sequence • create a pattern • describe sequence or pattern • creating symmetrical structures	• choosing construction pieces to copy a sequence or pattern • making ABAB patterns with construction kit pieces • making structures with a pattern in their design • building symmetrical structures such as robots
Block play	• copy a sequence • create line patterns • create a sequence • create a reflective pattern • create a pattern • describe sequence or pattern • creating symmetrical structures	• choosing blocks to copy a sequence or pattern • making a sequence or pattern using at least two different types of block • making structures with a pattern in their design • building symmetrical structures such as houses or castles
Role play	• describe sequence or pattern	• describing fabrics, wallpapers in the home area
Small world play	• describe sequence or pattern • create a sequence or pattern	• putting cars in straight lines of alternating red/blue/red/blue . . . • lining up the animals to go into the farm: cow then pig then horse, cow then pig then horse . . .

Outside play	• repeating patterns over time	• helping to grow plants in the garden: observe the repeating cycle of planting, growing, dying, planting . . .
Cooking	• create line patterns	• icing cakes and biscuits with lines
Information technology	• copy a sequence • create line patterns • create a sequence • create a reflective pattern • create a pattern • describe sequence or pattern	• using art software to copy sequences and patterns • using art software to create sequences and patterns

Assessment

What to look for

Regular observations of individual children, noting their use of language and how they create, continue and copy patterns, will give useful evidence of what children can do and what they understand, and identify aspects of pattern where children lack confidence. Use the assessment checkpoints and key questions in Table 4.1 to help with assessment. The questions include both closed (how many?) and open (how do you know?) types. Observations, with evidence of the child's behaviour to support their understanding, can be recorded. Where evidence of achievement in a standard form is required, the observational evidence can be supported by a note of the assessment checkpoint, with date and comment attached to show when the evidence of achievement was noted. Regular observations will show whether a child can:

- Recognise and take an interest in pattern.
- Begin to use repeating, ordering, positioning and balancing in their creative play.
- Recognise and use symmetry.
- Describe an order, using appropriate language of position.
- Describe and make line patterns, using language of size, shape, position and movement, and of thickness.
- Copy a sequence, making an exact copy.
- Create a sequence, discussing the start, position of elements and its finish.
- Create a pattern, by repeating a sequence and checking that the pattern repeats are correct, or by making a growing or shrinking pattern.
- Recognise and describe patterns in number.

Opportunities for assessment will occur through discussion with children about their pattern making, encouraging them to use the language of position correctly. Outcomes from children's activities, such as printed patterns and threaded bead patterns, can be used as part of the assessment process, especially where this is accompanied by the children's comments about their work.

There will be incidental opportunities for assessment as well as those arising from planned activities.

Children respond well to questions such as 'Can you make a new pattern using these. . .?', especially where they have been encouraged to respond using the mathematical vocabulary that they hear the adults using. Gradually they begin to respond in sentences and this should be encouraged. Indeed, when these questions were trialled the children responded eagerly to this question, and although they found it difficult to respond verbally, they showed with the pattern pieces that they understood what to do and could respond appropriately.

Three- and four-year-olds find it more difficult to answer questions which ask 'How do you know?' such as 'What comes next/before/after? How do you know?' and tend not to respond. However, with practice, and with examples of how they might answer given by adults, they do begin to answer the 'How do you know?' type of question in a satisfactory way.

Possible errors in concepts of pattern

Most pattern errors are developmental rather than due to misconceptions and will improve with more experience. Possible errors may include:

- Thinking that pattern only indicates attractive colouring.
- The inability to reproduce a sequence of items in a particular order. They may choose the correct items to copy the sequence, but then place them in a haphazard order. They do not yet understand proximity (nearness) and will identify the individual items but not their relative order. As the children mature they will begin to understand proximity and so both choose the correct items and put them in order.
- Inconsistency in copying a pattern. Children may copy part of the sequence correctly, but not do so consistently. This shows that they are beginning to understand proximities, but not with consistency.
- Inability to copy a sequence unless the original is directly above the copy. The children at this stage can only make direct comparisons. Where the sequence to be copied cannot be placed directly above the copy, the copying may well be inaccurate.
- Ability to make a sequence, but not to reverse it, that is red, blue, green; green, blue, red. Children lack left-right coordination until they are about five to six years old. However, with adult help, and careful comparison of their pattern, and with a mirror to observe the reflection of the pattern, children's ability with reverse patterns will improve.

Where a child consistently confuses colours in patterns this may be due to colour blindness. If this is the case, then instead of making colour patterns the child can make patterns from shapes.

Working in partnership with parents and carers

Children learn through play but also by observing and working alongside adults in everyday situations. At home, children will have real-life experiences of pattern. Whilst shopping for wallpaper or clothes children will see repeating patterns and hear these discussed, perhaps hearing language associated with pattern. They will see patterns in the environment, perhaps a repeating pattern of wall tiles or wrought-iron railings, or they may become aware of short life cycles, such as those of the butterfly or frog. These experiences, and those specifically designed for use at home, will provide an enriched pattern experience to encourage children to recognise, copy and create patterns.

Activities at home for developing understanding of pattern

These activities do not require any special equipment as they make use of everyday items in the home.

Pattern walks

- *At the shops:* observing and describing patterns on dress materials, packaging materials; observing tile patterns on walls and the ground.
- *Houses:* observing and describing patterns in roof tiles, bricks, railings, fences, manhole covers, windows.
- *Going to the park:* observing and describing patterns in flowers, fir cones, birds' feathers.

Line patterns

- *Cutting out:* making repeating patterns.
- *Making line patterns in dough:* straight, curved, zigzag, wavy, wiggly lines.
- *Drawing and painting:* making line patterns, using different thicknesses of crayons or paintbrushes.

Patterns in the home

- *Tiles:* describing repeating patterns in floor and wall tiles.
- *Wallpaper:* finding the pattern repeats; looking for similar patterns, same shapes, different colours; finding line patterns.
- *Clothing:* finding repeating patterns on socks and jumpers; finding patterns of colour, shape, line or a combination.
- *Wrapping paper:* describing the patterns; finding the repeats.
- *Packaging:* describing patterns on cans, boxes and bags.
- *Using mirrors:* observing patterns, then observing them in a mirror and describing what has changed.

Making patterns

- *Using construction kits:* making staircase patterns, making towers with alternating coloured pieces blue, red, blue, red...
- *Using small items:* lines of animals, buttons, conkers, acorns or marbles, to show ABAB, or ABCABC patterns.
- *Cooking:* making icing patterns on cakes and biscuits; putting food on the plate to make a repeating pattern such as carrot, peas, carrot, peas.

Time patterns

- *Ordering events when cooking:* making sandwiches and describing the order.
- *Ordering events during the day:* describing what has been done in order.
- *Days of the week:* repeating the sequence of the days.

Movement and dance patterns

- *Dancing:* moving to a repeated sequence of movements.
- *Music:* making repeating rhythmic sequences using homemade instruments such as cans or boxes with dried peas or rice inside, tapping with spoons, scraping wood on sandpaper.

Rhymes and stories

- *New and favourite stories:* re-telling the story, remembering the order of events. Story books often have patterns in their borders or end pages which can be explored.

5

Shape and space

What is the study of shape and space?

Shape and space is the area of mathematics that will develop as geometry in later schooling. Haylock and Cockburn observe that many adults do not see a relationship between the study of shape and space, or geometry, and the study of number. However, the two basic ideas in the study of shape are classification which is a form of equivalence and changing shape which is a form of transformation, so that 'the fundamental notions of transformation and equivalence are common to understanding both number and shape, and it is this that makes these two into a unified subject' (2008: 179). Studies of children's mathematical achievements have shown that young children who understand shape and space concepts are better at arithmetic as well as geometry in later years (Assel *et al.* 2003; Sarama and Clements 2009).

Understanding shape and space is essential for making sense of the world since all physical objects possess three-dimensional shape and are located in spaces within our environment. We should note that we only see two-dimensional shapes as faces of three-dimensional ones in the real world; as soon as we create a 2D shape, even from the thinnest paper, it possesses thickness and becomes 3D. Also, the shapes that we think of as being mathematical shapes (squares, triangles, cubes and spheres etc.) are not perfect when seen in the environment and are essentially abstract notions that we create in our minds. So, Mason (1991: 76) defines geometry as 'the dynamics of the mind; what is "seen"'. He describes geometry as being apparently in the physical world, but actually in the mind, and recommends that it is taught so that children have a means of organising their mental sense of shape and space.

The term space refers here to the position and orientation of objects and changes in position including translation (sliding), rotation (turning) and reflection (flipping). In the early years it begins as a developing understanding of spatial orientation; a child knowing where they are in relation to the things around them and the language of position and movement, and this understanding will later be extended to changes in geometric shape.

Shape and space concepts will also be experienced and used in other areas of the curriculum including the expressive arts and knowledge and understanding of the world.

How children learn about shape and space: research findings

Shape

Much of the early research into how young children develop concepts of shape and space refers back to Piaget's theories and research (Piaget and Inhelder 1967). Piaget's theory of constructivism emphasises the need for a wide variety of practical experience in order for a child to construct shape concepts. Furthermore, Piaget concluded that early shape concept formation was topological, describing the way in which shapes can be transformed by squeezing and stretching (see Figure 5.1). If a three-year-old is asked to copy a drawing of a triangle, they may draw a circle. From the topological perspective, this is correct, as a triangle can be stretched and squeezed until it forms a circle. Both shapes have the same property of being closed; that is the drawing begins and ends at the same point (Copeland 1979). Open shapes such as crosses are more accurately drawn, but straight lines are unlikely to be straight. Since young children find it difficult to draw accurate two-dimensional shapes, which distinguish between a circle and a square for example, Piaget concluded that the children saw all closed shapes in the same way.

Studies of babies show that from birth they are able to distinguish between an open shape (for example a cross) and a closed shape (a square) but cannot distinguish between two closed shapes (a square and a circle). This would seem to confirm Piaget's topological view, however by four months they were able to distinguish between two different closed shapes (Quinn et al. 2001; Turati et al. 2003). Older children may not be able to draw these shapes accurately, but this could be due to limited drawing skills. Indeed, Lovell (1971) observed that young children found it easier to construct straight-sided shapes using matchsticks than to draw them, while Golomb (1990) found that children could model in clay shapes which they were unable to draw in recognisable form. Samara and Clements (2009) conclude that Piaget's topological theory was restricted by the limited variety of shapes used in his research and also by a lack of attention to the role of language in shape learning.

In an detailed study of young children's understanding and development of shape concepts, Clements et al. (1999) found that although they use visual matching to identify shapes they also begin to recognise components of shapes and simple properties, so that by the time that they are six they become quite sophisticated in their ability to sort and classify 2D shapes. The range of children's understanding was based not so much on the age of the children as on their opportunities for learning, emphasising the role of the more competent adult in moving the children's thinking on (see also Coltman et al. 2002 on scaffolding learning of 3D shape) as well as the practical experiences advocated by Piaget.

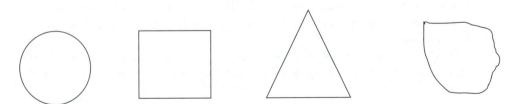

FIGURE 5.1 All these shapes are closed. They can be squeezed or transformed into each other

Since children who are offered only a limited understanding of shape often have fixed incorrect views by the age of five, Clements and Sarama (2011) also emphasise the importance of the practitioner's own understanding, since they will not be able to move children's thinking on if their own understanding is still at a low level. Indeed the following discussion may challenge your own understanding of shape due to the way that you were taught in school.

Clements *et al.* (1999) emphasise three essential elements of teaching about shape: regularity, orientation and the use of non-examples (see also Tsamir *et al.* 2008).

Regularity

Human beings have a preference for symmetry and regularity and this is true even in very young children and in peoples who have not received any formal schooling (Sarama and Clements 2009). This means that children will generally recognise circles and squares before other shapes because they are the most regular shapes (one square is identical to every other square except in size, having four equal sides and equal angles, whereas two triangles may have different shapes). There is therefore a tendency to use only regular examples of other shapes in teaching, perhaps in an attempt to simplify the curriculum, as a result of which many children will have a very limited understanding of the concept and will not recognise irregular shapes as examples (see Figure 5.2).

Children therefore need to experience a wide variety of examples of common shapes: long thin rectangles as well as short fat and square rectangles (note: a rectangle is any four-sided shape with right angles and therefore the square is a special, regular, rectangle); and all sorts of triangles: isosceles (two equal sides), right angled and scalene (all sides different lengths) as well as the more regular equilateral form, and the opportunity to talk about the shapes and their attributes (Figure 5.3).

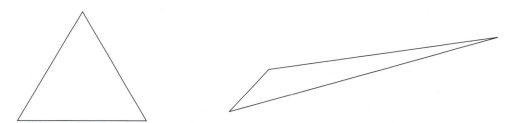

FIGURE 5.2 Two examples of triangles; both have 3 sides yet many children will not recognise the second as a triangle

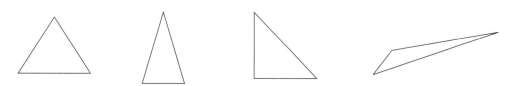

FIGURE 5.3 A range of triangles (from left to right): equilateral, isosceles, right angled and scalene triangles

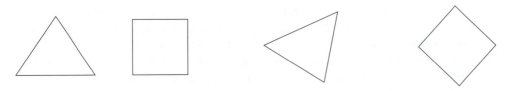

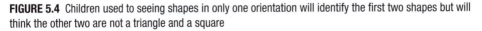

FIGURE 5.4 Children used to seeing shapes in only one orientation will identify the first two shapes but will think the other two are not a triangle and a square

Orientation

Orientation describes the position of a shape in relation to its context and is not a critical attribute of a shape. However many practitioners will always present polygons (straight-sided shapes) with one side parallel to the edge of the table or to the ground or draw it parallel to the edge of the paper or board. If children are only presented shapes in this way many will see the orientation as a critical (essential) attribute of the shape and therefore will not recognise the shape when it is presented differently (Figure 5.4).

Children need to experience a wide variety of shapes, in different orientations and to talk about their properties in order to develop higher level concepts.

Use of non-examples

The use of non-examples i.e. shapes that are not members of the set encourages children to look at the attributes in more detail (Clements *et al.* 1999). Young children asked to identify triangles are able to pick out clear non-examples, for example a square in a set of triangles, but not a near-example, for example an incomplete shape with three sides or a shape that has four sides, one of which is much smaller (Figure 5.5). Discussion about such shapes will encourage reasoning about which attributes are critical for a particular shape and which are non-critical (Tsamir *et al.* 2008).

Space

Research shows that children oriented themselves in space as the basis of a personal reference system using their own body; firstly towards themselves and later towards an object, then begin to consider relationships between objects and other people (Leushina cited in Thorpe, 1995). Their understanding grows as they learn first to reach out to grasp

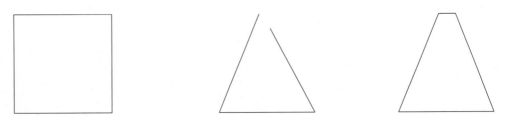

FIGURE 5.5 Non-examples of a triangle: children will recognise that the square is not a triangle but may think that the two near-examples on the right are triangles because they are visually similar to a triangle

objects, then to move around their environment and are then given greater freedom to explore their surroundings (Sarama and Clements 2009). Drawing children's attention to landmarks (next to the settee, or past the post box) will help them in this. There is some evidence that boys have better special abilities than girls (Casey *et al.* 2008) and it has been suggested that this is due to their preference for construction toys that encourage attention to relationships and shapes and to them being given more freedom to roam outdoors (Clements and Samara 2009). This would indicate that girls should be encouraged to engage in such activities in preschool.

Young children's understanding of shape and space

Unless otherwise noted, much of this section draws on the work of Sarama and Clements (2009, Clements *et al.* 1999). It should be noted that children's development is heavily dependent on the range of learning opportunities offered to them.

Babies

From birth babies begin to make sense of shape and space in their environment: they recognise familiar faces and objects; they are able to distinguish between open and closed shapes (e.g. between a cross and a square). By four months they can tell the difference between circles and squares (Quinn *et al.* 2001) and between different 3D shapes (Poirer *et al.* 2000) and as they get older they will explore these for themselves (Figure 5.6). They learn to stack 3D shapes and begin to make arrangements of them e.g. lines indicating spatial understanding.

FIGURE 5.6 Libby at 14 months enjoys exploring shape

In relation to the spatial environment, at first babies will learn patterns of movement, for example if they are used to looking right out of the cot to see who is coming in the door they will continue to look right even if turned round. However as they begin to get a sense of their own bodies they will develop an understanding of direction and distance, recognising and reaching out for things around them. From the age of about six months, as babies learn to move around they begin to develop a sense of the wider environment and develop 'path integration' – the ability to learn the path between one place and another. By the age of 15 months children can understand some of the position words especially on, in and under (Meints *et al.* 2002).

Two to three years

At this age children's concept of a particular shape may be too wide and include other, related shapes; e.g. 'circles' will often include oval shapes and 'rectangles' include parallelograms without right angles as they focus on one attribute but not all the critical attributes. Although they are able to distinguish between circles, squares and triangles, they are not yet able to show this in their drawings, but they can use sticks to create linear shapes and clay or playdough to create 3D models. By the age of two they can build towers and walls with blocks and are able to match two identical 3D objects even though they may not have names for these.

As they explore their environment further they are able to build up a mental image of the space they inhabit, locate familiar landmarks (stationary objects in the home as well as outdoors) and remember short journey sequences.

During their preschool years, the children will gradually learn about a wider range of positional concepts including up and down, next to, between and behind, although left and right may not be understood until the age of six. They become more competent at moving a shape in a straight line to match it (for example in placing a shape into a jigsaw or posting box) but may find it more difficult to rotate the shape. As they develop these concepts it is important that adults use the appropriate language with them so that they become fluent in positional language.

Four to five years

Children by this age are able to recognise a range of common shapes though their drawings, whilst distinguishable as triangle, circle, square, may not clearly show different types of triangles. They begin to recognise some parts of a shape (e.g. number of sides), usually paying more attention to side length than angle size. They can use flat shapes to create pictures and by five are able to choose appropriate shapes with attention to length and angle.

In their block play they create more complex arches, crosses, corners and enclosures and can visualise shapes in order to predict building outcomes. Drawings of solid shapes are usually not 3D representations but are of a face of the shape until children are five or six years old, for example drawing a square for a cube, a rectangle for a cuboid, and a circle or triangle for a cone.

They have developed a more complex understanding of space and can imagine what an object looks like from another person's viewpoint. They are more competent at rotating a shape to match it and by five are learning to flip the shape over where necessary.

Experiences and key concepts in shapes and space

Having outlined what children may be able to do by the time they start mainstream school, the key concepts and experiences to explore in preschool settings can be summarised as:

- exploring and describing natural and manufactured shapes
- constructing and deconstructing shapes
- exploring lines
- simple properties of 2D shapes
- simple properties of 3D shapes
- reflection and symmetry
- position and movement
- interpreting pictorial representations of spatial relationships.

These concepts overlap each other; the same experience can be used to encourage development of understanding across a range of concepts, such as, whilst making models with junk packaging, describing the shapes, discussing the shape in relation to what the packaging originally contained, and exploring how the boxes best fit together.

Exploring and describing natural and manufactured shapes

Young children will have explored their environment through touch, taste, smell, sight and sound. Through adult intervention in their play and through focused activities they can be encouraged to use new language to describe shapes, using the language of classification. They can investigate natural objects, such as leaves, bark, stones, shells, flowers, seeds and mini-beasts, as well as manufactured items. They will enjoy making their own objects from clay and junk materials and can be encouraged to describe those, classifying them according to their attributes:

- *Texture.* Children respond to touching an object by describing what they feel, whether it is smooth, soft, hard, rough, bumpy, sharp, has points . . . This may link with scientific exploration, especially when children are observing natural items which they have collected, such as crinkly autumn leaves, soft petals on flowers, or sticky clay.
- *Colour.* Children will be beginning to use colour names to describe objects. They can sort by colour for both natural and manufactured items. Sorting autumn leaves by colour, they can find reds, yellows and browns of differing hues. They may separate toy cars by colour, putting red ones on one road and blue ones on a different one on the floor plan.
- *Features.* Children can make collections by what is common, and can be encouraged to use shape properties such as things with holes in them (airflow balls, colanders, lacing board, slotted spoon . . .), rings (hoops, quoits, bracelets, necklaces . . .), things with lids (saucepan, box, jar . . .). Other features which children will encounter include:
  - shapes with 'insides': boxes, tins, bottles, shells
  - twists and turns: telephone cable, rope, liquorice or barley sticks, some shells, screws, pasta spirals

- knots: tied shoe laces, parcels tied with string, fastenings on dolls clothes
- flat surfaces: cube dice, bricks, boxes
- curved surfaces: balls, spoon bowls, wheels
- solid shapes: bricks, blocks, table tops, dolls . . .

■ *Differences*. When sorting, children may find items which do not belong in a set. They can be encouraged to find the odd-one-out from collections. Using a feely box with a collection inside, children can find the piece of velvet amongst the rougher fabrics, the ball amongst the bricks, the doll's cup amongst the plates . . . They can make their own collections of similar items and then add something which does not belong. It is the discussion of why something does not belong, using shape and other classifying language such as colour, texture or size, which will help children to develop the concept of difference as well as the concept of 'the same' or 'similar' as they identify the common and different features.

■ *Size*. As they compare two or more items children can be encouraged to describe the differences using size, such as larger and smaller balls, longer and shorter plank, thicker and thinner twig . . . Comparisons of size are considered in detail in Chapter 6.

When children are investigating they will probably use a mixture of the above ways of classifying shapes in order to describe what they have found. Tammy was four years old and had picked up a conker.

TAMMY: What's this?

ADULT: It's called a conker. Where did you find it?

TAMMY: There. (Points to under a chestnut tree.)

ADULT: Look up. Can you see those prickly balls? Those are conker cases. Let's pick one. (Pulls a conker case from a lower branch.)

TAMMY: It hurts!

ADULT: Yes. It's a special case to keep the seed safe. There should be a conker inside. Shall we look? (The adult opens the case to show the conker.) What does your conker look like?

TAMMY: My conker is bigger . . . brown . . .

ADULT: Yes and it's round . . . smooth . . . hard. And the case is green with prickles on it. Feel inside the case.

TAMMY: Lovely. Smooth.

ADULT: Does your conker fit in this case?

TAMMY: (Tries the case for her conker). Too big (referring to her conker).

Here Tammy uses colour, shape, size and texture to describe what she has found. She spent some more time that morning trying to find a container for her conker so that it was safe and returned to the adult later with a doll's teapot.

TAMMY: Look. Fits.

Constructing and deconstructing shapes

As young children develop so they become increasingly aware that some things will come apart and can be fitted together again. They may use trial and error methods to find what fits, such as pushing a jigsaw piece around until it falls into place. They will fill jars with treasures, pour sand into buckets to make sandcastles and play with jigsaws. These are all examples of putting together or taking apart to explore how shapes fit and how new shapes can be made. Children will benefit from opportunities to explore:

- *Fitting shapes together.* They will put scissors in the scissors holder, felt pens in their box, stack rings on a post, nest beakers one inside the other, play with jigsaws, build with blocks and construction kits . . . Each of these activities offers opportunities for looking at fit, whether there are gaps and whether the pieces are in the correct place. They can describe the fit using language such as on top, underneath, next to . . . They can also talk about items which do not fit together and why this is so, developing their observation skills.

- *Taking shapes apart.* In many settings children will have opportunities to build large constructions which they can climb inside, or make large models which they can sit on and move. Through these activities they can explore how the pieces fit together and which pieces fit in particular places to make their model. They may take apart one model and make something different with it, so that they explore the range of shapes which can be made with the same pieces. Using questions such as 'How else can the pieces fit?' or 'Where will this one go?' children can be encouraged to build mental images of their models whilst they are being made, and of the likely finished product.

When building models, children will frequently take them apart to make changes. Encouraging them to describe what they plan to do, are doing, or have done, will assist them to use mathematical language of shape and of position. When making playdough models children will reshape their dough to change what they are making, so that a ball of dough becomes a snake or a cat.

- *Rearranging objects.* Children move pieces in a construction to change its shape or its function. As they become more aware of how the pieces fit together they will begin to recognise whether or not a piece will fit in a different position. They may move objects such as doll's house furniture, changing its position. They may build a high tower with blocks, then use the same blocks to rebuild into a wall. Describing these changes, using language of shape and position, will help children to build mental images of shapes and where they will fit, especially if questions of the 'what if. . .' type are used.

- *Reshaping objects.* Changing the shape of dough models, folding pieces of paper or doll's clothes, stretching rubber bands, making and changing a necklace from poppet beads, are all examples of ways in which children can alter the shape of an object. They can be encouraged to try new changes, again by asking 'what if. . .?' questions. They can be encouraged to copy shapes, for example when making a pot from dough, and to describe what they are doing.

FIGURE 5.7 The boys made 'transformers', which can change shape from robots to machines

These experiences encourage children to consider how shapes can be made and changed, where pieces can fit, and to use language of shape and position. They may begin to explore volume, particularly through activities such as making and reshaping a piece of dough into something new or using construction kits (Figure 5.7). They may make straight lines, curves, shapes with holes or insides, and change them so that they, or a toy, can fit inside the shape they have made.

Tim and Ben (four years five months) made a truck with the Quadra. When it was finished, they sat in it for a while, pretending that they were in an aeroplane. They discussed their model with an adult and both expressed interest in helicopters. With help, they made a top for their truck, with blades. Another adult asked about their work.

TIM: It's a big helicopter now. The top goes round and round.

ADULT: How did you make it?

TIM: We made a car. It was boring.

BEN: We made a top for it. Sally (an adult) helped make the top.

TIM: Where we sit. It's the same.

ADULT: Do you both fit in?

BEN: Yes and we're going to fly away.

Exploring lines

Exploring lines will provide understanding of the sides and edges of 2D and 3D shapes. Painting, drawing, printing and sewing with lacing cards all offer opportunities for children to explore lines which are straight, curved, zigzag, loops, thick and thin. Making lines of different widths, and of various shapes, then discussing the shape, thickness and direction of the lines, will encourage development of the following concepts:

- *Line shape* which includes straight, curved, zigzag and loop. Using different printing materials will produce a variety of lines, such as straight with the edge of a piece of card, curved with string, zigzags and loops with felt pens, paint or crayons.

- *Thickness*, developing ideas of thick, thin, wide and narrow. Thick brushes will produce a different line from thin ones, and different again from a toothbrush or nail brush. Printing with a feather can give a very thin line, or a thick one depending whether the fine edge or flat face of the feather is used.

- *Outlines*, developing the ideas of shape, turn, straight and bend. Tracing around the outer edge of a shape will encourage awareness of the shape enclosure. This can be achieved through tracing around shapes in the sand tray, using sewing cards, drawing around shapes and printing with objects which will make a clear outline, such as the inside of a jam jar lid.

- *Direction*, including forward, backward, straight on and turn. The language of movement can be developed through exploring lines. This can be achieved through painting and printing, and also through the use of painting and drawing software, which enables children to produce different types of lines, a variety of shapes, with outlines or filled in. Most of this software has the facility to alter shapes, by stretching and turning. Programmable toys, such as Beebot and Roamer, can be programmed by the children to explore movement. If a pen is attached to Beebot or Roamer children can see the trail of the line of movement which is left and can re-program it to move back along the same line or to make different line patterns. Similarly, children's own movements can be used to explore lines, through nursery action rhymes such as 'Farmer's in his den', or 'Looby Loo', or through moving on trucks and tricycles outside, in different directions and using straight, curved and zigzag movements.

In all of these experiences, it is the interaction between child and adult that enables the use of new language to develop. Children's schema for 'straight', 'curved' and so on will develop through activities such as those suggested above, and through copying, repeating and devising their own patterns with lines and shapes (see Chapter 4 on pattern).

Simple properties of 2D shapes

Making pictures with shape tiles, Fuzzy Felt or magnetic tiles are regular early years activities. Children can describe the shapes which they have combined to make their picture, perhaps begin to name some of them, such as circle and square, though it should be remembered that children are really working with 3D objects, not 2D, and they are recognising, and later naming, the face of the object as circle etc. Where children use shapes to make repeating patterns there are strong links with their work on pattern (Chapter 4). They can cut shapes out of flat sheets of playdough or clay and describe them. Concepts to be developed here are:

- *Combining 2D shapes*. At first, children may use shape tiles which are recognisable as objects, such as Fuzzy Felt people and animals, flower heads and pieces of fencing. They will enjoy combining different pieces to make recognisable pictures, putting wheels onto a car body outline, or making an owl, with ears and eyes. Mosaic tiles, which have mathematical shapes including circles, triangles, squares and rectangles, can be used to make patterns. Children may explore which shapes will fit together, leaving no gaps (tessellation) and, through discussion, begin to name some of the shapes, particularly circle or 'round'. They may use these shapes in drawings, perhaps making a picture of a cat with a 'round' body, or the sun as a circle.

■ *Sorting 2D shapes and naming them.* Choosing shape tiles for a picture offers opportunities for sorting and naming 2D shapes. Shapes used should include everyday shapes as well as mathematical ones. Children can sort stars, moons, animal templates, transport and house templates or sorting toys, so that they have experience of making a set with common features and the opportunity to discuss what is common, such as 'points' on stars, that the sun is 'round'.

■ *Faces of 3D shapes.* Posting boxes are a good example of this concept, with their posting slots which match one face of a 3D shape. Children find, by trial and error to begin with, which shape fits where. As they become familiar with the task, they compare the surface shape, the 2D outline of the 3D shape, with the posting slots, and find a fit. Printing with objects such as bottle tops, corks, potatoes offers opportunities to explore the surface shape of these objects. They can compare the cork with the print left by its circular face and by its side, and consider which part of the cork has made this shape.

Simple properties of 3D shapes

From experiences of sorting and classifying objects, fitting shapes together and taking them apart and rearranging and reshaping objects, children will have had opportunities to explore some of the properties of 3D shapes (Figure 5.8). From their experience of 3D objects, which can be handled, children can make observations which will help them to begin to understand about 2D shapes, for example, that the tin of baked beans has 'round' or circular end faces, that the tins can be stacked one on another if the 'round' faces are put together and that if they turn the tin on its side it will roll. They usually sort and classify

FIGURE 5.8 Exploring 3D shape through building with wooden blocks

according to shape before they use shape names. Adult intervention may well include the use of more formal language, which will help the child to begin to give a name to the concept of 'square' or 'circle'. Children may draw, paint or model flat shapes and pre-fives can often recognise and name boxes, cones, cylinders (tins, cans) and pyramids.

Through experiences of working with shapes, and discussion, children will begin to recognise the following properties of shapes:

- *Face shapes* including curved, straight, flat, points and edges. These can be flat or curved. Some shapes have corners or points, for example cubes and cuboids, others do not, such as cylinders and spheres; the cone has both. Through finding shapes which fit particular criteria from a selection on display or from inside a feely box, they will develop the concepts of flat and curved, points, and edges. Using the 3D shapes for printing will emphasise their 2D faces.

- *Movement*, or rolling and sliding. Through throwing balls and quoits, and sliding toys down a ramp, children will have opportunities to explore properties of movement. Although in theory rounded shapes roll and shapes with flat faces slide, some flat-faced shapes can be made to roll if the gradient of the slope is steep enough. This property can be explored through encouraging children to change the gradient of the slope until all the objects they are using will roll down the slope.

- *Arrangements*, through stacking 3D shapes and building strong structures. By choosing shapes to fit together when building a model, children will have discovered that flat faces fit together and form strong structures; that cylinders will only stack with circular faces together and that some shapes are not good for building except as decoration, such as spheres, cones and pyramids.

- *Properties* of solidity and hollowness, exploring insides and outsides, and unfolding and folding nets of 3D shapes. These properties may be easier to explore as part of a focused activity, so that children are encouraged to discuss what they observe. Commercial packaging, such as sweet boxes and cereal boxes, will unfold if undone along the seams. Sweet packaging is particularly useful for this as it comes in so many different shapes and sizes. Children can take the boxes apart, fold them flat, look at the shapes of the flattened packet, then fold it up again. They may use construction kit pieces such as Polydron to make their own boxes and take them apart and put them together again.

Reflection and symmetry

Pushing shapes into a posting box, placing shapes into an inset puzzle board and seeing their reflection in the mirror as themselves are all examples of experiences which children may well have had by the time they are three years old. Young children do not discriminate between left and right, so that mirror images of objects such as shoes have little meaning for them. Until children are five or six years old they are as likely to put their shoes onto the correct feet as the wrong way round. By trial and error they may find how a puzzle piece fits into an inset tray or into a simple jigsaw, turning pieces around and over until there is a fit. When outside, or going for a walk, they can be encouraged to observe symmetry in nature, such as butterflies, or in manufactured items, for example symmetry in railings, wire fencing, or manhole covers (Figure 5.9). The following examples give an

FIGURE 5.9 Exploring symmetry in manufactured items

indication of the range of experiences which are appropriate for preschool children and which will help them to begin to understand about reflections and symmetry.

- *Turning*: developing ideas of movement, turning and flipping over. Using posting boxes offers early ideas of symmetry, as children find how to turn the shapes in order to fit them through the holes. As they look at the face of the shape they will see a mirror image of the hole through which it has to pass in order to fit. Similarly inset boards can be used. Some of these have been made so that shapes will fit in just one way; for others the shapes will fit in more than one way (Figure 5.10). Children experience matching the shape by turning it until it fits, and sometimes flipping it over. Jigsaws can be used as a later development. Here the pieces fit together and there are picture as well as shape and symmetry clues.

- *Reflections.* Using mirrors helps children explore the world around them in reflection and consider similarities and differences. Discussion with an adult can encourage them to make observations about people and objects that they see in the mirror. They can compare the 'sameness' of the two sides of their bodies. Where there is still water there may also be reflections and children will enjoy seeing their reflection in a puddle or in the water tray.

- *Making symmetrical patterns* (Figure 5.11). 3D constructions and 2D tile pictures can be explored for symmetry. When painting, children can make blot and fold patterns, open out their sheets of paper and discuss the symmetry of the pattern. Paper can be folded then cut and opened out to reveal a symmetrical design.

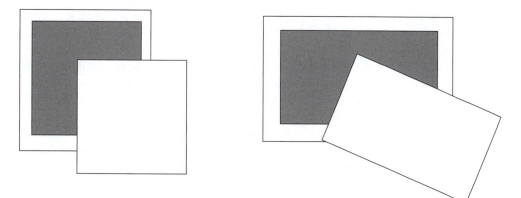

FIGURE 5.10 The square piece will fit back into its outline in four ways, whereas the rectangle piece will only fit back in two ways

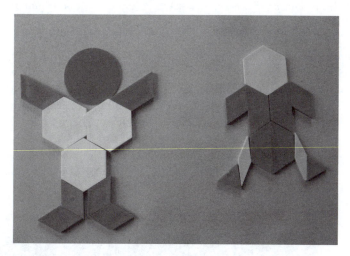

FIGURE 5.11 Symmetrical pictures made from shape tiles

Position and movement

Young children will climb to the top of the climbing frame, hang upside down from a bar, lie on their tummies to view mini-beasts, wiggle through a plastic tunnel, or crawl around inside crates and boxes, all the time taking note of how the world around them appears to change as they take different positions. They will move in different directions and in different ways, moving backwards, forwards and sideways. They crouch down or stretch up tall, curl up tight or stretch as far as they can. They can be encouraged to develop language of position and movement through such activities. The following shows the range of experiences which will help to develop these concepts:

■ *Observing and describing things from different spatial viewpoints.* Encouraging children to observe and describe things they can see from usual and unusual positions, such as looking backwards through their legs, from the swing, from the top of the slide, lying on their backs and looking up, will help them to begin to see objects from different spatial points of view. Opportunities will arise spontaneously during children's play and during a focused physical activity, such as a movement session, or through action rhymes. If photographs are taken and displayed of everyday objects from unusual views, for example objects viewed from the outdoor sandpit, the swings, the plastic tunnel or from the top of the slide, children can look at the photographs and decide where they think they were taken. During a walk there can be opportunities to stop and view familiar things from unfamiliar positions and children can observe what looks the same and what looks different. When children have made a model, perhaps a tower with blocks, they can be encouraged to draw it from the front, then move their position and draw it from another position. Similarly, they may like to draw a favourite toy, the doll's house or a car from different positions. Through discussion with an adult they can compare their drawings for similarities and differences.

■ *Relative positions, directions and distances.* Children will be beginning to use position, direction and distance vocabulary such as on, off, on top of, underneath, in front of, near, far away, next to, from, into, out of . . . (Figure 5.12). Sometimes they will have opportunities to choose from a variety of appropriate position language to describe what they see, for example 'My teddy is under the blanket'; 'My teddy is in the cot' or 'My teddy is next to the rabbit'. Any of these sentences can describe the situation which they see. With sensitive intervention, an adult can extend the child's awareness of the range of position language that might be used.

There will be opportunities for adults to describe movement: 'Jamie is running towards the tree' or 'John is going into the tunnel'. Relative positions can be described so that

FIGURE 5.12 At the top she announced 'I'm going to go *down* the slide *backwards*'

FIGURE 5.13 The train track enables children to explore movements of straight and turn

children become aware of situations where language such as close to, next to and far away is used. Sometimes the language can be confusing, for example, if 'next to' is used to describe two children sitting together with a 30 cm gap between them or it is used to describe next-door houses, with a much larger distance between them. At this stage children may still be confused if a barrier is placed between themselves and an object and they will then perceive the object as being further away. The concepts of position, direction and distance can be explored through the children's movement, through the use of road mats and train tracks and when using programmable toys such as Beebot or Roamer (Figure 5.13). They can explore both their own position in relation to things around them and the position of an object in relation to other things, through treasure hunts and simple mapping.

Interpreting pictorial representations of spatial relationships

Through discussing pictures in books and photographs children will begin to understand the relationships between objects and pictures. At this age perspective is not understood and they are just beginning to see how 3D objects are portrayed on paper as 2D objects. Six- and seven-year-old children may still not understand 2D representations of 3D objects. However, when children have opportunities to study pictures and photographs, and make their own paintings and drawings, they can begin to interpret spatial relationships in 2D representations. They can be encouraged to develop their understanding through:

- *Describing pictures of 3D objects.* Children will usually describe what they can see; for example, a man, a dog or a car. They may describe a bird, but not its position in the tree or the sky. Through discussion with adults their use and understanding of positional language can be enhanced.

■ *Modelling things in pictures.* This will help children to make close and detailed observation of what is in the picture and to begin to interpret 2D representations in 3D modelling. They may copy the stance of a person in a picture, or make a model with blocks or construction kit pieces from a picture or photograph. They may wish to use the blocks from a tower and draw around them, using a face to represent each block, as a means of recording (Gura 1992).

■ *Describing their own pictures of objects.* Children will not produce drawings which take account of perspective at this stage. 3D objects will have a 2D view of them; a person will be drawn from the front view, a box will be an enclosure, a ball will be a circle and a house will be a front view. Discussion will help children to observe the position from which they have drawn objects and to relate this to distance and direction.

Problem solving

Through their block play, working with construction kits and building models, children will set themselves problems and find ways of solving them. They will make a model, then take it apart to make it in a different way, perhaps changing its shape or its size or both to make it fulfil its purpose. For model making they can be encouraged to:

■ describe and/or draw a plan of what they wish to make

■ choose the materials to make the model, refining their choice as they work

■ carry out their plan, with adult intervention to discuss how closely their model fits their original planning, and the reasons for changes made

■ review the finished model, describe how they made it, which pieces were chosen and why, and identify improvements which could be made

■ make and evaluate the improvements to their model

■ use appropriately the language of shape, position and movement in their discussions.

For other aspects of spatial awareness children can be encouraged to describe what they plan to do in order to solve a problem, such as where they intend to go on their bikes, or how they can transport items to another place or finish a jigsaw puzzle, using appropriate mathematical language.

Block play

Block play has been popular in preschool education for many years. Commercially produced blocks were available during the nineteenth century (Hewitt 2001). Playing with blocks offers children the opportunity to build their own structures and to explore the properties of both 3D and 2D shapes. Good quality provision for block play includes:

■ a generous supply of blocks, easily accessible and well presented

■ clearly defined and well sited block areas with smooth floor surfaces

■ adequate time and space to play

■ freedom of choice to choose where to play

- unit and hollow blocks the main focus in the area
- a rich display of books and/or pictures to stimulate children's ideas
- opportunities for risk taking
- adults who understand and appreciate the value of block play and what is needed to enrich it
- the regular presence of an adult in the block area to support the children in their play (Cubey 1999).

Block play can be enhanced by children bringing items from elsewhere into the play; for example, making a bridge and running toy cars across it.

Concept map

Table 5.1 shows the concepts outlined above in matrix form together with examples of vocabulary which can be developed. Some example activities are shown so that the map can be used as a basis for planning. Some assessment checkpoints and key questions are given to show possible learning outcomes from the activities (and see section on assessment).

Planning shape and space experiences

Adult intervention in children's play

Sensitive adult intervention is essential in order to introduce and extend children's shape and space vocabulary. Many of the experiences that children have will come from their own choice, such as working with the blocks, choosing to make a model with a construction kit, deciding they want to make plasticine cakes. All of these experiences offer opportunities for children's awareness of spatial concepts and language to be enhanced. It is important that adults' own understanding of the concepts outlined above is secure, so that children listen to the appropriate language from the adult.

Adult focused activities

Planned activities for developing spatial concepts will frequently include opportunities to develop several concepts, rather than just concentrating upon one aspect. The following activities demonstrate both planning for a range of concepts and activities which concentrate upon just one concept.

Making jigsaws

An activity for a group of four children.

- *Purpose:* to develop understanding of 2D shape, symmetry and movement.
- *Materials:* pictures from celebration cards, such as Christmas, birthday or Eid, safety scissors, envelopes to store each home-made jigsaw.
- *Language:* shape, turn, turn over, move, fit . . .

TABLE 5.1 Concept map for shape and space

KEY CONCEPT	VOCABULARY	EXAMPLES OF ACTIVITIES	ASSESSMENT CHECKPOINTS	KEY QUESTIONS
Explore and describe natural and manufactured shapes	Texture: smooth, soft, hard, rough, bumpy, sharp, has points . . .; colour names, features: inside, outside, holes, twists . . .; same, different, similar. . .	Sorting natural from manufactured items: shells, stones, leaves, dolls, cups, books . . .; sorting by colour; sorting by feature: curved from flat faces; shapes with insides from solids; describing similarities and differences	• Uses vocabulary of texture, colour and feature appropriately • Describes similarities and differences	• Which group does this belong to? Why? How do you know? • What is the same about these? How are they different?
Construct and deconstruct shapes by fitting together, taking apart, rearranging and reshaping	Position: on top, under, beside, next to . . .; it: inside, outside; same, different, similar	Using: stack/nest toys; jigsaws. Making and changing with: blocks; dough; construction kits; shape tiles; cooking; a tent from blankets . . .; describing similarities and differences; making decisions, asking what if . . .? questions	• Fits pieces together and takes them apart • Makes and describes models using appropriate mathematical vocabulary • Plans what to make and how; revises plan to improve model	• Which pieces fit together? Can you make them fit together in a different way? • Can you make a different model with the same pieces? • How can you make your model better?
Lines: shape and directions	Straight, curved, zigzag, loop . . .; thick, thin, narrow, wide . . .; shape, turn, straight, bend . . .; forward, backward, straight on, turn	Sand play, printing, painting, drawing, computer art software, sewing: making lines, patterns, thicknesses, directions, outlines . . .; using Roamer or Beebot to tell a story: moving in different directions; using the pen adapter to show the pathway	• Discriminates between line shapes and patterns • Uses shape and movement vocabulary to describe line patterns	• What patterns can you make in the sand? What other patterns could you make? What could you use to make them? • How could you make Beebot go over there?

Simple properties of 2D shapes	Circle, triangle, square, rectangle, star; round, straight, flat, point, curved, edge, face, circle, square, triangle . . .	Making shape tiles pictures and patterns; describing the shapes; using 3D shapes: comparing their faces; using posting boxes, printing with 3D shapes to compare faces; Creating shapes with sticks, straws, clay or playdough	• Chooses appropriate shape for picture • Uses shape vocabulary to describe properties	• Describe this shape to a friend: can they guess what it is? • What shape will you see if you print with this? • How many sticks did you use?
Simple properties of 3D shapes	Shapes: ball, box, can, tube; cube, pyramid, sphere, cone; face: curved, flat, straight, points, edges. . . Movement: rolling, sliding Arrangements: stacking, building, hollow; insides, outsides, unfolding, folding	Building constructions: finding good shapes for making models; making models: solid, hollow; folding and unfolding paper, blankets; unfolding and refolding packaging; throwing balls, quoits	• Uses shape vocabulary to describe properties • Uses appropriate vocabulary to describe how shapes move	• Which shapes have flat/curved faces? • What could you make with these shapes? What else could you make? • Which shapes do you think will roll? How could we find out?
Reflection and symmetry	Turning: move, turn, flip over	Using shape tiles, jigsaw puzzles: turning, flipping pieces to find a fit . . .; looking in the mirror: describing what can be seen; making symmetrical patterns: printing; blot and fold; cutting folded paper shapes; mirroring movements . . .	• Uses flips and turns to find a fit • Uses vocabulary of reflection and symmetry to describe patterns, pictures and shapes	• What can you see in the mirror? • (Blot and fold) What do you think you will see when you open up your paper? • Can you copy your partner's movements?

(Continued)

135

TABLE 5.1 *(Continued)*

KEY CONCEPT	VOCABULARY	EXAMPLES OF ACTIVITIES	ASSESSMENT CHECKPOINTS	KEY QUESTIONS
Position and movement	On, off, on top of, underneath, in front of, near, far away, next to, from, into, out of . . .	Climbing apparatus/ movement sessions: describing movements, positions from the top/ bottom/part way up the slide; lying on tummy; Using Roamer or Beebot: moving in different directions; predicting where Roamer will go . . .; Describing relative position of toys: in the doll's house, cars on the road plan . . .	• Uses vocabulary of position and movement • Follows instructions which use position and movement vocabulary • Makes observations from different viewpoints	• What can you see? What do you think you would see if you went round the back? • Where will you go if you move forward/sideways . . .? • How can we make Roamer go to the cupboard?
Interpret pictorial representations of spatial relationships	Describing pictures of 3D objects: describing their own pictures of objects	Looking at pictures in books/pictures they have drawn: describing objects using shape and position vocabulary; making a model from a picture	• Uses vocabulary of shape and position to describe objects in a picture • Observes/ draws objects from different positions and identifies similarities and differences	• What can you see in the picture? Where is it? What is next to the . . .? • What if you draw it from over there? How will it look the same/different?
Use developing understanding of shape and space to solve practical problems	Pattern, puzzle; What could we try next? How did you work it out?	Making models, pictures or patterns using 2D and/or 3D shapes; moving Roamer from one place to another	• Makes models or drawings and describes them using appropriate vocabulary • Moves from one place to another and describes what has been done	• What other models/pictures could you make? • What other materials could you use? • How could you make this even better? • What could we try next?

How to begin

Each child chooses a card and makes one cut across the card to make two pieces. The cuts can be straight, curved or jagged. They move the two pieces apart and fit them back together again, then swap their jigsaws with each other. Discussion can include:

- What shapes have you made?
- Who has a curved/straight/jagged edge?
- Where does this piece fit?
- What happens if we turn this over? Does it fit now?

This activity can be repeated, this time making two or three cuts in the cards to make three or four pieces.

Clearing up

An activity for a group or for everyone as part of carpet time. This can be repeated over time, with one or two new words introduced each time.

- *Purpose:* to develop understanding of the language of position and movement.
- *Materials:* items to be put away.
- *Language:* straight, turn, near, far, underneath, on top, over, behind, in front, up, down . . .

How to begin

The adult chooses an item and a child to put it away. The child follows the adult's instructions, whilst the others watch. All the children will need to face into the classroom so that they all observe in the same direction as the adult. Putting away a bucket under the sand tray could include:

> Go behind the doll's house.
> Now go round the paint table.
> Turn to the sand tray. Now walk to it.
> The bucket goes underneath. That's right. On the shelf under the tray.

Or, for putting a puzzle on a display table:

> Go to the blocks; they're behind the books.
> Now, turn to the window. Go to the table.
> Put the puzzle in front of the dominoes.

As the children become more confident, they can take turns to give each other instructions for putting things away. The activity can be adapted as a treasure hunt to find hidden objects.

I-spy

An activity for a small group or the whole class during carpet time.

- *Purpose:* to develop understanding of simple properties of shapes.
- *Materials:* items on a tray which can be seen by the children, such as a ball, box, spring; shell, bracelet ...
- *Language:* round, straight, curved, corner, edge, flat ...

How to begin

The adult describes an item on the tray and the children decide which one it is:

- I spy something which is round and smooth. It doesn't have any corners. What is it?
- I spy something which has flat faces. You can put things inside it. What is it?
- I spy something curved, smooth, with a hole in it. What is it?

Children can take turns to describe items on the tray for the others to recognise.

Alternatively, with a small group of children, a feely bag or box can be used, and either children find items to fit a description, or they describe what they can feel.

Block play

An activity for four children.

- *Purpose:* to design and build a structure.
- *Materials:* large wooden blocks, picture books, paper and pencils or crayons.
- *Language:* flat, curved, edge ...

How to begin

Children discuss with an adult what they will make. They give as detailed a description as possible, perhaps showing a picture in a book of what they would like to do. Sometimes children can draw a picture of their intentions. The adult asks questions to encourage the planning process:

- Which blocks will be best to make the wall?
- Why will you choose those?
- What will you put on top?

When the model is made, ask the children questions to compare the finished model with what was planned:

- You've used these blocks instead. Why did you choose these?
- I like the curved shapes on top of the wall. Did you try any other shapes?

Encourage the children to draw their finished model, helping them to observe which blocks they have used, so that their drawing is as accurate as possible. If time permits, they can draw their model from different views.

Making models

An activity for four to six children.

- *Purpose:* to explore making and reshaping 3D models.
- *Materials:* playdough or plasticine, boards, clay tools.
- *Language:* outside, inside, side, flat, curved, straight . . .

How to begin

Ask the children what they would like to make, perhaps using that week's theme as the starting point. As they work discuss their models using shape language:

- What a wiggly snake! He curves around the board.
- What will you put inside the vase?
- Do you want to make a pattern on the outside of your vase?

When the models are finished, encourage the children to describe their own and each other's models. Remind them of their original intentions; ask about changes they have made. Discuss possible improvements and as they make changes ask them to describe what they are doing:

- I'm making round apples for my tree.
- The dog needs a long, wiggly lead.
- Straight flowers for the vase.

Line printing

An activity for four children.

- *Purpose:* to explore lines.
- *Materials:* items for printing, such as feathers, sponges, strips of stiff card, toothbrushes, printing pad and paints, paintbrushes, paper.
- *Language:* straight, curved, loop, wavy, zigzag, thick, thin . . .

How to begin

Ask the children to make prints on the paper, choosing different items. Compare the shapes and lines that they make:

- What did you use to make the thin straight lines?
- How can we make zigzags?
- What sort of shapes will the toothbrush make?

As the children begin to recognise how they can make various types of lines and shapes, they can design their own line patterns.

Involving other adults in the planned activities

Language associated with spatial concepts is also language used in everyday life. This language should be used correctly and in appropriate contexts. The language to be developed can be included on the weekly planning sheet and discussed during planning sessions. You may wish to display a poster with key language as a reminder: Table 5.1 may help here. Some adults may well, in their everyday conversations, misuse spatial language. It is important to encourage its correct usage, such as not confusing 3D shapes with their faces (calling a box a square for example). Where adults are involved with helping children to plan or record their models by drawing it is important to remember that at this stage children will draw 2D representations of 3D objects, such as a square for a cube. Other recording methods can be used, such as taking a photograph of the final model. In order to ensure that all adults working in the setting during that week are aware of any specific requirements with regard to language and recording, it is helpful to spend a few minutes before the start of each session agreeing the strategies to be adopted.

Setting up environments for shape and space activities

Table 5.2 shows suggestions for contexts across the setting which could offer opportunities for discussions about shape and space during child initiated learning, or be set up for adult initiated or focused activities.

Assessment

What to look for

Use the assessment checkpoints and key questions in Table 5.1 to help with assessment. The questions include both closed (how many?) and open (how do you know?) types. Observations, with evidence of the child's behaviour to support their understanding, can be recorded. Where evidence of achievement in a standard form is required, the observational evidence can be supported by a note of the assessment checkpoint, with date and comment attached to show when the evidence of achievement was noted. Much of the evidence will be physical and may be best captured as photos. Regular observation of children's use of spatial concepts will identify their current knowledge and skills. This may identify whether children can:

- describe natural and manufactured shapes, using appropriate mathematical and everyday language
- construct and deconstruct shapes, describing what has been made and the shapes used and formed
- make and name types of lines, such as straight or curved
- identify and name simple properties of 2D shapes

TABLE 5.2 Shape and space activities across areas of the setting

ENVIRONMENT	CONCEPT/SKILL	CONTEXT
carpet time	• explore line shapes and patterns • properties of 2D and 3D shape	• playing traditional nursery games, e.g. Farmer's in his den, Looby Loo . . . • I spy games
art and craft areas	• sort by shape • explore symmetry • fit together, take apart • explore line shapes and patterns • explore properties of 2D and 3D shapes • interpret pictorial representations of spatial relationships	• choosing printing block to produce shape • choosing item to print particular line • making symmetrical blot and fold pattern • making and reshaping dough models • taking apart/remaking cardboard boxes • folding sheets of paper • making line patterns by drawing, printing, painting . . . • making pictures and patterns by painting, drawing, printing . . . • making pictures of real objects
table top games and collections	• fit together, take apart • explore properties of 2D shapes • explore symmetry	• making jigsaws • making pictures and patterns with shape tiles • threading and changing beads, making and changing 'poppet' necklaces • using shape posting boxes
sand play	• sort by shape • explore line shapes and patterns • explore properties of 2D shapes	• sorting sand play items by shape • making line patterns in the sand • making shape outline patterns in the sand
construction	• sort by shape: same and different • sort by properties of shape • fit together, take apart • interpret pictorial representations of spatial relationships	• choosing construction pieces by shape • choosing construction pieces by property of shape, e.g. 'curved' • exploring which pieces make 'strong' structures • making a model, taking it apart and re-making in a different shape • making a drawn plan for a model • using a drawing/picture to make a model • drawing a picture of a model
block play	• sort by shape: same and different • sort by properties of shape • fit together, take apart • explore properties of shapes • explore line shapes and patterns • interpret pictorial representations of spatial relationships	• choosing blocks by shape • choosing construction pieces by property of shape, e.g. 'curved' • exploring which pieces make 'strong' structures • making a model, taking it apart and remaking in a different shape • running items down a ramp • making lines of blocks: straight, turn . . . • making a drawn plan for a model • using a drawing/picture to make a model • drawing a picture of a model

(Continued)

TABLE 5.2 *(Continued)*

ENVIRONMENT	CONCEPT/SKILL	CONTEXT
role play	• sort by colour, texture, • explore reflection • explore properties of shapes • explore position and movement	• choosing dressing-up clothes • choosing jewellery by shape of beads • observing reflection in a mirror • folding blankets, sheets, tablecloths • moving furniture and goods to rearrange the shop/cafe/kitchen . . .
small world play	• explore position and movement	• building train tracks or roadways • moving dolls and furniture in the doll's house/ boats on the marina/cars on the road plan . . .
outside play	• explore properties of shapes • explore line shapes and patterns • explore position and movement	• throwing and rolling balls, hoops, quoits . . . • painting lines with water and different width brushes • climbing/swinging from apparatus • moving on trucks and tricycles • moving toys using trucks
cooking	• explore lines and shapes	• making cakes and biscuits in different shapes • cutting out pastry and biscuit dough using various shaped cutters • decorating cakes with different shaped items
information technology	• explore 2D shapes and their properties • explore line shapes and patterns • interpret pictorial representations of spatial relationships	• using an art software package to draw lines, shapes • making Roamer/Beebot travel in a straight line/turn • using pen adapter with Roamer and observing Roamer's path

- identify and use simple properties of 3D shapes to sort, classify and identify suitable shapes to solve problems
- recognise reflections and symmetry in patterns and pictures, using appropriate language
- experience, observe and describe using the language of position and movement.

Opportunities to make such assessments may occur incidentally during children's chosen activity or through specifically targeted focused activity.

Children respond well to questions such as:

- What is the same about these? How are they different?
- Who has more/fewer?

especially where they have been encouraged to respond using the mathematical vocabulary that they hear the adults using. Gradually they begin to respond in sentences and this should be encouraged. Three- and four-year-olds find it more difficult to answer questions which ask 'How do you know?' such as 'Will this shape roll? How do you know?' Young children do not initially cope well with this sort of question and tend not to respond. However, with practice, and with examples of how they might answer given by adults, they do begin to answer the 'How do you know?' type of question in a satisfactory way.

Misconceptions in concepts of shape and space

Children's understanding of shape and space concepts will be limited by their experiences and adult scaffolding of the language. These misconceptions include:

- Enclosures used to represent any closed shape, such as circle, square, triangle, due to limited drawing skills.
- Judgements of proximity and separation are influenced by barriers. A child may say that the blocks are near the window until a chair is placed between the window and the blocks. Then they will believe that the blocks and the window are further apart, even though these have not moved.
- Fitting things together, such as completing a puzzle, may still be by trial and error, rather than observing the shape and how to turn it to make a fit.
- A line with bricks or buttons may not be straight unless there is a straight edge to act as a guide, for example the table edge. Children may not perceive that their line is crooked, and may have difficulty distinguishing 'straight' in 2D and 3D shapes.
- Misunderstanding of language of distance, unless the context is clear: 'near' relating to two children sitting next to each other, and 'near' as in relation to grandma living nearby, perhaps in the next street.

The above misconceptions are to do with developmental processes and children will understand these concepts in time. Further experiences of the concepts and opportunities to explore materials will enable children to begin to build their schemas for these concepts to enhance their understanding.

Working in partnership with parents and carers

Parents will be involved in helping their children to develop concepts of shape and space throughout the early years. Children learn through play but also by observing and working alongside adults in everyday situations. Children will hear language of shape, position and movement being used, and will begin to use it themselves, both through activities in the setting and through the home.

Activities at home for developing understanding of shape and space concepts

These activities do not require any special equipment as they make use of everyday items in the home.

Sorting shapes

- *Putting away the shopping:* sorting out the tins, the boxes, and noting how they stack or fit together in the cupboard.
- *I-spy games:* finding shapes the same such as cylinders, balls or spheres.

Exploring shapes

- *Using construction kits:* Lego and Sticklebrick models; describing the shapes.
- *Building bricks:* noting how the bricks fit together and stack; discussing which brick is used for a particular representation e.g. which one shall we use for the chimney?
- *Cooking and playdough:* making pastry shapes; using pastry cutters.
- *Cutting out:* cutting around pictures, following the outline; cutting up pictures to make a jigsaw puzzle.
- *Puzzles:* using posting toys, inset puzzles, simple jigsaws.

Drawing

- *At home:* drawing favourite toys, family members, the trees in the garden, the view from the window.
- *Lines:* drawing line patterns: straight, curved, wiggly, zigzag.

Reflections

- *Mirrors:* describing what can be seen in looking glasses, car mirrors and the bowls of spoons.
- *Outside:* looking in puddles and ponds and describing reflections.

Small world play

- *Doll's house:* describing where the furniture and the people are going.
- *Cars and garage, or train set:* talk about the routes taken and relationship between toys: next to, between, behind etc.

Going for walks

- *Position:* looking at things and describing where they are: the house on top of the hill; the chimneys on the roof; the tunnel under the road; the things in the shop, including looking at the same landmarks from different directions.
- *Movement:* using language to explain where we are going, for example, out of the door, across the street, turn the corner and down the hill.

Stories

- *Shape: All Shapes and Sizes*: Shirley Hughes; *The Blue Balloon*: Mick Inkpen; *I Can Build a House*: Shigeo Watanabe.
- *Position: Bears in the Night*: Jan and Stan Berenstain; *Rosie's Walk*: Pat Hutchins.

6

Measures: making comparisons

What is the study of measurement?

To be able to measure is an important skill that will be used in many contexts throughout life. Comparisons of size are important to a child, such as who has the longer pencil or larger teddy or made the taller sandcastle. A teenager will be concerned with clothes and sizes and prices, finding a good fit, understanding the sizing system and how that applies to them, and being able to measure with reasonable accuracy, and making estimates of size. For an adult, good measuring skills are important in industry, where very fine degrees of accuracy are used. Adults use their estimation skills when making purchases for the home, and will measure for household items such as curtains, carpets or shelving, in order to make successful purchases. In Britain the complexities of measuring are compounded by our use of a dual system of measuring units; although industry now uses metric units (metres, grams, litres . . .), many adults still use imperial measures (feet and inches, pounds and ounces, pints . . .) in their everyday lives.

Measurement is an important aspect of mathematics which 'bridges two important realms of mathematics: geometry and real numbers' (Sarama and Clements 2009). It also has important links into science and geography, and applications in technology. Measuring differs from counting, in that objects that can be counted are discrete (separate) whereas measures are continuous. So, measurement links well with ordinal number as represented on a number line where fractions and decimals can be represented as well as whole numbers.

Measurement is essentially about making comparisons. The dictionary defines measure as:

> ascertain the size, amount, or degree of (something) by comparison with a standard unit or with an object of known size.
>
> (*Concise Oxford English Dictionary* 2002)

It is not possible to measure something without comparison, as can be seen from this discussion between four-year-old Martha and her five-year-old brother, Tom. They had been watching 'The Littlest Hobo', a television programme about a dog which travelled around the USA helping people.

MARTHA: I don't think that is a very little hobo.

TOM (after some thought):   It depends what a regular sized hobo looks like!

It turned out that neither child knew what a hobo was, so it makes the point well. When we describe something as little, or big, or heavy etc., we are comparing it, mentally, with a 'regular sized' one. Comparison is more obvious when we compare two things directly such as by lining them up to see which is longer or using the balance scales to see which is heavier. It is slightly less obvious to children when they use some standard measures that they are comparing with a standardised object, for example when measuring weight with a digital balance.

Two ideas are fundamental to our everyday use of measure: estimation and approximation. First, in the real world we use estimation much more than we use measuring instruments. As babies learn to move around they estimate distances and spaces between the furniture as to whether they can crawl between them. Similarly, adults use a range of estimation skills. When making a cup of coffee we estimate the amount of milk we add and do not get the measuring jug out. On parking the car we do not get out and measure the space but estimate and, when we are new to driving, tend to over-estimate to be on the safe side, because good estimation requires a lot of prior experience.

Second, measuring can never be exact, an aspect which is not always understood by adults. A measure is always an approximation, and the degree of accuracy used, such as to the nearest kilometre, metre, centimetre, millimetre, tenth, hundredth or thousandth of a millimetre, reflects the notion of approximation. Town planners, dress-makers, microchip manufacturers and atomic scientists will all be working on a different scale and therefore the degree of accuracy required will be different. Copley (2000) therefore suggests that early years educators emphasise the language used for estimation and approximation such as about, nearly, just over, almost . . .

Measuring is complex, in that it involves a range of different concepts including:

- length (including height, width, and depth)
- weight (we use the term 'weight' rather than 'mass' as it is the one that the children are more likely to hear used in everyday life)
- capacity (how much something holds)
- area
- volume (the space taken up by an object)
- time
- temperature
- angle (a measure of turn)
- money
- and compound measures, such as density (weight per volume), and fuel consumption (litres per kilometre) and speed (kilometres per hour).

Some of these are more abstract than others: we can see length and feel weight but the passing of time is not visible, and many people struggle to see money as a measure of commercial value. To be able to make informed and effective decisions in adult life, children will learn about each of these aspects of measures, their units of measure and the use of the appropriate measuring tool. Whilst there are links between some of the measures, such as length and area and volume, the skills of measuring will need to be learnt for each. Because of the relative complexity of the different measurement concepts these aspects will be learnt at different times and at different rates. A child who has learnt to use a ruler may not be able to read a weighing scale or thermometer in a meaningful way. Compound measures such as speed require consideration of two measures simultaneously, distance and time, and are therefore very difficult for small children.

To be effective at measuring, children will eventually need to acquire skills of estimation, choosing units, using measuring instruments and making measures to an appropriate degree of accuracy for the task. Measuring using some form of units involves using numbers and number operations in real situations. But in preschool settings the focus is on understanding the measurement concepts and using appropriate language to describe and compare. By the time children start preschool, they will already be using notions of measuring in everyday life. They will discuss questions such as 'How old are you?' 'Have you older brothers and sisters?' Three- and four-year-olds will use measuring language for themselves, such as:

- I'm big! (Meaning I'm tall, or sometimes I am older.)
- I'm strong; I can lift it by myself.
- Put some more juice in; I'm thirsty.

Some children will have their growth marked regularly on a height chart at home, and some may help to weigh out ingredients in the kitchen. Preschool experiences will build upon these.

How children learn about measuring: research findings

Piaget (Piaget *et al.* 1960) studied children's acquisition of concepts of measurement, in particular length, area and volume. He concluded that children have a different understanding of these measures than adults and are unable to understand these aspects fully until they had mastered two key aspects: conservation and transitivity.

Conservation

The concept of conservation is that while one attribute of an object may be changed, another may stay the same. So when considering length, a piece of string is the same length whether stretched out or bent round; if two pieces of plasticine are taken of identical weight and one is flattened out, its weight does not change; two containers can have the same capacity even if they are different shapes. Children find it difficult to conserve measures before the age of about seven and will be deceived by appearances, thinking that the measure will have changed if the shape has changed, even if they are shown that it is still the same (see Figure 6.1). Understanding of these

FIGURE 6.1 Children who cannot conserve will think the straight line is longer, that the longer roll of plasticine has a different weight and that the taller (or sometimes the fatter) container contains more water, even if they are shown the transformation

measures will depend on the children's experiences but they will usually understand conservation of:

- length at between six and a half and seven years
- area at about seven to seven and a half
- volume at about eight and a half to nine
- capacity at about seven
- weight at about nine or ten.

Transitivity

In order to use any measuring tool a child needs to understand that if one doll is 20 cm long on the ruler and another doll is 20 cm long on the ruler than the two dolls are the same size. The ruler is being used as a transitional object to compare two things that cannot be compared directly. The relationship between the two sticks and the ruler can be described as:

if	length of first doll	=	20 cm on ruler
and	length of second doll	=	20 cm on ruler
then	length of first doll	=	length of second doll

This logical reasoning is known as transitivity.

Piaget reasoned that until children could understand these essential aspects of measuring, conservation and transitivity, they should not be taught to measure; however subsequent research has shown that children can sometimes conserve in context (Schiff 1983) and will use transitivity in context (Nunes and Bryant 1996). Furthermore it appears that children will learn these aspects more quickly through being taught to measure than if we wait until they are ready to do so.

The measurement of capacity, angle and weight appear to follow similar paths of progression; however the development of time is considered separately from the other measures, as the concept is abstract, rather than based upon physical objects and experiences.

The following discussion is a summary based on Sarama and Clements (2009) and Piaget *et al.* (1960) with other authors cited in the text.

Length and distance, area, volume, capacity, angle, weight

Birth to three years of age

From birth babies appear to be sensitive to concepts of quantities including length, area, volume and angle (Hespos *et al.* 2008; Lourenco and Huttenlocher 2008). As they learn to explore, reach out, move, turn, to cover and uncover things they develop these concepts in context. Through experience, they learn about weight as they try to lift and move objects, and about capacity as they fill and empty containers in the bath and sandpit. They begin to use language such as big and long and may describe capacity using everyday language such as gone (empty) and lots (full up).

From three to about four years of age

At this age children use one of three standards to judge size:

- perceptual – what the object looks or feels like
- normative – comparing it with a mental image of what is normal
- functional – comparing it with what it is used for e.g. 'this hat is too big' (for me).

They may make errors due to choosing the wrong standard to make the comparison: 'it must be heavy because it looks big' or 'she is older than me because she is bigger'.

Once children understand a measure concept they begin to make comparisons and use comparative language. They compare lengths, heights and distances, though proximities are not always understood, so that children may believe that distances are changed when something is placed between two objects, perhaps because the distance from one to the other now includes going round the object. Longer distances which cannot be seen are often measured in time rather than distance and are therefore more difficult to compare. Experienced time is subjective so children can believe that a journey which is travelled regularly is a short one, whereas an unfamiliar journey is perceived as being longer. The measurement of length includes distance, width, height and depth with the complexities of different language about each.

Four-year-olds may compare two equal areas and agree that they are the same size, especially if it is possible to superimpose one on the other to compare. However, an experiment with two card fields of equal area and houses placed on them showed that there was an intuitive response to questions about area, and that children did not perceive two areas as still the same where the same number of toy houses had been placed on both fields, but in different arrangements. When dividing up volumes, such as cakes for dolls, children of this age did not make equal shares; a cake might be cut so that each doll received a piece, but either the pieces were of different sizes, or the dolls were given small quantities and a large piece was left.

Children will begin to compare capacity directly by pouring from one container to another though they may think that a smaller container contains more because it is fuller. They explore concepts of angle through their own physical movements and in block building.

At about four to five years of age

Children can align objects to compare their lengths and can learn to use a third (transitive) object, such as a piece of string, to compare lengths at a distance, or a stick to compare depths (Nunes and Bryant 1996). Children who see adults using measuring tools will begin to use these, such as using a ruler to measure length, though they may not yet understand the need to start at zero. Some five-year-olds may also begin to order more than two items according to length and to use the superlative language: longest, shortest, tallest . . .

They understand weight in terms of themselves, 'can I pick it up easily', though they may be deceived by the size of the object, thinking all big things must be heavy, and whether it can float or not, thinking that all light things float and heavy ones sink (MacDonald 2010). They can begin to use a beam balance to compare the weights of objects but may not know that the heavier item will make that side go down, so will need a lot of opportunity to explore.

They will compare capacity directly by pouring from one container to another and can begin to measure capacity in cupfuls etc., though they may still make conservation errors when tested. In their play, especially construction with blocks and train tracks, children will use ideas of angle including parallel lines and right angles.

Time

The concept of time is an abstract one which attracts much discussion from philosophers, even as to whether it exists at all! For children learning about time there are two related concepts:

- the measurement of time on a watch or clock, that is 'the time' that something occurs, such as 4.30 or half past four
- the passing of time, measured in seconds, minutes, hours, days, weeks, months, seasons, years. Age is an example of this which young children readily accept, for example, that they are a year older with each birthday.

Most children do not conserve time until they are about seven or eight years old (Althouse 1994). Preschool children believe that they control the passing of time by the speed of their movements, so that if they run quickly time passes quickly, but if they move slowly so does the passing of time. Until they can separate time from their own movements, children cannot make sense of standard units of time. Concepts of the passing of time have been further analysed into three categories (Charlesworth and Lind 1990):

- *Personal time.* This refers to past, present and future. Young children find understanding of past and future more difficult than the present, as they are not part of the child's immediate experience.

- *Social time.* This refers to the sequence of events which makes up the child's daily experience, for example, getting up in the morning, having breakfast, and so on, significant days of the week and times in the year such as birthdays.
- *Cultural time.* This is time measured by clocks and calendars.

As discussed above, time is subjective and without an external measure (clock) it is difficult to talk about a long or short period of time. Many settings talk about yesterday, today and tomorrow and use calendars to talk about days of the week and months (cultural time). However, before children understand these they need to understand their own personal and social time sequences and the language of before and after, earlier and later (Beneke *et al.* 2008). Preschool children will begin to understand years in relation to their birthdays and days in terms of 'sleeps'. However, a study of three- to five-year-olds in the USA (Flores 2007) found children from low socioeconomic groups had significant delay in understanding time, emphasising the importance of early years education for these children.

Measurement of time using a clock is a difficult concept for children even in the first years of primary school, since it requires an understanding of circles and fractions, and numbers in multiples of 60 and 12. Children can be introduced to a measured length of time through the use of sand timers (Copley 2000).

Temperature and money

Little has been written about how young children develop ideas about money and even less about temperature. One study on money found that at three children recognised money and knew it was for 'paying', but had little awareness of exchange or value. By the age of four some children understood that different things cost different amounts of money, at five that there was a match between the cost of the item and the money to be paid and at six they understood the concept of giving change (Berti and Bombi 1981).

Measuring and key concepts

Conservation of measures is not acquired during the preschool years. However, building upon their experiences from home, children begin to understand concepts of comparison and order related to size; they experience time passing and begin to understand that this can be measured, and to sequence events. The key concepts for most measure are common, though they develop at different rates. The key concepts in time are different and will be discussed separately.

Key concepts for measures of objects

The key concepts for measures of objects are:

- understanding the concept of a measure and using descriptive language
- comparing and using comparative language
- ordering and using superlative language
- using non-standard units and then standard units to measure and using cultural measuring tools in real world contexts.

Because of the different rates of concept development, only the first key concept and the experiences that can help to develop understanding will be considered for angle and temperature, the first two for area and volume, and all four for length, weight and capacity. Further development of concepts of area, volume, angle and temperature are usually left until children are older.

Key concepts for time

Not only is time abstract but adults often use the language of time inaccurately. An adult may say 'I will be with you in a minute' but come five minutes later; another will say 'I had to wait hours for a bus' when it was a five-minute wait on a frequent route. We experience time subjectively: time spent at a party will feel different from the same time spent in the hospital waiting room. It is therefore difficult to compare time without using a direct measure.

In the early years the key concepts for time include:

■ sequencing events and using comparative language
■ recognising time events in the child's personal history
■ comparing different units of time.

Understanding the concept of each measure and using descriptive language

Language such as big, little, small, long, thin and wide can be used to describe attributes of the experienced world (Figure 6.2). However, for the very young child, or one whose vocabulary is not well developed, this language needs to used regularly by the adult so as to become part of the child's everyday speech. Descriptive language often depends upon the child's experience: a parcel which is heavy to one child may seem light to another. Adults tend to use the 'large' words: tall, heavy, long., more often when describing objects, even describing short things as 'not very tall', so children may need to be taught the 'small' words: short, light. . .

"I think the big fish eats the little fish."

The children were really interested in the size of the plants and trees, "It's massive, up to the sky."

Dinosaurs at the Museum.

FIGURE 6.2 Visits to the Botanic Gardens and the Natural History Museum stimulated a lot of discussion about size ('I think the big fish eats the little fish', 'The children were really interested in the size of the plants and trees, "It's massive, up to the sky"', 'Dinosaurs at the Museum')

Length

Children enjoy sorting objects and using the language of length to describe what they have found, such as big, little, long, short, thin, wide and tall. Opportunities may arise in all areas of the setting including block play, small world play, model making and painting. Children can be encouraged to follow instructions which use the language of length, such as making a block roadway long enough to reach the garage, or cutting long strips of wool to make hair for the puppet. It should be noted that where children make drawings their representations of objects may well not be accurate in terms of height or width. Other considerations seem to come into play here, as demonstrated by Cox and Wright (2000), who looked at five- and seven-year-olds' representations of men and women. It seemed that the children perceived women as taller when they wear a skirt. However, it is important to discuss drawings with children and, where appropriate, to make direct comparisons between their drawings and the objects themselves in order to compare for length. In this way children will begin to make more accurate observations, even if they cannot yet show that in what they draw.

Weight

They will pick up items and say whether these are heavy or light. They may use scales or a beam balance to 'weigh' what they have collected.

Capacity

When filling containers, pouring water or sand through sieves, funnels or wheels, children will use the words 'full' and 'empty' (Figure 6.3). Discussion with them as to what is meant by 'full' is helpful, as the mathematical meaning is different from the social one. A cup

FIGURE 6.3 Sand play: 'It's full up to the top'

of tea is full to the point where it can still be safely lifted, whereas when playing in the sand or water, full may mean to the brim. This can be discussed during snack time, when children pour out their own drink. Capacity of other containers can be discussed such as 'is this box big enough to put all the toy cars in?'

Area

Putting a cloth on the table, covering the table with newspaper before painting or covering a defined area or surface with paint or collage materials are examples where children can be encouraged to use early language of area, such as cover and fits. Older children may enjoy playing with shapes which tessellate (fit together without spaces) to create a larger shape.

Volume

Language such as big, little, large, small and tiny may be used at first to describe the size of containers and boxes, or of models which the children have made. They might sort out the tiny buttons to fit in an egg cup, or put the large pebbles into a pile in the garden.

Angle

Children will begin to understand angle as a property of the corners of shapes, and as a measure of turn through physical activity. They will use concepts of angle, including parallel and perpendicular lines, in their play when constructing with blocks and creating train tracks. The language of angle is more difficult and attention can be drawn to turning a short or long way round, and to 'square' corners (right angles) and 'sharp' corners (acute angles). Attention can also be drawn to the amount of turn in physical activity and when using a programmable toy (see Chapter 5), and adults can help develop the language of turning corners, or half way or all the way round.

Temperature

Language such as hot, cold and freezing is used to describe how the children are feeling, the weather and in connection with cooking. Having warm (not too hot) water in the water tray on a cold day or ice on a warm day will initiate discussion about temperature and what happens over time: warming and cooling. Comparative language such as hotter or colder may also be introduced in context though direct comparisons of temperature are difficult.

Comparing and using comparative language

In order to give more meaning to the language of size, children should be encouraged to make comparisons of two objects and to consider which is longer, heavier, more full and so on. Again, the opposite of each of these words needs to be used too, so that children can begin to use words such as shorter, lighter or nearly empty. This language, being used in practical situations, will become familiar and understood as its meaning becomes apparent. Children can use the language when estimating, and then make a direct comparison to check.

Length

There is a wide range of comparative vocabulary about length which can be developed including longer, taller, shorter, wider, narrower, thicker, thinner, about the same, deeper, shallower ... Children can be encouraged to make these comparisons, during their play, such as when dressing up and finding a longer or shorter scarf, or when using woodworking tools and looking for a wider piece of wood. They can use different length sticks to make holes in wet sand and discuss the depth.

Weight

Children can use their hands to make estimations of comparisons of weight, lifting an item then another, or holding one in each hand. They can decide which is heavier and which is lighter, though this is difficult unless the objects are quite different weights. They can use a simple balance, putting an object in each side and observe which is heavier or when they are about the same weight. Using a balance and pouring sand or water into one then the other pan allows the children to experiment with weighing and to observe how the balance operates; that as more is poured into the lighter side it will become heavier than the other. Putting a balance by the sand and water trays encourages children to explore the weight of free-flowing materials.

Capacity

When working in the sand or water, pouring drinks in the home area or cafe, or at snack time, children can make comparisons of how much is in a container. Language such as more, less, about the same, empty, full, nearly full, nearly empty can be developed. Children can compare two containers and say 'This is nearly full; this one has less'. The comparisons will not necessarily be opposites, as the language of full and empty without some qualification is unlikely to be appropriate. They can pour from a jug into two cups to make both have the same capacity. The difference between filling a cup for drinking, and filling a cup to the brim should be discussed since they may spill drinks if cups are too full.

Area

Children's understanding of area develops later than that of length. Language which can be developed at this early stage includes more than, less than, cover, fit, too much, not enough ... Children can be encouraged to place one book on another to see if they take up the same amount of space, or to choose a sheet of paper to cover another. They can discuss which one is larger or smaller. Children can match lids to boxes and jars, making comparisons of size to find which fit. Sponge printing irregular shapes of paper emphasises the idea of covering areas of different sizes (Figure 6.4).

Volume

Comparing two models to see which one is larger or smaller will help children to begin to develop the concept of size and volume. In sand play, a colander can be used to separate buttons or small stones from sand. Children will not conserve volume until they are much

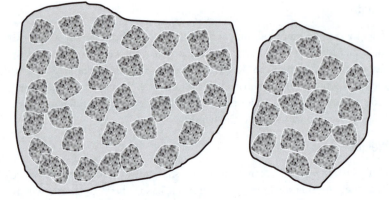

FIGURE 6.4 Covering areas with sponge printing

older but making models from playdough, then using the same piece of playdough to make another model will help their understanding. They can use some bricks to build a model and then use the same number of identical bricks to build a different model. They can use language of same, more, different . . . when comparing volumes.

Ordering and using superlative language

Length

Children can compare the lengths of objects by matching one end of each in line and use the language of longest, shortest, tallest, widest . . . It is important to check that they are lining the objects up, as they may look to see which one is furthest in front without considering the starting point. They can sort and order a collection of ribbons or scarves by length or by width. They can cut lengths of paper to show the size of their models, to compare the longest, shortest and widest. They can also compare length and width for the size of an object, for example when making a 'bed' for the teddy with blocks.

Weight

Children fill tins or boxes and make their own heaviest or lightest parcel. When working in the shop, they compare parcels with their hands to estimate which is the heaviest. They will learn that the weight of an item is not directly related to its size if adults draw attention to things that are larger and lighter (balloons, sponges) or smaller and heavier (paper weights, metal tools).

Capacity

When filling containers, children fill one to the top, another half full and a third with hardly anything in it. They can describe how full they are, using language such as most, least, nearly empty, nearly full to the top, half full, empty . . . When putting buttons or beads into containers, they can be encouraged to use similar language, so making comparisons, and putting into order how full the containers are.

Using non-standard and standard units and cultural measuring tools in real world contexts

Once the children have a secure understanding of the concepts and associated language they can begin to learn about units of measure. Traditionally this has been introduced with non-standard units such as hand spans and paces for length, fir cones or conkers for weight, cup- and spoonfuls for capacity. Children were encouraged to find lengths by counting units, for example, putting out a line of bricks which matches the length of a model. They poured from a jug to find how many cups it would fill (Figure 6.5) and compared the weight of a toy with a number of conkers. Then in primary school, once the children understand the need for a uniform unit size they would be introduced to standard units: centimetres, litres, grams . . .

However, recent research indicates that, rather than starting with non-standard measures, introducing children directly to standard measures of length – centimetres on a ruler and with centimetre cubes – may be more effective. Children taught length in this way were found to prefer using a ruler and be more accurate than children using non-standard units.

This approach may need more research especially in relation to other sorts of measure, but would fit with an apprenticeship view of learning (see Chapter 1) and would suggest that children should have access to a wide range of measuring tools – rulers, metre rulers, tape measures, beam balances with weights, dial and digital scales, measuring jugs and thermometers etc. – and see adults using these in real contexts including craft work, woodwork, cooking, preparing snack food. The children will initially 'play' at using the tools but will also be learning about what and how to measure. They will understand that adults use specific tools for measuring and talk about the results in terms of numbers.

FIGURE 6.5 Exploring capacity indoors and out

They may 'measure' length with a ruler, or count along a length with their finger and talk about it being a number 'big' or a number of centimetres. In the shop they may discuss buying litres (or pints) of milk and kilograms (or pounds) of fruit. When baking, children can begin to use a 100 g weight and add flour until it balances the weight. They may also use a dial or digital scale, and pour flour until the pointer or display reaches 100 g though this does not allow them to see what they are comparing the weight of flour with.

Time

Sequencing events and using comparative language

The concept of time passing, past, present and future, is difficult for young children to grasp, as it is the immediacy of 'now' that is most important to them. Recalling events in order, using past experiences to predict future ones, can be very difficult. Teachers of young children will recognise Mark, aged four years six months, and his request:

MARK: Miss, Miss. Can I put my coat on? It's time to go home.
TEACHER: Not yet, Mark. It's time for milk. Then you can put your coat on to go out to play.
MARK: Isn't Mummy coming?
TEACHER: At home time. She'll be here later on. Now, it's time for milk.

During milk time, Mark's teacher discussed with all the children the format of the school day, encouraging them to remember what had happened so far that morning and to predict what was to come.

Sequencing regular events

Sequencing regular events will help children such as Mark to recognise features of the day in order to remember what has just happened and predict what is likely to happen next. A series of photographs could be taken throughout one day and displayed to refer to when questions are asked. Children may remember events, but not the order in which they occur. Language such as today, yesterday, morning, afternoon, next, before, after, then, now ... should be used so that this language becomes familiar in context to the children.

Describing past events

What happened yesterday? When was your birthday? How old were you? What did you do at the weekend? are examples of social questions that are asked. Young children may not remember the sequence of events, nor have a relevant vocabulary so that a holiday was 'yesterday' rather than some months previously. Children can be encouraged to recall past events, describing what they have done or seen. When special events occur in the setting it can help children to remember this at a later date if photographs are taken, then placed in sequence in a book. A photographic record of individual children and their activities over time can be very useful as it will lead to discussions of changes in height and appearance, clothing changes with the seasons, recalling past events and what occurred. Language of the past, including days of the week, ages, special events and festivals, before, then, next, after ... can be developed to help children to be more precise in their recall (Figure 6.6).

FIGURE 6.6 Sorting pictures of themselves when younger prompts discussion about past events

Predicting future events

Discussion of tomorrow, next week, future days of the week, at the weekend, where children describe what they hope will happen, encourages understanding of what is meant by the future. Children can be encouraged to plan what they intend to do next, orally or by drawing a picture, then to recall what they have done and compare it with their prediction, Similarly, they can predict what they will do when they get home, then compare their prediction with their recall of events the following day. They can help to plan special events, or celebration of festivals, through discussion, photographs of past events and making drawings of what they would like to happen. A count-down chart to a special event, such as an Advent calendar, will help to mark how many days have passed and how many are still to come.

Recognising time events in the child's personal history

Calling attention to the clock at snack time or at home time will give children experience of clocks as a measure of the time. The numbers on the clock may be read, and the position of the hands noted for important times. Children can begin to recognise certain times, such as 'twelve o'clock and it's time to go home'. A calendar, marking the days of the week, and perhaps the date, may help children to recognise the regular sequence of the days. Birthday charts, with the months marked, will introduce the months in order. A count-down calendar, to mark the timing of a future special event, will help to show the passage of time. This is just the beginning of recognising that clocks and calendars are used by society to mark the passing of time and that such instruments can be read. Children will not yet understand these standard units of time. However, such language is part of everyday conversation and children will begin to use some of it with understanding, such as 'today is Tuesday and tomorrow will be Wednesday'. Language to be introduced can include days of the week, the months, o'clock times, minutes, hours, days, etc.

Comparing different units of time

Telling the time is a skill which most children do not acquire until about eight years of age. But certain times of the day will be very important to them, representing something special such as a favourite television programme or the time that they will be collected from preschool. With digital timers in household appliances such as video recorders, hi-fi systems and cookers, many young children will be aware that timers are used to ensure that certain events happen, such as recording a favourite television programme, or ensuring that food is reheated properly in the microwave oven. They may be aware that the time is 'told' on clocks by numbers, but they are unlikely to have any sense of what this means.

A six-year-old at school, who had just had his birthday, showed his teacher his new watch:

JAMIE: Look. It says 10.59.
TEACHER: What will it say in one minute?
JAMIE: 10.60.

Jamie had learnt to read the numerals, and knew that 60 followed 59 but this did not mean that he understood how to tell the time.

Children can play with clocks, watches, sand timers, rocker timers and water timers as part of everyday life. Repeatedly watching the sand pour through the sand timer to see how it works then using the timer to mark a well-defined period of time, such as putting some toys away, will help them to begin to appreciate the duration of that period of time. A clock in the home area may be set by the children to show breakfast time, or lunch time, and be included in their play. Expressions such as 'in about an hour' or 'in two weeks' time' have little meaning but relating periods of time to real events helps children to begin to appreciate time intervals, such as 'by the time you have put the toys away it will be milk time' or 'when the daffodil bulbs have grown their flowers it will be your birthday'. A regular, recurring sequence of events in the day will help children to make sense of the passage of time when they are away from home.

Problem solving

Children will use their growing understanding of measures to solve problems. If they choose to make a roadway for some cars, they will make decisions about how long it should be, how wide, whether there is room for two cars to pass each other, how to turn corners to avoid obstacles. They will choose which blocks to use, deciding upon their size: length, width and height. When using a Beebot or Roamer they will make estimates of how far to send the programmable toy in order to reach its destination, and may use addition to help them: 'We put in 3, but it wasn't enough, so then we put in another 2. That was just right. So we'll do it again and put in 5.' They will estimate, when choosing a block to make a bridge, whether it is a suitable length. When loading up a truck, they will make decisions about how much it will hold, and whether they are strong enough to pull it when it is loaded, or if it is too heavy. They may set themselves a problem using a sand timer: 'Can I finish the jigsaw before all the sand runs through?' Adults can encourage the use of appropriate measures language in discussing their solutions.

Concept map

Table 6.1 shows the concepts outlined above in matrix form. Example activities are shown so that the map can be used as a basis for planning and assessment checkpoints and

TABLE 6.1 Concept map for measures

KEY CONCEPT	VOCABULARY	EXAMPLES OF ACTIVITIES	ASSESSMENT CHECKPOINTS	KEY QUESTIONS
Use descriptive vocabulary	Big, little, long, short, thin, wide, tall, weigh, heavy, light, full, empty, cover, fit, large, small, tiny, turn, hot, cold, freezing . . .	Using blocks, construction kits; picking up parcels, using a balance, cooking; pouring and filling with sand, water, beads; putting the tablecloth onto the table; fitting items into a container using descriptive vocabulary	• Uses descriptive vocabulary of size appropriately • Understands that different objects have differences of size	• Can you find a big brick? Is this too small? • Can you find a big box to hold all the beads?
Compare and use comparative vocabulary	Longer, taller, shorter, wider, narrower, thicker, thinner, about the same, heavier, lighter, nearly, full, empty, more than, less than, cover, fit, too much, not enough, size, too big, too small, hotter, colder . . .	Dressing up; making models; pouring sand to balance a parcel; weighing out ingredients; pouring drinks at snack time; pouring and filling in the water or sand tray; finding a sheet of paper large enough to cover a box; fitting lids to saucepans; putting away the blocks by matching them to their outline drawn on paper; using comparative vocabulary	• Uses descriptive vocabulary of size appropriately • Uses opposites to compare sizes	• Can you find me a long scarf? • Can you put these in order of size? Which is bigger . . .? How did you decide how to do it? • If this one is heavy how could we describe this one?
Order and use superlative language	Longest, tallest, shortest, widest, heaviest, lightest, about the same, most, least, nearly, full to the top, half full, empty . . .	Putting ribbons, pencils, scarves, in order of length; putting parcels in a bag for the postman, with the heaviest at the bottom, the lightest at the top; finding the cup which holds the most, the one that holds the least; using superlative vocabulary	• Puts items in order of size • Uses superlative vocabulary appropriately • Makes estimations and approximations	• Can you put these in order? Which is the tallest? How did you decide how to do it? • How much do you think this holds? How could you find out?

(Continued)

TABLE 6.1 *(Continued)*

KEY CONCEPT	VOCABULARY	EXAMPLES OF ACTIVITIES	ASSESSMENT CHECKPOINTS	KEY QUESTIONS
Begin to use non-standard and standard units and measuring tools	As above; same as, measures, weighs, balance, holds, covers, grams, litre, metre, centimetre . . . Ruler, metre rule, tape measure, scales, weights, measuring jug	Finding things longer or shorter than a metre ruler; filling containers with sand or water using a cup or jug; exploring weighing by putting one large thing on one side and several smaller ones on the other; using measuring tools in context in play	• Compares lengths using an intermediate tool • Uses e.g. handspans to measure length, cupfuls for capacity or conkers to weigh items • Uses measuring equipment appropriately in play (though not necessarily accurately)	• How do you know it is longer/ shorter? • If this is 6 handspans long and this one is 4, which is bigger? • Have you ever seen anyone using this at home (at shops etc)? What were they doing?
Sequence events	Today, yesterday, tomorrow, morning, afternoon, next, before, after, then, now, days of the week, weekend . . .	Sequencing photographs, pictures in event order; recalling events in order; predicting what will happen next; changing the daily calendar; marking off the days on a count-down calendar . . .	• Puts events in time order • Uses vocabulary of time appropriately • Recalls events of significance • Makes reasonable predictions of the future	• What did we do after we added the eggs? • What do you think will happen next? Why do you think that? What else might happen? • What do we do next?
Recognise time events in the child's personal history	As above plus: days of the week; the months, o'clock times . . .	Discussing birthdays, holidays, special occasions in week (visit Granny) and times (home time, favourite TV programmes)	• Knows age and age on next birthday • Uses language of months, days and times • Recognises special times on clock	• How old will you be next birthday? • Which day do you . . .? • Is it time to go home?

Compare different units of time	Days of the week; the months, o'clock times, minutes, hours, days . . .	Turning the hands on clocks; observing and using sand timers, rocker timers, water clocks, competing to do most jumps/hops in one minute	• Uses vocabulary of time appropriately	• What day is it today? What day will it be tomorrow? • What can we do before the sand runs through?
Use developing understanding of measure to solve practical problems	Measures language as above; puzzle, test, find out What could we try next? How did you work it out?	Making a tower as tall as themselves; finding which is the heaviest teddy; finding two containers which hold about the same amount; using a sand timer to see what they can do before the sand runs through	• Explains the plan and describes what was done • Uses appropriate measures vocabulary to explain	• How could you make this even better? • How did you work it out? • What could we try next?

key questions are given to show possible learning outcomes from the activities (and see section on assessment below).

Planning measuring experiences

Adult intervention in children's play

Children will naturally use concepts of measures in their play and can be encouraged to explore these further and use the language of measure. Many of the experiences which children will have of measures will come from their own choice of activities, such as deciding to dig a hole in the sandpit large enough to hold a pick-up truck. Here an adult can encourage children to make an estimate, and to use appropriate language in their questioning: is the hole deep enough? How much sand have you dug? Does the lorry fit in the hole?

Adult focused activities

Planned activities for developing concepts of measuring may include opportunities to develop across more than one aspect of measuring, rather than just concentrating upon one aspect. The following activities demonstrate both planning for a range of concepts, and activities which concentrate upon just one concept.

Goldilocks and the three bears

An activity for four children.

- *Purpose:* to make comparisons of size.
- *Materials:* three of each of these of different sizes: teddies, chairs, bowls, a doll about the size of the smallest bear.
- *Language:* small, smaller, smallest, tall, long, high, low …

How to begin

Remind the children of the story (read it if you have not done so recently) and tell them they are going to look at some of the things in the story. Each child chooses a teddy or the doll. They compare the teddies and by making direct comparisons put them in order of height. The child with the doll can be asked to check that they are doing it correctly. If they lay them down to compare, ensure that the feet are level. Ask questions such as:

- Which is the tallest teddy?
- Which is the shortest teddy?
- How can you tell?
- What happens when I stand this teddy on the chair? Is this one still the tallest?
- Which one is higher than this one?

The child with the doll compares Goldilocks with the teddies too. The children choose a chair for their teddy. Ask them to explain how they have decided which chair each teddy has. Accept their responses, and, if they have not done so, encourage them to think about ordering the chairs by size and placing the teddies on them according to teddy height. Which chair do you think Goldilocks will fit? The bears want some breakfast – which bowl should they each have? Which would Goldilocks want?

Look out for other stories which could be used as the basis for a measuring activity.

Baking

An activity for four children.

- *Purpose:* to experience balancing.
- *Materials:* self-raising flour, eggs, soft margarine, castor sugar, old fashioned kitchen scales and weights, bowls, wooden spoons, paper cake-cases, bun tin, oven temperature 180°C.
- *Language:* weigh, balance, more, less, about the same, enough, heavier, lighter . . .

How to begin

Encourage the children to hold the unbroken egg carefully and to feel how heavy it is. They can compare its weight to other things, and decide whether it feels heavier or lighter than those. Then the children take turns to balance their egg, still in its shell, with flour, then margarine, then sugar, putting the ingredients into the bowl each time. Ask:

- How much flour do you think we'll need?
- Is there enough yet? How can you tell?
- What happens if we pour some more?

When the children have weighed out their ingredients, the egg is broken into the bowl and the mixture beaten to make cake batter. The cakes are baked in the usual way.

Instead of using the egg to balance the other ingredients, a balance with metric weights can be used to weigh out ingredients for a recipe. Encourage children to feel the weight first, before pouring out the ingredients. A balance with weights allows the children to see what they are comparing the flour with. Dial and digital scales are more abstract. With these, allow each child to observe how the pointer or display changes to find the given weight.

Snack-time drinks

An activity for a group of children (Figure 6.7).

- *Purpose:* to make fair shares of liquid.
- *Materials:* snack time drink, large jug, identical beakers for each child, with straight sides and an elastic band on the beaker.
- *Language:* Pour, enough, more, less, empty, full, half full.

FIGURE 6.7 The elastic band can be moved to mark the level for pouring

How to begin

Discuss with the children how much of the drink they think they can each have so that everyone has the same. Talk about fair shares, where everyone has an identical beaker with about the same amount of the drink. The children move their elastic band so that it marks a point of more than half full and then compare where they have marked. Pass the jug around the group so that everyone has a turn at pouring. Ask:

- Do all the beakers have the same amount? How can we tell?
- What happens if we fill the beaker right to the top? (It will spill!)
- There is some drink left, how many more beakers can we fill like these? Let's pour and see if we made a good guess.

Ask the children to move the elastic band to about half full, then drink some and see if they have half a beaker of drink left. Ask if they made a good guess for half full. Then ask them to drink until their beakers are empty. Instead of using drinks at snack time, water coloured with food dye can be used.

Making models

An activity for four children.

- *Purpose:* to compare models with the same volume.
- *Materials:* interlocking cubes, small boxes.
- *Language:* size, same, big, bigger, biggest, larger, smaller, different. . .

How to begin

Children choose some cubes and make a line. Ask them to compare their lines. Ask if they have all used the same number of cubes. Ask them to choose the same number of cubes again and make a different model. Ask:

- Whose model is the biggest/smallest? How do you know?
- Which models used the same number of cubes?

Each child chooses a box and packs their cubes into it. Ask if they can find a different way to pack the cubes.

As an extension, children make models using five cubes each time. Ask them to make different models. Discuss how the models all have different shapes, but use five cubes each time, that is, they are the same overall size.

Recalling a special event

An activity for all the children at carpet time.

- *Purpose:* to sequence events.
- *Materials:* large photographs of a very recent special event.
- *Language:* before, next, after, then, now . . .

How to begin

With the children sitting in a circle, so that all will be able to see the photographs, show them one photo and ask what was happening. Encourage children to recall the events of that day. They can explain:

- Why the day was so special.
- Who any special visitors were and why they came.
- If it was an outing, where they went and how they got there.

Show the photographs. Ask individuals to come out and hold the photos so that everyone can see them. Then ask which photo shows the first part of that special day, and the next and so on, until they are in event order.

Children can take it in turns to tell the story of the day, using the photos to remind them of what happened. The photographs can be mounted in sequence as a display, or placed in an album, which children use to remind themselves of what happened. The activity could be carried out with digital photos on an interactive whiteboard.

A similar activity can be designed around a task all the children have taken part in such as baking a cake.

Rocker timers

An activity for four children.

- *Purpose:* to mark and compare the passage of time.
- *Materials:* coffee jar lids, card, glue, felt pens or crayons, plasticine.
- *Language:* first, last, longest, shortest time . . .

How to begin

Help the children to cut out a piece of card to fit the coffee lid, with a triangular extension to fit above the lid (Figure 6.8).

The children can decorate their piece of card, making a clown, Father Christmas or patterned decoration. They stick the card to the front of the lid and place a small piece of plasticine at the base of the back of the lid. When the glue has dried the rocker timer is ready for use.

Show the children how to set the timer rocking, by pulling down on the point until it touches the table, then let go. Ask:

- Which timer rocks for the longest/shortest time?
- Can you put all the felt pens back in the box before the timer stops?
- What do you think you can do which lasts for a longer/shorter time than the timer?

The children can order their timers, from shortest to longest lasting. They can use their timers to time short activities, such as:

- building a tower until the timer stops
- see how many times they can jump
- see if there is time to write their name.

Alternatively, children can make water timers (a plastic cup with a hole in the bottom for the water to run though), or use commercially available timers, such as sand, water and rocker timers, which they set going, and then try to finish a short activity before the timer is finished.

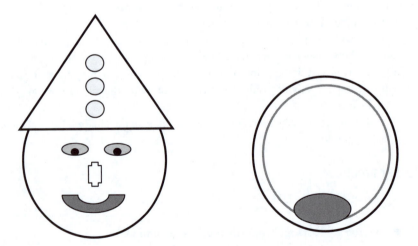

FIGURE 6.8 To make a rocker timer: put a lump of plasticine at the base of a coffee jar lid, then stick a piece of card to the front of the lid

Involving other adults in the planned activities

The skills of measuring and the associated language are used in everyday life. The language should be used correctly and in appropriate contexts and can be included on the weekly planning sheet so that all adults are aware of the language focus for the week. You may wish to display a poster with key language as a reminder: Table 6.1 may help here. It is important to use the language of time in such a way that children can make sense of it from their personal experience. References to, for example, a holiday still to come should be linked to something within the child's experience, such as 'You see Grandma every Saturday. Three more visits to Grandma, then it will be holiday time.'

There will be many incidental opportunities in the setting to develop children's use of language for measures, such as dressing up and comparing the lengths of the clothes; seeing how much the guinea pig weighs and if he has become heavier; watching plants grow and marking a chart to show the growth each week (a strip of paper can be cut to match the size each time). Care should be taken when using personal data as some children may be sensitive about being the shortest in the class or having the biggest feet, etc. Recording for measures can include photographs, charts, and keeping a simple calendar which is changed every day to show the day and date. To ensure that all adults working in the setting during that week are aware of any specific requirements with regard to language and recording, it is helpful to spend a few minutes before the start of each session agreeing the strategies to be adopted.

Setting up environments for measures activities

Table 6.2 shows suggestions for contexts across the setting which could offer opportunities for discussions about measures during child initiated learning, or be set up for adult initiated or focused activities.

TABLE 6.2 Measures activities across areas of the setting

ENVIRONMENT	CONCEPT/SKILL	CONTEXT
carpet time	• compare and order heights • sequence days of the week	• playing lining up games: ordering heights • changing the calendar; saying what day it is today, tomorrow . . .
art and craft areas	• compare and order lengths, widths, sizes, areas	• making dough models: making a longer, fatter, wider worm • painting wider, shorter lines • covering an area with paint or collage; wrapping presents • making models: larger, smaller, taller . . .
table-top games and collections	• compare volumes, capacities • compare timing devices	• fitting beads, buttons, cotton reels, shells into boxes • ordering nesting and stacking toys • using sand, water, rocker timers

(Continued)

TABLE 6.2 *(Continued)*

ENVIRONMENT	CONCEPT/SKILL	CONTEXT
sand and water play	• compare and order capacities and volumes • explore balancing	• making sandcastles in size order • filling and pouring sand and water; • estimating and checking how many cups can be filled from a container using a bucket balance with sand or water play
construction	• compare and order lengths • discuss angles e.g. on roofs, ramps or tracks layouts • measuring and exploring time	• making models: comparing to find longer, shorter, taller . . . • running cars down slopes • using a timing device when making a model and finding who finishes building their tower first • taking apart old clocks: turning the hands; as part of a 'clock repair shop'
block play	• compare and order length and comparing angle	• making models: estimating which pieces will fit; making a roadway longer, shorter, wider, go round the cupboard . . .
role play	• compare and order length, weight, capacity, sizes • use the language of time	• dressing up: wearing a longer dress or scarf, smaller shoes, wider cloak • sharing out drinks in the cafe • weighing the dolls at the baby clinic • using a clock in the home area
small world play	• compare and order sizes • estimate capacity	• ordering the play people by height, the cars by length • choosing two different containers to hold all the large animals and the small ones
outside play	• explore distances and heights • using units of time	• who is nearest/furthest away from e.g. the sandpit • who is highest, lowest on climbing frame • running races, who can run furthest in a set time
cooking	• explore weight and capacities	• weighing out ingredients • balancing ingredients • pouring out spoonfuls, cupfuls
information technology	• compare and order lengths • estimate and explore lengths and angles	• using art software to draw larger, smaller, longer, wider lines and pictures • moving Beebot or Roamer

Assessment

What to look for

Observing children while they work, encouraging them to discuss what they are doing and asking them to review what they have done will give insights into their understanding of concepts of measurement. Use the assessment checkpoints and key questions in Table 6.1 to help with assessment. This will identify whether children can:

- use descriptive language for length, weight, capacity, area, volume and temperature
- use comparative language for length, weight and capacity when comparing two or more objects; use opposites appropriately
- make ordered arrangements of length, capacity and weight and using superlative language
- sequence events: recognise that there were events that happened in the past and that there will be things happening in the future; use language of time, such as days of the week
- talk about significant times, days and dates which are special to them
- compare different units of time, and explore the use of simple timing devices.

Opportunities to make such assessments may occur incidentally during children's chosen activity or through specifically targeted focused activity.

Children respond well to questions such as 'can you put these in order of size?' or 'which is bigger ...?', especially where they have been encouraged to respond using the mathematical vocabulary that they hear the adults using. Gradually they begin to respond in sentences and this should be encouraged. Three- and four-year-olds find it more difficult to answer questions which ask 'How do you know?' such as 'How do you know that one is the longest?' and tend not to respond. However, with practice, and with examples of how they might answer given by adults, they do begin to answer the 'How do you know?' type of question in a satisfactory way.

Possible errors in concepts and skills of measuring

Children's understanding and use of measuring will be limited by their ability to make direct comparisons and to conserve; these are concepts which will be developed when they are older. They may use the wrong words when describing such as saying something is long when they mean heavy. Early misunderstandings include:

- *Length.* Not comparing both ends of an object with both ends of another. To overcome this, it is helpful to ask children to place one end of each of the objects to be compared level so that the other ends can be compared for differences in length.
- *Capacity.* Children may believe that the container with the highest water level has more in even if they pour all the water from one into the other. This is because children do not conserve the capacity of the container or the volume of liquid in it.
- *Weight.* Large objects will be regarded as heavy; small objects as light. Children will need encouragement to pick up and compare a wide range of sizes, shapes and weights of objects before they begin to understand that the size does not necessarily reflect the weight. Children, and some adults, often confuse weight with the ability of an object to float or sink, saying that heavy things sink and light things float. Sinking is not directly related to weight as can be seen by looking at a cruise liner.

- *Angle.* Especially when using Beebot or Roamer, children may believe at an instruction to turn left or right will result in a sideways move rather than a turn.

- *Sequencing time events.* Children find the notions of past and future far more difficult to understand than the present. Often language of time is imprecise, so that all past events are 'yesterday', and future events may all be 'tomorrow'. Some children, whose second language is English, may not have words in their home language for describing past and present, so that such concepts will not be explored in the same way at home.

- *The passing of time.* Although children may begin to recognise special clock times, such as noon or home time, they will have little concept of a regular passage of time and will not be able to tell the time for some years yet.

These misunderstandings are to do with developmental processes and children will understand these concepts in time. Further experiences of the concepts, and opportunities to explore materials, will enable children to begin to build their schemas for these concepts to enhance their understanding.

Working in partnership with parents and carers

At home, children will hear the language of measures used in many different contexts. They will see their parents making comparisons, such as 'have the curtains shrunk?', 'how heavy is the new baby now?' or 'how long will the car journey take?' They will be aware that clocks are set for recording video programmes and that the alarm clock wakes everyone in the morning. Thus, both at home and at preschool they will hear this rich language used in a variety of contexts.

Activities at home for developing understanding of measuring

These activities do not require any special equipment as they make use of everyday items in the home.

Length

- *At home:* completing a growth chart on a regular basis for all the children; making cheese straws (long ones, short ones, wide ones); making paper chains at Christmas to go right across the room.
- *In the garden:* comparing the heights of plants and trees; planting a sunflower seed and noting the height of the plant over time, seeing who can throw a beanbag toy the furthest distance.
- *In the park:* finding the tallest tree, the shorter path; finding who can jump the furthest.
- *Shopping:* finding the longest cucumber; finding a dress or a pair of trousers just long enough; measuring height on the shop's height chart; buying a new pair of shoes that are wide enough.

Capacity

- *In the bath:* filling up the bath, watching the water level rise; making bubbles; using squeezy toys in the bath; filling up containers until they sink.

- *In the kitchen:* helping with the washing up; talking about water levels; pouring out drinks and talking about how much.
- *Shopping:* looking at the different shaped bottles which hold one litre; watching the meter display turn as the petrol tank is filled.

Weight

- *At home:* weighing out ingredients for cooking; using the bathroom scales; comparing the weights of different food packets by hand.
- *Shopping:* observing items being weighed; helping to put items into the bag and weighing them at a serve-yourself counter, choosing the heavier items to go in the bag first.
- *Health clinic:* watching how the babies are weighed.

Sequencing events

- *Recall:* recalling a story in order; recalling an exciting event in order; remembering the sequence of the day; looking at the family photograph album and talking about the people and past events.
- *Predicting:* what will happen next; what will we do next week; deciding on what to do to celebrate a birthday or plan a holiday.

The passing of time

- *Clocks:* finding the different types of clock in the house: video timer, cooker timer, wall clock, digital watch. . .; looking for clocks when at the shops; watching the hands move on a watch; watching the numerals change on a digital watch; knowing when it is time to go to bed.
- *Timing events:* helping to set the video timer; setting the kitchen timer; winding up an old-fashioned clock; referring to the calendar to see when appointments are scheduled.
- *Time words:* using the days of the week, birthday months; recognising the changes in season; special celebrations which mark the year.

Story

- *Traditional rhymes and stories:* Goldilocks and the three bears, The three billy goats gruff, Jack and the beanstalk, Monday's child is fair of face.
- *Story books: You'll Soon Grow into Them, Titch*: Pat Hutchins; *Who Sank the Boat?*: Pamela Allen; *What's the Time, Mr. Wolf?*: Colin Hawkins; *Time to Get Up*: Gill McLean; *Five Minutes Peace*: Jill Murphy.

CHAPTER

Sorting, matching and handling data

The skills involved in sorting, matching and handling data are crucial across the mathematics curriculum and in other curriculum areas, especially science and the humanities. In many settings adults will also involve children in early graphing activities in order to find the answer to relevant questions, enabling the children to take greater responsibility for such tasks as they move into more formal schooling.

What is handling data?

Handling data is a crucial aspect of mathematics which relates to collecting, representing and analysing data in order to solve a particular problem or question. Through primary school it teaches different ways to represent data in the form of graphs and diagrams, discusses issues of probability and leads into the mathematics of probability and statistics.

Handling data is an integral part of real life and of the everyday activities of a preschool setting. Tidying up at the end of a play session by sorting toys to go into the correct storage containers (Figure 7.1), organising items on shelves in the 'shop', collecting information about how many children are present at a session, finding out how many are staying for school dinners or having packed lunches or asking who wants which fruit at snack time, are all examples of handling data for real world purposes.

This chapter on handling data is new to this edition of the book. Chapter 2 discussed how the activities of sorting and matching, which were seen as crucial to a Piagetian view of understanding number, have been superseded by a greater focus on counting. However, sorting and matching are still important mathematical skills and are discussed here in relation to the early stages of handling data since, in order to be able to make sense of any data, it is important to be able to sort and classify the data.

Take, as an example, the question 'What is the most popular type of cake?' There are many different ways in which data could be collected so that this question could be answered, depending on the reason for asking. The manager of a national chain of supermarkets, the owner of a local cake shop or someone planning a party for the children in their class would each want to ask a different group of people and be looking for a different kind of answer. One way to collect the data might be for everyone involved to answer to the question 'What is your favourite cake?' However there might be a wide

FIGURE 7.1 Suitably labelled boxes (words and pictures) offer opportunity for sorting when tidying up

variety so these answers would need to be sorted into types of cake using some form of categories for example: plain sponge cakes, chocolate cakes, fruit cakes, carrot cakes.

Once this data has been sorted it may be possible to put the data onto a table or to draw a graph of the results which can then be analysed to see which was most popular (Figure 7.2). The graph indicates that more people liked chocolate cake and flapjack but no one likes carrot cake, and can interpreted to decide what kinds of cake to buy for the party.

Which are our favourite cakes?

Plain sponge	2
Chocolate	12
Fruit	4
Carrot	0
Shortbread	3
Flapjack	6

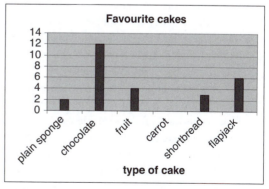

FIGURE 7.2 Table and bar chart of favourite cakes data

This whole process is sometimes known as the PCRAI cycle – which stands for:

- Pose the question related to the problem identified
- Collect the data
- Represent the data
- Analyse the data
- Interpret the data in terms of the original question and if there is still a problem a new question may need to be formulated and the cycle repeated.

Opportunities for sorting and classifying permeate the curriculum so that, although this chapter focuses on mathematics, there will be aspects of sorting and matching in other areas including:

- putting small world and construction toys away in their appropriate boxes or baskets e.g. all the bricks in the brick box
- sorting objects found on a nature walk (science)
- matching word cards to a particular letter or sound (literacy)
- choosing materials to make a collage (art).

How children develop understanding about sorting, matching and handling data: research findings

Two theoretical perspectives underpin this area of the mathematics curriculum: concept formation and the progression from concrete to abstract representation.

Concept formation

In order to sort and match objects children need to have a concept of the attribute they are using for comparison. Early research into concept formation indicated that understanding concepts, as shown by the ability to sort, was rudimentary in preschool children (Meadows 2006). For example Inhelder and Piaget (1964) and Vygotsky (1986) concluded that young children were unable to sort in a stable and consistent way. Using structured materials (Inhelder and Piaget used wooden blocks which varied in colour and shape, and Vygotsky used blocks which varied in colour, shape, height and area) they found that very young children would first make 'figural collections' which did not have any common characteristic obvious to the observer. Later they would start to collect according to a chosen criterion, e.g. red, but get distracted by another, e.g. round, and so produce 'chain complexes'. Still later they could sort consistently according to one criterion but were unable to subdivide the set using a different criterion. Vygotsky found that height and area were more difficult concepts than colour and shape for young children to understand.

However subsequent research has found that very young children are developing real world concepts at an earlier age than the structured mathematical concepts used in the testing materials. Children as young as two will have a concept of 'dog' which may be limited by their own experience of dogs but excludes, for example, the cats and rabbits they know.

Babies

Working with very young babies and using a methodology similar to that used to understand babies' ideas of number (see Chapter 2), Quinn *et al.* (2001) showed that even in the first three months of life babies are able to categorise shapes that are similar from ones that are different. Sugarman (1981) observed how children manipulated objects and found that at 12 months, babies would choose objects belonging to the same group in sequence but without forming a group of them. For example a child could pick out animals one by one from a mixed set of toys in a basket but might replace them or drop them haphazardly on the floor rather than placing them in a group. By 18 months, toddlers were able to pick out objects and form a group of them, using their own choice of items.

Between one and two years of age there is some relationship between a child's skills in sorting and their ability to name objects but this is not directly related – they can sort items they cannot name and vice versa (Gopnik and Meltzoff 1992). However Ricciuti *et al* (2006), studying children between the ages of 16 and 23 months, suggest that being able to name the items helped focus the children's sorting and conclude that it is important for adults to engage toddlers in discussion of the items used.

Two to three years of age

Sugarman (1981) found that by 30–36 months children are able to move objects from one group to another in order to sort them. Much of this sorting is purposeful in that the children were making collections for their own purposes: a collection of ribbons that a child finds attractive, of cars to play in the garage, of cuboid bricks to build a tower; it is more difficult for them to sort according to an attribute chosen by someone else.

Four to six years of age

Copley (2000), with reference to her own work and that of Markman and Seibert (1976), found that children developed through the following stages when carrying out more formal tasks:

- *Sorting by one attribute:* the children are able to sort out a set that matched a particular attribute e.g. all the red shapes from a set of shapes, though they will need help to express that those left behind are 'not red'.
- *Sorting by more than one attribute:* the children can use two attributes at the same time to sort e.g. all the shapes that are red and square. They may not, however, be able to identify the attributes chosen by another child for such sorting.
- *Stating the rule:* the children are able to state the rule used to sort a collection with more than one attribute even when the sorting has been done by someone else.

Copley does not offer age boundaries for her stages and research by Inhelder and Piaget (1964) and Kemler (1982) indicates that the final stages may be beyond the expectations for many children before the age of six or seven.

The progression from concrete to abstract

The progression in data representation follows the theoretical perspective developed by Bruner (1966). First the concept is experienced through an *enactive* form, through experience and physical interaction with the environment. Second, it may be represented in an *iconic* form, an image that can be called to mind which represents the absent object or concept. Finally the concept may be represented in spoken word or written symbols – a *symbolic* form. Here the word or symbol will call to mind the concept directly. As the concept moves from the concrete to the abstract it no longer is connected with a particular example but becomes generalised; for example we use the number 2 in arithmetic without needing to know what it is two of.

In Chapter 1 we considered the work of Worthington and Carruthers (2006) on how young children develop mark making in mathematics. Worthington and Carruthers (2006; drawing on Hughes 1986) describe five categories of marks:

■ Dynamic
■ Pictographic
■ Iconic
■ Written
■ Symbolic.

Of these the pictographic and iconic are particularly relevant to recording data. A child using pictographic marks will draw either what they see in front of them, for example record three sheep by drawing three sheep, or sometimes draw the same number of another object, for example drawing four houses to represent four bricks. Iconic representations are more abstract marks such as tallies which have a one-to-one relationship with the original objects.

When we apply this to data representation, the children move from manipulation of the real objects as they do when sorting, to understand that the data can be represented by other objects or pictures which still have a one-to-one correspondence with the original, to a block graph where it is no longer possible to identify which square represents the individual object. So, as we move from concrete to abstract representation, a child's eye colour could be represented by standing in a line of children with blue eyes, a blue coloured brick in a tower with others, a picture of the child's eyes coloured blue (pictograph), a square coloured blue on a block graph or part of the bar on a bar chart at which stage the one-to-one representation is lost (Figure 7.3).

Just as children find it difficult to interpret someone else's sorting, they find it difficult to interpret a graph created by others, a skill which is not developed until around the age of eight (Leavy 2008). It is essential in the early years that children are engaged in sorting and data handling tasks which are related to their own experiences. Where possible the initial questions should be their own and they should be involved in all stages of the data collection and representation in order to be able to interpret the data.

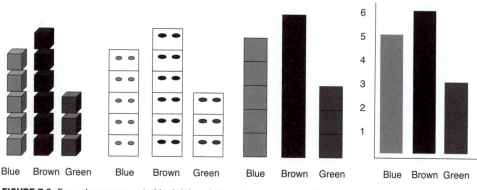

FIGURE 7.3 Eye colour represented by bricks, pictures, block graph and bar chart

Key concepts in sorting, matching and handling data

It can be seen from the research outlined above that children will come into the preschool setting already skilled in some aspects of sorting and matching. They will, from birth, have been making sense of the world by categorising and identifying attributes of objects in the world around them. They will have experienced sorting and matching when playing and when helping around the home e.g. laying the table, sorting the clean washing, or putting the toys away.

How children's understanding of sorting, matching and handling data can be enhanced by an appropriate early years curriculum is the focus of this section. The development of data handling skills and concepts is considered under the following headings, though these should not be considered to be sequential stages:

- recognising the attributes of familiar objects and using these to compare and match
- creating purposeful groups
- creating a set of all the objects with a given criterion
- representing and interpreting data using concrete materials:
    - reordering materials to compare
    - understanding the importance of unit size when comparing line length
- representing and interpreting data using pictographic and iconic materials.

Recognising the attribute of familiar objects and using these to compare and match

Attributes that may be used for sorting and matching tasks include colour, size, shape, and position (see also Chapter 6 on pattern), but also attributes of elements in the natural world including plants (colour, size, number of petals), rocks (colour, texture hardness), animals (fur colour, size, habitat, type) and people (eye colour, number in family, favourite cakes). Further attributes may be used in sorting tasks which have more abstract connections such as 'things which are used to bake a cake', or 'my favourite toys'.

While the children will have developed many of these concepts they may not have the appropriate language to express their ideas. A sensitive adult can, by commentating on what they are doing and by asking open questions, help develop their language skills which will also encourage a clearer understanding of sorting tasks. At first children will often focus on one particular attribute, say colour, and working with other children as well as adults will help them to recognise that there are other attributes that they could use.

Their understanding of attributes can be enhanced by focused tasks such as asking children to find something the same as a chosen object from a larger group of varied objects. If there is nothing identical they will need to select something which is similar in some way, and can be asked to say what is the same about it. In a nursery setting the children were playing with a basket of ribbons of varying colours, patterns, length and widths. The student teacher selected a long, wide red ribbon and asked the children to find one which was like this. At first some children tried to find one identical. Mary found another red ribbon and said that hers was the same colour. Habib chose another red ribbon and said 'red'. The student teacher commented that her ribbon was very long, so David found a long yellow ribbon and said 'mine's long ribbon'. If any children are still trying to find one that is exactly the same they may find it easier to find one that is different from the given item and say what is different about it. This will help them to focus on similarities and differences. Understanding attributes is a skill that they will continue to develop throughout childhood and through their adult life.

Creating purposeful groups

A purposeful group is a set of objects which have been chosen for a particular purpose. Even very young children are able to create purposeful groups, for example Libby (13 months) was given a mixed bowl of Shreddies, bite-sized Shredded Wheat and raisins for breakfast instead of the usual bowl of just Shreddies. After eating some of the Shreddies she encountered a Shredded Wheat, took it out of her mouth and laid it on her highchair tray. She then looked carefully at what she was eating and found a raisin. This she tasted, then rejected. By the end of the meal she had eaten all the Shreddies and had two carefully sorted piles on her tray, one of Shredded Wheat and the other of raisins.

Athey (2007) describes young children using two schemas which are related to sorting and creating purposeful groups. The first is transporting which results in a heap of items which have the attribute 'things I brought here'. The second is that of containing and enveloping, when children will make collections of items by wrapping them or placing them together in a bag or box.

Children can be observed during their free play for their ability to create purposeful groups (Figure 7.4). A discussion of why they have selected these objects will indicate their understanding of the purpose; this may be simply 'because I like them' rather than 'because they are all the same size and shape'.

Creating a set of all the objects with a given criterion

Creating a set according to a criterion given by someone else is more difficult than creating a purposeful set (Figure 7.5). It is essential that the child understands the attribute

FIGURE 7.4 Creating purposeful groups: 'all these cars open'; 'for the bathroom'

of the object – a child cannot sort ribbons by width without a concept of width and some understanding of the related language. It is also helpful if a reason can be given for the criterion used, for example sorting a set of fruit is given meaning if 'we need to find if there are enough oranges because lots of people like them'. For this reason such tasks do not need initially to be created as special activities but can be part of the normally running of the setting. For example, a group of children are making Mother's Day cards. At the end the adult asks one child to collect all the scissors, another the coloured pencils, another the rubbers, another the rulers and another the spare paper and card. The collection task is still purposeful but the criteria are set by the adult.

A set of structured materials such as Compare Bears® could be used to create a more formal task. These small plastic bears were created to focus the children's attention on the attributes of colour, size and weight. Children could be given a small coloured box and asked to fill it with all the bears which match that colour. To focus on a different attribute, a story could be created which involves one child collecting all the baby (small) bears to go to preschool, another the mummy (medium sized) bears who are going shopping, and another the daddy (large) bears who are going to play football.

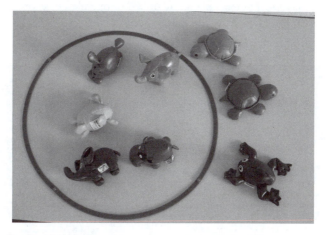

FIGURE 7.5 Sorting for animals with ears

Representing and interpreting data using concrete materials

The focus of each of the stages above is on sorting according to attributes. This relates to the *collecting data* stage of the PCRAI cycle mentioned above. Once the children are confident in this they can begin to *represent* the data in some way in order to compare (*analyse and interpret*) it more effectively.

Reordering the sorting materials

Another simple form of representation is to use the actual objects being sorted but to organise them in such a way that comparison is possible. This is usually done by lining them up in rows so that the group with the most and least items can be identified. Starting with small numbers of objects and using, for example, egg boxes or chocolate box trays will ensure that there is a one-to-one (1:1) match of the items (Figure 7.6).

Understanding the importance of unit size when comparing line length

One of the important issues at this stage is to understand that objects need to be the same size or evenly spaced in order to compare the line length. While the use of egg boxes etc. suggested above will help this, at some stage the children will need to learn for themselves the importance of unit size by comparing objects of different sizes.

Working with an adult, four children had sorted a group of farm animals and were finding which group had most by lining them up (Figure 7.7). Amil said that there are most cows because the line was longest. However Laura said that the cows were just bigger and you couldn't tell by looking at the ends. David said that the sheep and the chickens were the same. Haris was not sure and wanted to count them to find out. The children counted each group and the adult wrote a number label for each. David was still not sure, arguing for the same numbers of sheep and chickens. The adult spaced the animals out so that there was one cow and one sheep to each chicken. David agreed that there were now more chickens. The children were beginning to understand the importance of unit size when comparing line length.

To aid comparison we often represent the objects themselves with objects or pictures of equal (unit) size. For example lining up a class of children according to eye colour will create several lines which are difficult to compare, especially for the children who are in

FIGURE 7.6 Using an egg box to compare 1:1

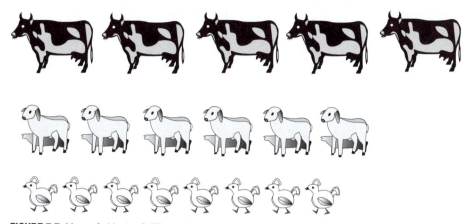

FIGURE 7.7 Lines of objects of different sizes are not helpful for comparison

the lines. Allowing each of the children to select a coloured cube to represent their eye colour and add it to a tower of matching colours will create towers of cubes which are much easier to compare. Having been involved in the process the children will recognise that one of the cubes 'stands for' their own eye colour.

Representing and interpreting data using pictographic and iconic materials

As children begin to use pictures to represent their mathematics (Worthington and Carruthers 2006) they can also begin to use pictures to represent data. A class of 4–5-year-olds were asked to draw a picture of their favourite pet (actual or yearned for) on a small piece of paper and these were ordered and compared to find which sort of pet is most popular. As with the coloured cubes there is still a one-to-one correspondence between the picture and the person choosing it allowing the children to see how it represents their own data. Alternatively children may use a small card with their name on it to represent their choice and place it in a box or on a pile labelled with the options.

Lists are very simple records of a set of objects. So, a collection of things used for a particular purpose, for example the ingredients for a sandwich, can be recorded on a list which is used to check everything before making the sandwich. Lists can be in the form of pictures or written, in which case it can be linked with literacy (Figure 7.8).

More complex data can be simply represented by counting the items in each set and representing them as a number in a simple table (Figure 7.9). It is then possible to discuss which pets are most and least popular by comparing the numbers. It is also possible to use tallies to record how many, although tallying is best reserved for data that develops over time, for example recording how many birds visit the bird table, or which cannot be collected all in one place.

For most children in preschool settings this will be sufficient representation. In the later school years, the data will be represented iconically by a coloured square to create a block graph, progressing to the use of a bar chart where the individual piece of data is subsumed into a single bar (as in Figure 7.2 above).

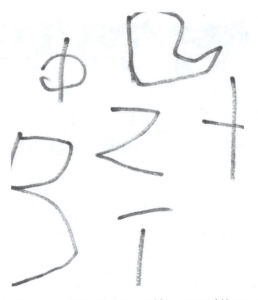

FIGURE 7.8 A list in emergent writing: 'What we need for our game' (4-year-old)

Oak Class: favourite pets	
Cats	5
Dogs	7
Rabbits	4
Hamsters	3
Gerbils	6
Fish	2

FIGURE 7.9 A simple table recording children's favourite pets

Problem solving

All areas of sorting, matching and data handling have the potential to be problem solving if we start from the first element of the PCRAI cycle outlined above with identifying a problem or question to be answered. At its most basic, tidying up by sorting the various toys into the correct containers solves the problem of a messy floor and the need to be able to find particular toys in the future.

It is good if the questions come from the children themselves or at least relate to things that they are interested in. James (three years nine months) was fascinated by cars and loved to play with the cars in the garage at preschool. He could talk about the cars in relation to colour and to other attributes such as those with doors that could be opened, which fascinated him. He was asked to share the cars with George so that they could both play. He carefully separated out those with opening doors, which he kept, and gave the rest to George. Later, he noticed that one of the cars he had given to George had a boot that opened. 'That's mine', he argued, ''cos it does this', demonstrating the opening. James had showed himself able to sort the cars according to a self-chosen criterion (opening doors) for a particular purpose (sharing) and even to extend the criterion.

Mary (four years six months) came into the setting bursting with the news that she had a new baby sister. Many of the other children wanted to share that they too had baby sisters or brothers. The practitioner asked whether they thought that there were more baby brothers or baby sisters, and how could they find out? Susan suggested that they could count. Children were asked to put up their hands if they had a baby sister and the practitioner helped one of the children count how many. She recorded this on a flip chart. They repeated the process for baby brothers and for no babies resulting in a table:

Baby sisters   6

Baby brothers   7

No babies   10

and the results were discussed. Later, Laura (five years two months), who had no babies in her family but did have an older brother, was found going round the class asking about older brothers and sisters and recording the results. She found that some children had both sisters and brothers and added an extra row to her list. Laura was able to extend the class activity to solve a question of her own.

Using ICT in sorting and handling data

Many ICT packages provide opportunities to sort and handle data. The simplest of these involve simple sorting, where objects can be moved around the screen and placed together in a group or dropped into a box. As with any ICT application, children will need to have some experience of manipulating actual objects before doing so in a virtual environment on screen.

Software packages are also available which create simple graphs. In their most basic form each child clicks on the icon of their choice and the programme builds a pictograph of the data so that the children can see the graph growing as the data is entered and then discuss the result.

Concept map

Table 7.1 shows the concepts outlined above in matrix form together with examples of vocabulary which can be developed. Example activities are shown so that the map can be used as a basis for planning and assessment checkpoints and key questions are given to show possible learning outcomes from the activities (and see section on assessment below).

Planning sorting, matching and handling data experiences

Opportunities for sorting and matching will naturally occur in all areas of the setting including outdoors. Through observation, practitioners need to recognise these and to extend the children's vocabulary and understanding through careful, sensitive commentating, questioning and challenging.

TABLE 7.1 Concept map for sorting, matching and handling data

KEY CONCEPT	VOCABULARY	EXAMPLES OF ACTIVITIES	ASSESSMENT CHECKPOINTS	KEY QUESTIONS
Recognises the attributes of familiar objects	Colours, sizes, shapes etc.	Free play with small world toys	• Can find a toy with a specific attribute • Can name that attribute	• Can you tell me something about your . . .? • Can you find something the same colour?
Compares more than one object	Same, different, not (plus all the attribute vocabulary above)	A set of cards with pictures of mini-beasts. Each child had two cards and has to find one thing the same and one thing different about their two mini-beasts	• Can identify something that is the same • Can identify something that is different • Can talk about why	• Can you find one the same/one different? • What is the same/ different?
Matches two or more objects	Same, different (plus all the attribute vocabulary above)	Any collection of small world objects. Each child selects an object and then chooses one which matches it in some way	• Can match two or more objects • Can describe why they match	• Can you find one the same/one that matches? • How do you know it is the same?
Creates purposeful groups	Same, different (plus all the attribute vocabulary above), all	Any play objects which can be put into sets. Notice when a child collects a set	• Can choose an attribute/ sort by • Can select all the objects which match that attribute	• Why have you put those ones together? • Do you have all the (red) ones?
Creates a set of all the objects with given criteria	Same, different (plus all the attribute vocabulary above), all, not	Any play or structured mathematical objects which can be put into sets. Ask the child to collect of one type (e.g. all the red triangles)	• Can find all the red ones or all the triangles • Can find all the red triangles	• Why are they all the same? • Why are these ones not in your set?

Learning objective	Vocabulary	Activity	Assessment	Questions
Counts or reorders objects in order to compare	More, most, fewer, fewest	Children having sorted objects into 2 or more sets are asked to find out which set has most/fewest	• Can count to find answers • Can reorder sets to compare (not necessarily successfully)	• Which set has most/fewest? • How could we find out?
Understands the importance of unit size when comparing line length	More, most, fewer, fewest	Children having sorted objects into 2 or more sets are asked to find out which set has most/fewest	• Can reorder sets with 1:1 matching to compare	• Why have you matched them up like that?
Can represent own data using concrete materials and interpret data	Most, least	What is the most common eye colour in our class? Choose the colour of cube and place it on the tower labelled with that colour	• Can place their cube on the appropriate tower to represent their eye colour	• Is your eye colour the most/least common? • If not which is?
Can represent own data using pictographic materials and interpret data	Most, least	What is your favourite pet? Draw a picture and place it in the line labelled with that. In which month is your birthday? Make a birthday train (Figure 7.10)	• Can place their picture on the appropriate line to represent their choice • Can place picture in correct carriage	• Is your pet the most/least popular? • If not which is? • When is your birthday? Where should your picture go?
Can represent data using iconic materials and interpret data	Most, least	Where shall we go for our class outing? Children 'vote' by placing their name card on their choice	• Can place their name card on the appropriate line to represent their choice	• Which outing was most/least popular? • Can explain their answer (zoo line is longest)

FIGURE 7.10 Birthday train (part): children put their picture or photo on the appropriate carriage for their birthday

Adult focused activities

Opportunities for more focused data handling are best related to the everyday contexts of the setting and to other areas of the curriculum, especially 'knowledge and understanding of the world'. The following ideas can therefore be adapted to suit your own contexts.

Find one like mine

An activity for four children.

- *Purpose:* To focus on the characteristics of a set of objects.
- *Materials:* Any set of objects with varying characteristics – small world toys are often suitable.
- *Language:* Same, different, plus attribute vocabulary appropriate to objects chosen.

How to begin

Place the objects in the centre of the table or carpet area. Choose one of the objects and place it in front of you. Describe your object in as many ways as possible – size, colour shape, use, noise it makes etc. Ask the children to choose an object that is the same as yours in some way and ask them, in turn, to say what is the same about it.

Put the children in pairs and ask them to look at each other's object and find something the same about their pair. Can they find something different about their pair?

If you have. . .

An activity for a whole teaching group or class.

- *Purpose:* To focus on groups who have a similar attribute.
- *Materials:* None.
- *Language:* Same, not.

How to begin

The children all begin by standing up on the carpet area. Choose an attribute which some of the children have and say, for example, 'sit down if you are wearing black shoes'. Ask the children what is the same about the children sitting down (they are all wearing black shoes), and about the children standing up (they are not wearing black shoes). This can also act as a check that everyone has it right.

Repeat using a different attribute and trying to allow different children to sit down each time.

This game can also be played in a larger open space by drawing a large circle on the ground and all the children who have that attribute run into the circle. It can also be used as a method to line the children up or send them off to get their coats on. In this case the children start by all sitting down and move when they match the chosen attribute.

It can be extended to more than one attribute e.g. sit down if you are wearing a blue jumper and white socks.

What did we find?

An activity for children in groups of 3–5.

- *Purpose:* To make a purposeful group from sort items found on a nature hunt.
- *Materials:* Collected on nature hunt.
- *Language:* Same, different, group.

How to begin

The children will have collected items on their nature hunt. Each child is asked to look at their own items carefully and to see if they can make groups of things that go together. The children are asked questions about their group of objects. Why do they go together? What is the same; what is different about them. At this stage we are looking for the children's ability to make a group according to their own purpose and not according to specific categories. So, 'I got these all in the woods' is an acceptable group; it does not have to be as specific as, for example, 'these all grow on trees'.

Colour collage

An activity for seven children (though these need not be working together).

- *Purpose:* To make a group according to a given criterion in order to create a colour collage.
- *Materials:* Paper of different rainbow colours, approximately 20 cm square (one per child). A large selection of collage materials – fabric, paper, ribbons, buttons, etc.
- *Language:* Same, matching.

How to begin

Explain that you are going to make a collage display about colour. Give each child a piece of paper and ask them to stick as many different things onto their paper which are the same colour as the paper. You may need to discuss that light and dark varieties of the same basic colour are allowed. In order to make sure that the children understand the task you may like to ask them to find six things which could go on their paper and check with you before giving them the glue. Use the collages to make a display about colours of the rainbow. To involve a greater number of children over a period of time the collages could be on arcs of paper which are combined to form a rainbow shape.

NB *note carefully any child who cannot create a set of matching colours as this may indicate that the child is colour blind.*

Egg box sorting

An activity for 3–5 children.

- *Purpose:* To sort two different types of objects and compare the results by column length.
- *Materials:* Each child will need an egg box that holds 12 eggs in two rows of six and a collection of around ten small objects which can be sorted into two sets (for example four buttons and six toy dogs).
- *Language:* Same, different, how many, more, fewer.

How to begin

The children are given their set of objects to explore. Explain that we are going to sort them into the egg boxes. The things that are the same will go into the same row. Watch how the children place the objects. Are they clear about the sorting criteria? Are they able to sort into the two rows? Discuss the lengths of the rows. If any of the children have placed the objects haphazardly, draw attention to another, more ordered box and suggest reordering.

Which is more?

An activity for 3–5 children.

- *Purpose:* To identify the need for unit size when comparing line length.
- *Materials:* 24 objects: 11 small, 8 medium and 5 large sized (for example 11 buttons, 8 plastic cups and 5 long wooden bricks).
- *Language:* Most, least, longest, shortest.

How to begin

Let the children explore the objects and talk about their sizes. The children then work together to sort them into three groups: small, medium and large. Ask them which they think there are most of and which least. Explain that one way of comparing is to make lines of the objects.

Create three lines which start on a level but with the objects placed close together so that it is not possible to match objects one-to-one across the lines. Ask the children which line is longest. Does that mean that this has the most items? Ask the children which line is shortest. Does that mean that this has the least items? Discuss why. Issues of 'fairness' may arise, e.g. 'it's not fair because the buttons are only little'. If so ask how they could make it fair. The children may suggest spacing out the smaller items, if not you may wish to do so.

Yes or no

An activity for up to 20 children (or more if the children's counting is good).

- *Purpose:* To represent the answer to a question using concrete representational materials in different ways.
- *Materials:* Each child has an identically sized wooden block; two boxes labelled 'Yes' and 'No'.
- *Language:* More, same, how could we find out?

How to begin

A question is posed about an area of the setting, for example discussion of what sorts of snacks are popular could result in the question 'Do you like carrots?' Try to choose a question that will not be too one-sided. Children take it in turns to come up and place their brick in either the Yes or No box. Ask whether more children like carrots or don't like them. How could they find out? The children may suggest counting, or making matching rows and seeing how many left over, or making towers and seeing which is higher. If one way is chosen can they think of a different way? Suggest a different way if none is forthcoming. Having tried different ways, discuss which is easier to see the answer. Discuss also the implications of the findings. Should we buy extra carrots or not buy any? Is this group representative of the whole class?

One reception class had a questions box where children would post questions. Adults gave help with writing where necessary. Some of these could be used in the Yes or No activity.

How many brothers and sisters do you have?

An activity for between 5 and 20 children.

- *Purpose:* To begin to form graphs with more than two columns using pictures.
- *Materials:* Each child has an identically sized small card with their picture on it.★ Small boxes labelled 0, 1, 2, 3, 4, more than 4.
- *Language:* More, fewer, how many, compare.

★These can be self-drawn at the start of the activity. In settings where similar activities are carried out regularly, special cards may be produced with the child's photograph.

How to begin

Explain that we want to find out about the number of brothers and sisters everyone in the class has. Each child counts how many brothers and sisters they have and represents the answer by holding up that number of fingers.

Hold out the 0 box and ask all those who have no siblings to put their card in the box. Repeat this with the other boxes.

Taking one box at a time lay out the cards in a line to form a graph, leaving the box as the column label.

Discuss the results. You could use closed questions such as: What is the most common number of brothers and sisters? What is the least common? How many people have one brother or sister? When the children are more experienced at this type of graphing use more open-ended questions such as: What does this tell us about the number of brothers and sisters of the children in our class?

Some of the questions in a question box (see Yes or No activity above) may also be suitable for this activity.

Voting

An activity for the whole class.

- *Purpose:* To begin to form graphs with more than two columns.
- *Materials:* A voting slip for each child with a list of options and a box against each.
- *Language:* More, fewer/less, most, fewest/least.

How to begin

The context for this voting task must come from an issue current in the classroom and which will be acted on as a result of the data collected. This might relate, for example, to a place to visit for the summer outing, the theme for a fancy dress party, the buying of new equipment for the setting or deciding what sort of shop to have in the 'home corner'. Where possible connections may be made with real world examples of voting: e.g. for elections or for TV personalities.

Once the context is decided the options are discussed, three or four agreed on which to vote and voting slips drawn up. Each child is given a voting slip on which they record their vote by colouring in a square next to their choice. (The traditional method of voting by placing a cross in the square can confuse children since they see a cross as wrong rather than right.) The voting slips are sorted and used to create a graph as indicated in the 'Yes or No' activity above.

The children are asked which option has the most votes and this is discussed and acted on where possible.

Some of the questions in a question box (see Yes or No activity above) may also be suitable for this activity.

Involving other adults in the planned activities

Sorting and matching occur all around us and there will be many incidental opportunities to discuss such activities with children. Much of the language associated with sorting and matching concepts is also language used in everyday life, however the logical language of, for example, 'not red' is rarely used. This language should be used correctly and in appropriate contexts. The language to be developed can be included on the weekly

TABLE 7.2 Sorting, matching and handling data activities across areas of the setting

ENVIRONMENT	CONCEPT/SKILL	CONTEXT
Carpet time	• Collecting data	• Choice for lunches, snack time
Art and craft areas	• Attention to attributes • Sorting and matching	• Painting and drawing • Collage, crafts
Table top games and collections	• Attention to attributes • Sorting and matching • Making collections	• Tidying up; making groups
Construction	• Attention to attributes • Sorting and matching	• Tidying up
Block play	• Attention to attributes • Sorting and matching • Comparing line lengths	• Building especially lines and towers
Role play	• Sorting and matching	• Shops e.g. groups of similar items; home corner e.g. setting table
Small world play	• Attention to attributes • Sorting and matching • Making collections	• Tidying up • Making groups, families
Outside play	• Making collections	• Nature trail • Tidying up balls etc.
Cooking	• Making collections • Making lists	• Listing and collecting all the things needed to make a fruit salad
Information technology	• Sorting • Graphs	• Use specific sorting and graphing software suitable for early years

planning sheet and discussed during planning sessions. You may wish to display a poster with key language as a reminder: Table 7.1 may help here. In order to ensure that all adults working in the setting during that week are aware of any specific requirements with regard to language and recording, it is helpful to spend a few minutes before the start of each session agreeing the strategies to be adopted.

Setting up environments for sorting, matching and handling data activities

Table 7.2 shows suggestions for contexts across the setting which could offer opportunities for discussions about sorting, matching and handling data during child initiated learning, or be set up for adult initiated or focused activities.

Assessment

What to look for

Observations, with evidence of the child's behaviour to support their understanding, can be recorded. Where evidence of achievement in a standard form is required, the observational evidence can be supported by a note of the assessment checkpoint, with date and comment attached to show when the evidence of achievement was noted. Regular observation of children's use of data handling concepts will identity their current knowledge and skills. This may identity whether children can:

- show an interest in the attributes of objects and match together things that are alike
- begin to make purposeful collections
- describe the attributes of objects
- explain why two or more things are the same
- explain why two or more things are different
- create a group according to a given attribute
- explain why the things in a group go together
- recognise the need for even spacing or unit size when comparing line length
- represent their own data or choice using a concrete object
- represent their own data or choice using a picture
- interpret the data.

Opportunities to make such assessments may occur incidentally during children's chosen activity or through specifically targeted focused activities. Children develop different skills at different rates so the above list should not be seen as a developmental sequence.

Children respond well to questions such as:

- What is the same about these? How are they different?
- Which has more/fewer?

especially where they have been encouraged to respond using the mathematical vocabulary that they hear the adults using. Gradually they begin to respond in sentences and this should be encouraged.

Three- and four-year-olds find it more difficult to answer questions which ask 'How do you know?' such as 'How do you know more people like carrots?' and tend not to respond. However, with practice, and with examples of how they might answer given by adults, they do begin to answer the 'How do you know?' type of question in a satisfactory way.

Possible errors in concepts of sorting, matching and handling data

As with concepts of pattern making (see Chapter 4), children's early understanding of sorting and matching will be limited by their awareness of attributes of objects. Most errors are developmental rather than due to misconceptions and will improve with more experience. Some may also be due to the child's egocentricity, seeing the world only from their own point of view. For example, a child who continues to make purposeful groups rather than using an attribute given by an adult may need further experience of discussing attributes and looking at groups made by others.

Possible errors in the development of graphing may include:

- not recognising that in order to compare line length to identify which is more, the objects need to be the same size and/or equally spaced.
- not seeing the data as a whole and instead focusing only on the child's own view so, when asked what the graph indicates, the child will reply that it shows, for example, that he has two brothers (Leavy 2008).

Note: where a child consistently confuses colours in sorting and matching tasks they may need testing for colour blindness.

Working in partnership with parents and carers

At home, children will have real-life experiences of sorting, matching and handling data both in their play and when helping around the home. Parents and carers may need help in seeing these activities as developing their children's mathematical understanding.

Activities at home for developing understanding of sorting, matching and handling data

These activities do not require any special equipment as they make use of everyday items and activities in the home and the wider world of the child.

Matching

- *At home:* setting the table by matching one fork one knife etc. to each place setting; matching up pairs of socks when sorting the washing; matching shapes to holes in a shape sorting box or jigsaw; matching one driver to each car etc. when playing.
- *Going shopping:* take part of the packaging from the used food items (cereal packet, tin label etc.) to match with a new item at the shop.
- *At the park:* choose something (for example a yellow flower or a type of tree) and see how many others you can find the same.

Sorting

- *At home:* tidying up toys by putting all the cars or Lego in to one box; sorting the washing either into types of clothes (all the T-shirts together) or by ownership (all the clothes belonging to the child), challenge to build a building using only one colour of brick; collect, for example, old Christmas cards and find all the cards with a snowman on.
- *Going shopping:* organising groceries in the trolley by food type or packaging type (tins, boxes, bags); putting the groceries away at home in the correct places.
- *At the park or beach:* make a collection of nature objects and sort into types.

Handling data

- *At home*: talk about preferences and which to choose if the family needs to compromise (e.g. what sort of biscuits to buy).
- *Cooking*: make lists of ingredients or equipment to make a cake (can draw pictures as well as words).
- *Going shopping:* shopping lists – specify how many of each item.
- *Going on a bus or train*: demonstrate how the timetable (a form of database) is used to help plan a journey.

Rhymes and stories

- *Choices: Would You Rather:* John Burningham.
- *Making lists: Don't Forget Bacon:* Pat Hutchins.

8

Planning, organising and assessing for mathematics

Mathematical activity in preschool settings

Many different activities can contribute to children's mathematical learning in a preschool setting and there are many different ways in which these can be described and categorised. This section will bring together a range of ideas, first to consider how activities might be organised and planned, and secondly to show the range of different types of activity in which children can engage in mathematical learning.

Activity planning

Play is central to the activity of young children and much mathematical learning will be in the context of play (Moyles 2005). However, many observers have found that, when playing, children do not often use arithmetic (number and calculations) in contexts where adults would; for example when playing 'shops' they will enact being shopkeepers and customers and carry out the social interactions due to these roles but left to themselves will rarely consider the prices of items or the need to pay and give appropriate change (Gifford 1997). Similarly with slightly older children, teachers trying to implement early years pedagogy with 5–7-year-olds found that calculation rarely arose spontaneously in play and therefore required careful planning (Fisher 2010).

This is because counting, the structure of number and calculation are not essentially elements of the environment but social constructs which, like language, must be learnt through interaction with more knowledgeable adults and peers and so require more structured adult intervention. But this should not mean introducing formal arithmetic through worksheets or workbooks, forcing the children too early into abstract symbols and resulting in the development of negative attitudes to mathematics at an early age. Activities which are planned and directed by adults should also be enjoyable and playful.

In order to ensure a range of appropriate learning experiences, Fisher (2008) recommends a balance between three different aspects of learning which should be considered when planning:

1   Child initiated learning: where the child is in total control of what they choose to do, how to do it and for how long.

2   Adult initiated learning: where a resource or activity is planned by the adult with a broad learning objective in mind and children engage with the activity in their own ways, which may mean the learning is taken in a different direction from that planned.

3   Adult focused learning: where the adult is in control of the learning outcomes, working with an individual, pair or group of children on a focused task.

Types of mathematical activity

A range of research has attempted to categorise mathematical activity. The REPEY research into learning in early years settings (Siraj-Blatchford *et al.* 2002) identifies 15 categories of learning activity, one of which they label *mathematics*; however this is restricted to calculation, number symbols or number concepts while many other categories also contribute to mathematics development, including using *structured materials*: jigsaws; pegboards; threading beads, the *manipulation* of sand, dough and water and *domestic activity* such as snack times. Sarama and Clements (2009) identify three types of play in which children engage with mathematics: sensorimotor play; symbolic or pretend play (which includes constructive play and dramatic play); and games with rules. The 'Big Math for Little Kids' project (Ginsburg 2006; Greenes *et al.* 2004) recognises three categories of mathematical activity: *mathematics embedded in play*, when the mathematics is incidental to the play focus; *play centring on mathematics*, when the mathematical concept is central to the activity such as pattern making; and *playing with mathematics* when the children are explicitly playing with mathematics they have been taught, perhaps playing 'teacher' in teaching others. Other researchers emphasise the importance of story and story books in helping children develop understanding of some of the abstract mathematical concepts in a context which they will recognise and enjoy and in introducing the language of mathematics in meaningful contexts (Van den Heuvel-Panhuizen and Van den Boogaard 2008).

Summarising this literature and for the purpose of this chapter the following categories have been developed: play; playfulness; games with rules; working together with adults and stories, rhymes and songs. Examples of each of these are given in Chapters 2–7.

Play

Play is a key element in young children's learning. It is through play that they explore social interactions, learning about turn-taking, discussion and sharing (Sheridan 1977). Play is purposeful and enjoyable. Two of the three types of mathematical play identified by Sarama and Clements (2009), come into this category (the third is considered separately under *games* below):

■ *Sensorimotor play*: this is the most common form of play in very young children, involving learning and repeating action sequences such as clapping or pouring water. Through sensorimotor play children will learn a range of mathematical concepts including space and position, pattern, size and distance, shape and number.

■ *Symbolic or pretend play*: using objects to symbolise other things such as pretending to drink from a cylinder block, which emerges in around the end of the baby's first year and develops during the preschool years, often moving through the stages of solitary, parallel and collaborative play (Bunker *et al.* 1982). Symbolic play may be:

■ constructive: manipulating natural (clay, water ...) and construction materials (blocks, Polydron ...) to create something new and reordering materials such as making patterns with threaded beads or making collections of like objects, or

■ dramatic (or socio-dramatic): entering into imaginary situations which are acted out.

Through symbolic play children can learn about a whole range of mathematical concepts including situations where they will practise the more formal mathematics they have been taught and play at being 'teacher'. (Note: symbolic does not refer here to mathematical symbols).

All these forms of play can contribute to children's mathematical learning whether child initiated, adult initiated or adult focused and all offer equally valuable opportunities for observation and assessment. Broadhead *et al.* (2010) emphasise the role of observation, arguing that in play the children are the experts and the adults are the learners. They observe that to facilitate play adults must recognise the child's right and ability to make choices and the adult's responsibility to provide environments to maximise opportunities for playful learning for individuals and groups.

Playfulness

Gifford observes that, while play is essentially child controlled, adults can also engage children in playful behaviours (1997) and identifies a range of interactions which she brings together under the heading of playfulness.

Playful activities might include:

■ pretending to be unable to do something and asking the child to help

■ deliberately misunderstanding a child's instructions in order to draw out a teaching point, for example drawing a triangle with three wavy lines

■ playful challenges such as 'I bet you can't count this many'

■ the use of puppets to model misconceptions and to promote risk taking (Figure 8.1)

■ 'tricking' the children by doing the unexpected, for example suddenly changing the direction of counting

■ using humour such as greatly over or under estimating how many.

These playful activities may be used as interventions in children's play, challenging the children in their thinking, but also offer ideas for adult focused mathematical activity. Compared to more formal teaching methods they are open to individual interpretation, are enjoyable for adult and child, and allow a high level of risk taking without the pressure to 'get the right answer'.

Games with rules

Many commercially manufactured games, including dominoes, playing cards and dice games, provide opportunities for mathematical activity including reasoning and problem

FIGURE 8.1 'One, two, three, it's four!' – using a puppet to make mistakes and model misconceptions

solving. Games can be adapted with new rules which extend the mathematics, for example placing the ends of the dominoes to add up to seven instead of matching them. Children can find board games with tracks difficult, often counting the square on which their counter starts as 'one' so that they lose one square for each turn, and jumping over a square when they pass another counter on the board without counting it (Hughes 1986). These issues can be discussed with children as they play board games.

Children will choose to play games which they have enjoyed with an adult or another child, and once they understand the nature of games they will adapt and invent games for themselves. Invented games can use almost any materials common to the setting and can be encouraged by providing numbers cards, spinners and dice (large dice made from sponge or fabric are less easy to lose), number tracks and 100 squares, shape cards and shape spinners alongside other resources. For example, leaving large dice in the block play area resulted in a game where the children took turns to throw a die and build a tower with that number of bricks, adding to it with their next turn. The aim was to build the tallest tower but if one fell down that child had to start again. The game seemed endless but was greatly enjoyed.

'People games', which require little or no equipment, can also offer mathematical learning such as following directions in 'Simon Says', a treasure hunt to see who can find the most shapes, or getting into a certain group size when the adult calls out a number.

Working together with adults

Some activities use an apprenticeship model of learning, as discussed in Chapter 1. Here the child is learning from the more knowledgeable adult by joining in an activity which the adult carries out as part of the daily life of the setting or in their everyday life at home.

Examples might include: preparing drinks and snacks for snack time, baking cakes, going to the shops to buy ingredients, measuring a space in order to fit new shelves or buy new carpeting. Where these activities are part of the adult's normal work in the setting a child might just stand on the edge and watch (legitimate peripheral participation) or they may ask questions or want to help. Such tasks can also be planned as adult focused activities to involve the children. Mathematically, many will involve aspects of counting and of measures: capacity, weight, length, money, time and temperature. It is through these activities that children will learn to use measuring tools (see Chapter 6) and understand how mathematics is useful in the real world.

Stories, rhymes and songs

Rhymes and songs are an everyday part of most settings and many will include aspects of mathematics. When planning to sing and learn a variety of songs and rhymes over time, care should be taken to look at the mathematics of these, as many will focus on the same mathematics (often counting back from 5 or 10: 5 little speckled frogs, 5 currant buns, 5 little ducks; 10 green bottles ...).

Story books offer enjoyable contexts in which mathematical concepts can be explored. These need not be specially constructed 'mathematical' stories'. Research has shown that adults will engage children in mathematical ideas when reading stories to them and furthermore, children will often make mathematical observations themselves (Van den Heuvel-Panhuizen and Van den Boogaard 2008; Anderson et al. 2004; Casey et al. 2004). Retelling the story allows children to practise using mathematical language in context. When using story books for mathematics it is important to choose good quality stories, appropriate for the children's stage of language development, in which the mathematical ideas are an integral part of the story and the mathematical connections are natural, not contrived (Thatcher 2001).

Equality of opportunity

Children can explore mathematics in a wide range of contexts in the setting; however, individual children will have preferences for what they wish to do. Some may not choose to work in every environment, restricting their opportunities for learning. Attention must also be given to equal opportunity across special needs, gender and culture. As a result of outside influences, some children perceive activities as gender-related, so that particular toys or environments are seen as being only for girls of for boys (Sheridan 1977; Ross and Browne 1993). Adults too may believe that particular toys or activities are best suited to one gender, for example, that boys spend more time with construction toys and produce more complex models than girls, despite research showing no innate difference in boys' and girls' abilities to manipulate materials (Walden and Walkerdine 1982). For children from ethnic minorities there are issues of language and culture to consider. It may be that a child's home language does not have equivalent vocabulary for some mathematical concepts, such as time concepts of tomorrow and yesterday, suggesting that practitioners will benefit from having some knowledge of the children's culture and language which differ from their own. Children may be less familiar with certain games, and resources in the 'home corner' should reflect their home backgrounds.

Adults in the setting should be aware of children's choices of activities, and the learning opportunities that these provide (Dowling 1988). From the full range of quality activities offered over time, adults will be able to offer all children access to the full range of mathematical concepts and skills. A simple observation checklist can be used to monitor how individual children access provision. The following list, originally developed for technology (Ross and Browne 1993), is here adapted for mathematical learning:

- the range of activities/environments which children choose
- how children use the materials provided or chosen
- how often individual children return to a specific environment or activity
- which activities or environments are dominated by particular children or groups
- the type of play which activities or environments encourage
- evidence of a gender bias in any activity or environment.

Such observations will identify any restrictions in individual children's choice of activity, and the children can then be encouraged to access a wider range of mathematical opportunities. Encouraging individual children to join in new activities may be sufficient. New resources may be needed to reflect the home culture of the children, or to help children whose movement or manipulation skills are restricted. Altering certain provision may help, for example hiding a dolls' house which is popular with the girls in order to encourage them to make their own dolls house in the construction area, or setting up the shop to sell dinosaurs instead of the usual groceries to encourage more children to play there.

Planning

Approaches to planning

There is a wide variety of provision for children between ages of two and five:

- buildings range from a family home to a purpose built foundation stage unit, a classroom in mainstream primary school, or a hall which needs clearing at the end of each session
- children's ages may be any combination of rising three to almost six with some settings grouping according to age and others across ages
- attendance may range from three mornings a week at a preschool to five full-time school days and additional afterschool care
- settings vary in the contacts they have with other settings and primary schools when considering the progression and transition of children
- practitioners will have a range of levels of training and experience; some may be trained teachers or nursery nurses, others may have early years professional status or CACHE children's workforce qualifications, yet others will be learning in the setting and some may also invite parents in to help out (subject to safeguarding checks).

All of these variations will affect the planning needs of the children and adults in the setting.

The contribution of this book to planning

The focus of this book is mathematics and it is beyond its scope to offer more than a broad brush approach to planning. However, it is important to emphasise that all planning for young children should start from the children's current understanding and interests and consider how to develop this further, rather than starting from a curriculum to impose upon them. Each chapter contains a theoretical discussion of children's mathematical development. Key concepts and skills are identified, with examples of planned activities. There are concept maps for each of the mathematical topics showing the key concepts, the language development, example activities and assessment checkpoints. For each mathematical topic there is a checklist showing the concepts and skills which can be developed in different areas of the setting and sample activities. All of these elements will be helpful in the planning process.

Identifying mathematics concepts and skills in topics from the chapters

The maps and checklists in each chapter give the basic ingredients for planning specific mathematical activities. These can be used for:

- *Long-term planning:* for a cycle of 1–3 years, depending upon how long children normally attend the setting. Fisher (2008) describes this stage as ensuring a broad and balanced curriculum for all children. It will show the range of mathematical concepts across all the topic areas of number, pattern, shape and space, measures and handling data, and identify where these will be covered in the given period. Some settings will collaborate with other provisions in this, for example a nursery class working with a reception class in a school to ensure effective progression in the provision for all children.

- *Medium-term planning:* for about a month to six weeks which should ensure continuity and progression of the children's mathematical learning. It may be based on a particular area of mathematics, for example shape, or may be based on a theme such as 'Toys' or 'Summer', but within it the mathematical content must be specific and the concepts and skills to be developed clearly identified. Good topic based planning can ensure a genuine cross-curricular experience for the children but Fisher observes that it is not easy and there is a danger that the links are 'engineered by teachers' rather than understood as cross-curricular by the children (2008: 43). Fisher also warns that topic/thematic planning can come too early in the planning cycle, before practitioners know children sufficiently well to know what will encourage their learning and understanding.

- *Short-term planning:* for a week, on a daily basis and for specific tasks, adult focused activities should be based on the needs of the individual children in the setting as identified through ongoing observation and assessment (Fisher 2008). The weekly plan identifies how individual areas of the setting will contribute to the mathematical concepts to be developed, and includes specific adult initiated and adult focused activities (Table 8.1). Details of resources needed and language development will help all adults to be aware of what the provision should encompass. A daily plan will show

TABLE 8.1 An example of a weekly planning sheet for mathematics

2–6 June			
KEY CONCEPT	ACTIVITIES	RESOURCES	ASSESSMENT
Count items which can be partitioned (moved)	Counting how many by touching and moving:		Does the child • count each item only once? • coordinate the count with the partition? • use appropriate language for: count words? comparisons? • can they also count the collage items once they are stuck on? (indicating next stage of learning: count items which can be touched but not moved)
Language	Adult initiated:		
Counting numbers one, two, three. the same, different, enough, more, not enough, too many, nearly the same . . .	Table top beads on laces; pegs on a pegboard; magnetic shape tiles	Table top beads, laces; pegs and pegboards; magnetic shape tiles, boards	
	Small world: cars, garage, road; play bus and people	Small world: cars and garage; play bus and people	
	Adult focused:		
	Baker's Shop pennies in purses; breads and cakes on the shelves	Shop pennies, purses, shopping bags, clay cakes and breads	
	Collage counting items for butterfly collage	Collage pasta spirals, shells, large sequins, glue, glue spreaders	

individual responsibilities for both routine tasks, with any mathematics to be drawn from these, and specific adult focused teaching. An activity plan may be used with different groups across the week, in which case it should identify differentiation across groups. Whether the adult focused teaching is intended for all children or for specific groups, needs to be clear in the weekly plan.

Mathematical learning will not just happen; careful planning is needed to ensure that opportunities for developing understanding of specific concepts are offered. The choice of materials in each area of the setting will need to be considered carefully, so that these reflect the learning outcomes identified in the planning. It would be impractical to resource every area to develop a particular concept or skill; however, it is helpful to be aware of ways in which the concept can be developed through play so as to be prepared to observe, comment or question as opportunity arises.

Some aspects of mathematics, especially counting in the early years, will be embedded in the everyday activities of the setting, rather than just focused on occasionally in order to provide opportunity for practice and consolidation. Number rhymes and songs, counting tasks and calculation should be built into the routines of the day including registration, snack time and carpet times.

The importance of language

Language is not only a vehicle for communication but also for thinking and learning and it is crucial that consideration is given to the language that will be used and how this will be introduced. It is important that adults use language correctly, so that children understand the meaning of new vocabulary, how it is used and the contexts to which it applies. It is not just a matter of using the correct words; adults must also think through how they will explain concepts and be prepared to extend children's understanding through careful questioning.

Each chapter identifies appropriate vocabulary and key questions in the concept map and you may find it helpful to make a poster for your current mathematical focus as a reminder to all adults in the setting and also to inform parents (Figure 8.2). This will also be useful for appropriate interactions during child and adult initiated play.

Role of adults

When children are working on child or adult initiated tasks there will be opportunities to observe their learning and to interact with them. Such interactions in children's play cannot be specifically planned by adults as they will arise from children's choice of activities, their questions and comments. However, adults need to be aware of the mathematical possibilities within each area as the quality of interaction depends upon the adult's understanding of the mathematical concepts enabling appropriate questioning skills and language.

1 2 3 4 5 ...	Number and counting	How many?
Number words:	count	**Key questions:**
one, two, three, four, five	sort	How many?
six, seven, eight, nine, ten	group	How many more/fewer?
then to 20 and beyond	order	What number comes next, before N, after N?
First, second, third, fourth ...	position	How do you know?

FIGURE 8.2 Poster showing key vocabulary and questions for number and counting

Careful and sensitive adult intervention in play can move children on in their thinking, working within their ZPD to scaffold their learning by:

- commentating: making an observation about what they are doing which may introduce appropriate language e.g. I like the way your pattern repeats itself, red, blue, green

- questioning: open-ended questions enable insight into the child's thinking 'Can you tell me about your model?'; or extend their thinking: 'Is there another way you could do it?'

- challenging: may be direct: 'Can you make it even taller?'; or indirect 'I wonder what would happen if . . .?'

- discussing: genuine discussions are more than a series of questions and answers and should allow an interchange of experiences or ideas (Siraj-Blatchford *et al.* 2002)

- modelling: if a child is stuck it may be appropriate to model how you would do something – but not do it for them. Adults also model language patterns, perhaps rewording a child's utterance in their response: 'I builded it more big'; 'Yes, I like the way you've built it even taller'

- playing: joining in the play needs to be done sensitively and it is usually best to wait until invited.

In order to intervene effectively, all adults working in the setting need to be aware of the mathematics teaching focus. If there are parents or carers who assist in the setting they can be informed using a daily plan showing the role of each adult for the day and outlining the teaching focus and any new or specific mathematical vocabulary. It is difficult to ensure that all adults are confident in their mathematical ability: whilst the majority of parents recognise that they have a positive and important role to play, many feel themselves to be deskilled when it comes to helping in more formal education settings (Caddell *et al.* 2000) and particularly with mathematics. Involving everyone in planning and evaluation discussions, where possible, will raise their awareness of the mathematical issues in the chosen topics and successful ways of tackling them. Parents who help out regularly could be invited to training sessions with the permanent staff, or a session run for all parents to raise awareness of early mathematics.

Mathematically rich environment

Mathematical resources should be freely available indoors and out. In order to encourage independence, materials must be readily available to the children including

- clear labelling of shelves and boxes for storage with words and pictures so that the children can access these and also clear them away providing practice on sorting and matching

- outlines of equipment for sand and water, cooking or carpentry encourage matching 2D outlines with their 3D objects

- equipment such as blocks stored by shape and size

- name tags available for all children which they place on a board in the area where they have chosen to work. Where there is a number limit, for example, four children to work in the sand, the children can check whether there is a spare peg for their tag, or count how many tags are already hanging on the board (see Chapter 2 Figure 2.13). This gives opportunities for interpreting data such as 'how many', 'how many more' and 'who' are working in specific areas.

High quality displays also offer children the opportunity to engage in focused mathematics. Displays may:

- introduce or reinforce mathematical ideas: a display about 2D shapes at the beginning of a fortnight's focus on shape
- celebrate children's work: physical objects (models, bead patterns) and photos as well as writings, drawing and paintings
- be interactive:
    - practical resources on a topic which can be played with e.g. pattern making
    - challenges such as a question for the children to answer: 'How old is Teddy?' with sticky notes to write answers on
- a poster of vocabulary as discussed above.

Planning for child initiated activities

For children to engage in learning through high quality play they require three main elements which should be considered when planning. First, they will need sufficient *sustained time* to play without being constantly interrupted for administrative tasks or to adult focused learning. Second, they need *high quality provision and resources* in and out of doors which are freely accessible. Chapters 2–7 suggest the sorts of play activities and resources required for each area of the setting, most of which will be common to many other areas of the children's leaning. Finally, they need *sensitive interactions* with adults to support their learning and move them on in their thinking (as discussed above).

Planning for adult initiated activities

Adult initiated activities will also require sufficient sustained time to play, high quality provision and resources and sensitive interactions with adults to support their learning and move them on in their thinking. They differ from child initiated activities in that specific resources will be set out with clear learning intentions identified by the adult. These learning intentions may be shared with the children depending on the purpose of the activity. The activities need to be clear to allow the children to work independently, motivating to sustain engagement and open ended (Fisher 2008).

Adult initiated activities provide opportunities such as:

- freely exploring new materials which are to be used in adult focused activities in the future, for example a range of shapes which will be used in a feely bag activity

- practising new understanding such as patterning with pegs and pegboards
- exploring a concept with a different medium such as creating different shaped triangles out of playdough
- playing games which have been introduced during adult focused activities.

The children may take these activities in a completely different way from that intended by the adult and the learning outcomes cannot be guaranteed. However, the lack of adult supervision can also enable more advanced learning than expected. A group of five-year-old children were making triangles from playdough, designed to reinforce learning about triangles. Most children rolled the dough into a thin sheet and cut out a triangular piece. One child rolled three pieces of dough into sausage shapes and laid them out to form the sides of a triangle, resulting in a heated discussion about whether a triangle had to have a middle and a greater awareness of the characteristics of shapes than had been intended.

Planning for adult focused activities

All planning must take account of the needs of children through suitable differentiation. While child and adult initiated activities will be mainly differentiated by outcome, with the child engaging in the activity at their own level, adult focused activities offer the opportunity for differentiated input to meet children's identified learning needs. The children may be grouped in similar achievement levels so that carefully targeted teaching takes place. Children need to know the purpose of the activity so that they understand what is expected of them and can reflect upon their achievement through discussion with the adult.

Experienced practitioners may be able to teach this in sufficient detail from the weekly plan but others may find an activity plan useful, which lists the children who will be involved, the intended learning outcomes, differentiation where necessary, details of the activity, resources needed, the language which will be used, key questions which will extend the children's thinking and space to note the children's levels of achievement against clear criteria (Figure 8.3).

Planning for progression and continuity

The planning cycle must ensure all aspects of mathematics are addressed. Few, if any, activities will ensure that children have a secure understanding of a concept the first time they encounter it. Planning must therefore revisit the same concepts, perhaps in different contexts over a period of time, to extend the child's understanding. Bruner (1966) refers to this as the spiral curriculum.

The balance between different aspects of mathematics is important when planning. Number and counting, and later calculation, will be a feature of each day, through counting rhymes, being involved in registration or snack time activities, putting out and putting away items, or deciding how many cars or play people to use. Activities involving shape and space, measures, pattern and handling data will also be

Activity Plan *Give a dog a bone*	Date and time September 24th 9.10 am; 1.10 pm	Children am: Caleb, Hajani, Carolina pm: Lee, Hannah, Bao Yu

Intended Learning: To practice counting out a number from a larger group and making a matching set	Key Language: Counting numbers, same, more fewer

Key questions:	Resources
• How many dogs do you have?	24 small cards with pictures of a dog
• How do you know?	30 matchsticks (without heads) to represent
• If the dogs each want a bone, how many bones will you need?	bones
• Ask 'have you got the same number of dogs and bones?	**Differetiation:** am group may extend to counting out 2 bones per dog pm Bao Yu will need clear demonstration and language
• How do you know?'	

Activity:
Ask each child in turn to count out 7 dog cards and place them on the table in front of them. Observe whether they know when to stop. When all have 7 cards, ask 'How many dogs do you have? How do you know? If the dogs each want a bone, how many bones will you need? Ask the children to take enough bones. Observe whether they use counting or 1:1 matching (dog to bone). Ask 'Have you got the same number of dogs and bones? How do you know?' Repeat with another number of dog cards.

Assessment:

Name of child	Can count out cards	Counts or matches bones	Comments on learning
Caleb	*yes*	*matched 1st time counted 2nd*	*did not want to try 2 bones*
Hajani	*yes*	*counted*	*stayed and counted out 2 bones per dog up to 10 dogs*
Carolina	*yes*	*counted*	*wanted to do more but time ran out*

FIGURE 8.3 Example of an activity plan (based on an activity from Chapter 6)

embedded in children's play, but adults may not be aware of these unless time is planned for observation.

A dated record should be kept, for individual children or small groups, of the adult focused activities which have been experienced, for example, Table 8.2 shows how the key concepts from a chapter can be adapted as a record of experiences. This is not a record of achievement: it does not show what has been understood but monitors the children's experiences. It will help adults to plan for progression and continuity and identify any omissions where a child has been absent or unwilling to take part. It can be used, together with assessment records, to plan their next stage of learning and may be passed on to their next setting or school.

TABLE 8.2 Record of experiences in number and counting

KEY CONCEPTS	EXPERIENCES	DATE
Can use structured representations of numbers and counting words to 10		
Can recite the number names to 5 (then 10, then 20 and beyond)		
Can enact movements in time with count words to reinforce 1:1 correspondence		
Can count items in a set which can be partitioned (moved)		
Can count items which can be touched but not moved (items in a picture) or seen but not touched (items at a distance)		
Can count sequences of sounds or actions		
Can count out a given number of items from a larger group		
Can recognise the numerals to 10 and beyond and order them		
Can count on from any small number		
Can count backwards from 10		
Can count in multiples of 2, 5 and 10		
Can use number and counting for real-world purposes and in problem solving		

Assessment

Assessment of the child's mathematical knowledge, skills and understanding should identify significant achievements in the child's understanding and skill development. Assessment must be manageable, include the child in the evaluation process and enhance the learning and teaching process (adapted from Hutchin 1996).

Planning for mathematics will identify both the learning objectives for individuals or groups of children and also assessment criteria related to their learning. Careful monitoring of children's learning will show whether they are making appropriate progress, enabling the practitioner to adjust subsequent planning (Stephen and Wilkinson 1999).

It is not possible to keep records of everything that happens in a child's day; however significant achievement needs to be identified and recorded. This will be individual to the child and could include:

- the first time that a child does or says something
- a child showing particular interest in an activity
- evidence that the child has thoroughly grasped a concept or skill.

Using assessment criteria

Tables 8.3 and 8.4 show key concepts, assessment criteria and key questions compiled from Chapters 2 to 7. They have been grouped under their mathematical topic and can be used to help to identity significant achievement. Settings which do not admit children across the whole age range may wish to use only a subset of concepts. Key questions can be used to probe young children's understanding of the mathematical concepts as they encourage children to think mathematically and to answer using mathematical language. At first, young children will find it easier to answer questions of fact. By encouraging them to move from one word answers to sentences, then to answer questions where they need to describe what they did, or what they were thinking, they will become more fluent in their thinking and speaking about their mathematics.

TABLE 8.3 Assessment criteria and key questions for number and counting, calculation and problem solving with numbers and pattern

KEY CONCEPT	ASSESSMENT CHECKPOINTS	KEY QUESTIONS
Number and Counting		
Exploring structured representations of numbers to 10 and use these counting words	• Recognises how many and gives correct counting word • Recognises numbers can be made in more than one way	• How many? • How do you know? • Why are these the same?
Consistently recite the number names to 5 (then 10, then 20 and beyond)	• Recites number names in order to five, ten, beyond ten to. . . • Identifies errors made by puppet and corrects these	• Why do we have to say the number names in the same order? • Which number comes after . . .?
Enact movements in time with count words to reinforce 1:1 correspondence	• Coordinates movement with the count • Can match one counting word to one action	• Can we count how many jumps we can do? • Why does sev-en only have one jump?
Count items which can be partitioned (moved)	• Counts each item only once • Coordinates the count with the partition	• How many have you counted now? • How many are there still to count? How do you know?
Count items which can be touched but not moved or seen but not touched	• Counts each item • Counts each item only once	• How many are there? • How do you know you have counted them all?
Count sequences of sounds or actions	• Counts each sound or move • Counts each sound or move only once	• How many did you count? • Board games – where did you start? How many did you count? Where did you land?

(Continued)

TABLE 8.3 *(Continued)*

KEY CONCEPT	ASSESSMENT CHECKPOINTS	KEY QUESTIONS
Count out a given number of items from a larger group	• Counts out required number of items	• How many do you need? • How many did you count?
Recognise the numerals to 10 and begin to order them	• Recognised numerals to 10 • Can identify missing one by order	• Which is missing? • How did you work it out?
Count on from any small number	• Can count on from any small number	• Which number comes after 7?; and after 8?
Count backwards from 10	• Can count backwards from 10	• Which number comes before 9?; and before 8?
Count in multiples of 2, 5 and 10	• Knows multiples of 2 to 20; of 5 to 50; of 10 to 100	• Can you count in 2s; 5s; 10s?
Use number and counting for real-world purposes and in problem solving	• Uses counting strategies to solve problems	• How many do you need? • How do you know that? • How do you work it out?

Calculating and problem solving with number

KEY CONCEPT	ASSESSMENT CHECKPOINTS	KEY QUESTIONS
Compare sets and discuss relative sizes Calculate difference between two sets	• Compares small numbers of objects visually or by counting • Uses comparative language • Can calculate difference	• Who has more/fewer? • Who has most/fewest? • How do you know? • How many more?
Explore the relationship between sequential numbers	• Knows how many for one more/fewer	• How many are there? (add/subtract one) Now how many are there?
Partition a set of objects and recombine them	• Can count each colour separately • Finds total	• How many of each colour? • How many altogether?
Develop strategies such as finger counting, mental imagery, for addition and subtraction of small quantities	• Adds and subtracts small unseen quantities with reasonable accuracy	• I put three pennies in the money box, and now two more. How many are there? How do you know? • Five people on the bus. Two get off. How many are left? How do you know?
Begin to relate addition to combining two groups of objects, and subtraction to 'taking away'	• Adds and subtracts using materials with reasonable accuracy	• How many cars have you each got? How many altogether? • You have six bricks. If I took three how many would you have? How did you work it out?

KEY CONCEPT	ASSESSMENT CHECKPOINTS	KEY QUESTIONS
Use language of addition and subtraction	• Can use appropriate language for addition, subtraction and equals	• Is there a different way we could say it?
Begin to solve addition by counting on and subtraction by counting back	• Counts on from the first number • Counts back to subtract	• Do you need to count those again? How many have you got here? • What would one less be?
Explore sharing an object or set equally and use vocabulary of division and fractions	• Shares a quantity into equal groups or cuts a whole into two similar (equal) pieces • Recognises when a sharing is unfair • Describes result as a share, half, same, etc.	• Share these between us; How many do you have? How many do I have? Is that fair? • How could we make this one cake between us? How much do we get?
Explore and discuss situations that involve dividing a set into equal groups	• Can put items into groups • Can say how many groups there are	• Is each plate/group equal? • How many plates/groups?
Explore and discuss situations that involve calculation in one-to-many relationships	• Understands that 2 or 10 need to be added each time • Finds ways to calculate	• How many would we need/ have if we had another person?
Use developing understanding of calculation to solve practical problems	• Uses number-based strategies to solve problems	• How many do you think there are? • How do you know that? • How did you work it out? • What could we try next?

Pattern

KEY CONCEPT	ASSESSMENT CHECKPOINTS	KEY QUESTIONS
Recognise pattern in the environment	• Identifies items with some element of pattern • Begins to talk about elements of pattern	• What do you like about this pattern? • Can you find another pattern with stripes?
Talk about an order	• Identifies positions within the order e.g. before, and uses vocabulary of order appropriately	• What comes next/before/ after? How do you know? • Can you make a new pattern . . .?
Make line patterns	• Describes the line shape • Uses a range of lines to make patterns and designs	• Which shapes have you used? • Can you make a different pattern using these lines?
Make symmetrical patterns	• Uses elements of symmetry	• Why did you put this one here?

(Continued)

TABLE 8.3 *(Continued)*

KEY CONCEPT	ASSESSMENT CHECKPOINTS	KEY QUESTIONS
Create a sequence	• Uses imagination to make a sequence • Describes the order	• Can you make a different pattern using the same pieces? • How is it different? • What will come next/ between . . .?
Copy and extend a sequence	• Copies a sequence accurately • Identifies any differences	• Are these patterns the same? • (Of a sequence with one piece different): Is this the same? What is different? Can you make these the same?
Recognise and create a growing pattern	• Identifies how the elements increase • Describes what the next element would look like	• What is different here? • What would come next?
Recognise and create cyclic patterns	• Describes a cyclic pattern • Finishes a cyclic pattern keeping repeats correct • Uses vocabulary of position and cyclic time	• What comes next? • Can you finish the pattern? • Tell me about you day: what did you do next? . . . and next?
Use developing understanding of pattern to solve practical problems	• Makes patterns and describes them • Can identify what is missing and complete pattern	• What other patterns could you make? • How did you work it out? • What is missing? How do you know?

As well as key concepts and assessment criteria for mathematical topics, skills in problem solving need to be considered and their acquisition assessed across a range of mathematical topics. Problem solving is an integral part of children's play and a core aspect of mathematics. Children can be encouraged to develop their problem–solving skills through:

■ identifying the problem and making a plan, either verbally or as a picture, or both

■ working at their plan, revising it as they go. Adults can help by asking open questions, such as 'What have you thought of so far?', 'What could you use to help you?' or 'What have you seen like this before?' (Early Childhood Mathematics Group 1997)

■ recalling what has been done. Children can discuss what they have made, or painted, or the solution to a problem, either with an adult or in a small group of children with an adult. They can develop their ability to use mathematical language and to ask and answer questions through discussion. Others can offer suggestions for improvement to the finished result.

TABLE 8.4 Assessment criteria and key questions for shape and space, measures and handling data

KEY CONCEPT	ASSESSMENT CHECKPOINTS	KEY QUESTIONS
Shape and space		
Explore and describe natural and manufactured shapes	• Uses vocabulary of texture, colour and feature appropriately • Describes similarities and differences	• Which group does this belong to? Why? How do you know? • What is the same about these? How are they different?
Construct and deconstruct shapes by fitting together, taking apart, rearranging and reshaping	• Fits pieces together and takes them apart • Makes and describes models using appropriate mathematical vocabulary • Plans what to make and how; revises plan to improve model	• Which pieces fit together? Can you make them fit together in a different way? • Can you make a different model with the same pieces? • How can you make your model better?
Lines: shape and directions	• Discriminates between line shapes and patterns • Uses shape and movement vocabulary to describe line patterns	• What patterns can you make in the sand? What other patterns could you make? What could you use to make them? • How could you make Beebot go there?
Simple properties of 2D shapes	• Chooses appropriate shape for picture • Uses shape vocabulary to describe properties	• Describe this shape to a friend: can they guess what it is? • What shape will you see if you print with this? • How many sticks did you use?
Simple properties of 3D shapes	• Uses shape vocabulary to describe properties • Uses appropriate vocabulary to describe how shapes move	• Which shapes have flat/curved faces? • What could you make with these shapes? What else could you make? • Which shapes do you think will roll? How could we find out?
Reflection and symmetry	• Uses flips and turns to find a fit • Uses vocabulary of reflection and symmetry to describe patterns, pictures and shapes	• What can you see in the mirror? • (Blot and fold) What do you think you will see when you open up your paper? • Can you copy your partner's movements?
Position and movement	• Uses vocabulary of position and movement • Follows instructions which use position and movement vocabulary • Makes observations from different viewpoints	• What can you see? What do you think you would see if you went round the back? • Where will you go if you move forward/sideways . . .? • How can we make Roamer go to the cupboard?

(Continued)

TABLE 8.4 *(Continued)*

KEY CONCEPT	ASSESSMENT CHECKPOINTS	KEY QUESTIONS
Interpret pictorial representations of spatial relationships	• Uses vocabulary of shape and position to describe objects in a picture • Observes/draws objects from different positions and identifies similarities and differences	• What can you see in the picture? Where is it? What is next to the . . .? • What if you draw it from over there? How will it look the same/different?
Use developing understanding of shape and space to solve practical problems	• Makes models or drawings and describes them using appropriate vocabulary • Moves from one place to another and describes what has been done	• What other models/pictures could you make? • What other materials could you use? • How could you make this even better? • What could we try next?
Measures		
Use descriptive vocabulary	• Uses descriptive vocabulary of size appropriately • Understands that different objects have differences of size	• Can you find a big brick? Is this too small? • Can you find a big box to hold all the beads?
Compare and use comparative vocabulary	• Uses descriptive vocabulary of size appropriately • Uses opposites to compare sizes	• Can you find me a long scarf? • Can you put these in order of size? Which is bigger . . .? How did you decide how to do it? • If this one is heavy how could we describe this one?
Order and use superlative language	• Puts items in order of size • Uses superlative vocabulary appropriately • Makes estimations and approximations	• Can you put these in order? Which is the tallest? How did you decide how to do it? • How much do you think this holds? How could you find out?
Begin to use non-standard and standard units and measuring tools	• Compares lengths using an intermediate tool • Uses e.g. handspans to measure length, cupfuls for capacity or conkers to weigh items • Uses measuring equipment appropriately in play (though not necessarily accurately)	• How do you know it is longer/ shorter? • If this is 6 handspans long and this one is 4, which is bigger? • Have you ever seen anyone using this at home (at shops etc)? What were they doing?

KEY CONCEPT	ASSESSMENT CHECKPOINTS	KEY QUESTIONS
Sequence events	• Puts events in time order • Uses vocabulary of time appropriately • Recalls events of significance • Makes reasonable predictions of the future	• What did we do after we added the eggs? • What do you think will happen next? Why do you think that? What else might happen? • What do we do next?
Recognise time events in the child's personal history	• Knows age and age on next birthday • Uses language of months, days and times • Recognises special times on clock	• How old will you be next birthday? • Which day do you . . .? • Is it time to go home?
Compare different units of time	• Uses vocabulary of time appropriately	• What day is it today? What day will it be tomorrow? • What can we do before the sand runs through?
Use developing understanding of measure to solve practical problems	• Explains the plan and describes what was done • Uses appropriate measures vocabulary to explain	• How could you make this even better? • How did you work it out? • What could we try next?

Sorting, matching and handling data

KEY CONCEPT	ASSESSMENT CHECKPOINTS	KEY QUESTIONS
Recognises the attributes of familiar objects	• Can find a toy with a specific attribute • Can name that attribute	• Can you tell me something about your . . .? • Can you find something the same colour?
Compares more than one object	• Can identify something that is the same • Can identify something that is different • Can talk about why	• Can you find one the same/one different? • What is the same/different?
Matches two or more objects	• Can match two or more objects • Can describe why they match	• Can you find one the same/one that matches? • How do you know it is the same?
Creates purposeful groups	• Can choose an attribute/ sort by • Can select all the objects which match that attribute	• Why have you put those ones together? • Do you have all the (red) ones?
Creates a set of all the objects with given criteria	• Can find all the red ones or all the triangles • Can find all the red triangles	• Why are they all the same? • Why are these ones not in your set?

(Continued)

TABLE 8.4 *(Continued)*

KEY CONCEPT	ASSESSMENT CHECKPOINTS	KEY QUESTIONS
Counts or reorders objects in order to compare	• Can count to find answers • Can reorder sets to compare (not necessarily successfully)	• Which set has most/fewest? • How could we find out?
Understands the importance of unit size when comparing line length	• Can reorder sets with 1:1 matching to compare	• Why have you matched them up like that?
Can represent own data using concrete materials and interpret data	• Can place their cube on the appropriate tower to represent their eye colour	• Is your eye colour the most/least common? • If not which is?
Can represent own data using pictographic materials and interpret data	• Can place their picture on the appropriate line to represent their choice • Can place picture in correct carriage	• Is your pet the most/least popular? • If not which is? • When is your birthday? Where should your picture go?
Can represent data using iconic materials and interpret data	• Can place their name card on the appropriate line to represent their choice	• Which outing was most/least popular? • Can explain their answer (zoo line is longest)

Gary (four years three months) decided to make a 'car' from a cardboard box which he wore on shoulder straps over his body. He planned this carefully, talking it through with an adult, made a model from cardboard and at recall time was unhappy with his model.

GARY: It's too small. I think I need a bigger box.

GEMMA: Longer straps.

GARY: I'll try that next.

The next day, Gary had three other children helping him. They made a new 'car', using a larger box and longer lengths of tape for the straps. All the children saw the finished 'car' at carpet time and were very impressed. Gary's problem solving involved him in exploring mathematical issues of shape and measure in a real context.

The following assessment criteria will be helpful in identifying significant achievement in problem-solving processes:

■ recognises which aspects of mathematics to use in the given context

■ makes and carries out a plan

■ evaluates the outcome and identifies possible improvements

■ has the confidence and motivation to complete the task, even when it proves difficult.

(adapted from Early Childhood Mathematics Group 1997)

Using assessment as a formative process: making it manageable

As can be seen from Tables 8.3 and 8.4, there are too many assessment criteria for each one to be assessed for each child and to attempt to do so would lead to an impossible workload for adults. Instead, the tables have two functions:

■ Guidance on what to look for in observation of children at work. The key concepts and assessment criteria for a specific topic can be identified and kept in mind for the duration of a mathematical topic. Adults will be able to keep these in mind and use them as a basis for their observation of individual children's significant achievement.

■ A summative check of what needs to be covered. A record for each child, with the list of key concepts and assessment criteria, can be checked on a regular basis and highlighted and dated when there is evidence of significant achievement. Over a period of time, such a record will also highlight those children who are not making progress and those for whom little assessment has been undertaken.

Observation

Much of the evidence of children's learning will come through observation during child initiated, adult initiated or adult focused activities. What the child is doing and how, and what they say during discussion or as a response to open questions may indicate significant achievement. The child will benefit from understanding that they have made a significant achievement which is being recorded. In order for there to be quality observation, adults must be aware of what the child has already achieved, which implies liaison between staff on a regular basis. It is important to observe not only what the child understands or can do but also how they learn and what their interests are since this information can also be used to plan effective learning for them.

Recording significant achievement

It is important to record what has been observed at the time of the observation, or it may be forgotten. In some settings notebooks are used as children are observed, so that a brief note is made there and then. Others make a brief record on sticky notes and the observation from the notes is written into the child's record at a later date. Sometimes conversations are taped, or photographs taken, perhaps of a model, or an adult may make a drawing of a child's model (Cubey 1999). Occasionally a video of activities may be made. On a regular basis, the child's mathematical record of achievement needs to be cross-referenced with the assessment criteria (both for mathematical topics and for problem-solving processes) so that a full range of mathematical topics is explored by the child and the quality of learning assessed. In this way, following assessment, planning for the individual as well as the group will ensure children's entitlement to the breadth and depth of the mathematical curriculum.

Once an assessment has been made and significant achievement acknowledged by the adult with the child, planning for the next stage of learning needs to be undertaken. Where children are grouped for focused teaching, the appropriateness of the planned teaching for those children needs to be reviewed. Those children who have not yet achieved will need to be given opportunity for learning. Those who have demonstrated their understanding will benefit from opportunities to use their understanding in problem-solving situations.

Keeping records

Recording achievement can be difficult especially in large settings. Three basic records can be kept:

- a record of activities experienced: where children are regularly grouped for focused activities, records of activities may be kept by group rather than individually
- a record of observations of significant achievement for individual children (some sticky notes or jottings will not record significant achievement and can be discarded)
- a record of assessment criteria, highlighted and dated to show understanding and skill development: this will help complete summative assessment forms such as the Foundation Stage Pupil Profile.

These records can be enhanced by a portfolio of evidence containing samples or photographs of children's work, for example, children's own recordings, pictures of models or patterns created, and notes of significant discussions. It is helpful to annotate the samples of work with the date of completion and why it is significant.

Records should be updated on a regular basis and used for forward planning. The records will also indicate areas of experience which the children have not yet had, and aspects which have yet to be assessed. The three record sheets will form the child's record of mathematical achievement and can be passed to the receiving setting or school.

Partnership with parents and carers

Parental contributions to records

Parents have a wealth of knowledge about their children. When children start in a setting it is useful to have a record of what children have already achieved at home, so that appropriate activities, which extend understanding and skills, are planned. Similarly, the evidence of achievement should be shared with parents so that parents are aware of which aspects of mathematics their child has understood and of areas where they may benefit from more experience.

Informing parents about mathematics in the setting

Parents may appreciate information on which aspects of mathematics will be covered during each week. This can be provided through informal discussion, by making the weekly planning sheet accessible to parents, perhaps on a notice board. A parents' newsletter could contain a list of key mathematical language that is the focus for the month or half term. The range of mathematical opportunities which children will have may not be immediately apparent to parents, nor will the importance of building understanding of number. It may be necessary to explain, in a sensitive way, that very young children are not yet ready to 'write sums' and that there is a wealth of mathematics to explore before written calculation has any meaning. Parents may appreciate an occasional parents' evening at the setting where they can try some of the activities which their children experience. With parents' permission, some activities can be videoed and watched at parents' evenings showing the range of activities which their children have enjoyed. This can encourage discussion about the purpose of the activities and so extend their knowledge about the range of desirable mathematical experiences which help to build concepts and skills.

Activities to do at home

Some parents or carers will ask how they can help their child at home. Suggestions at the end of each chapter can be used in discussion with parents, or incorporated into leaflets of ideas for home use. In order to encourage this partnership, children could bring back photographs of themselves at work or pictures from the activities or models, which could be displayed in the setting for others to see. Some nurseries have toy and book libraries run by parents, which could be extended to include mathematical games, toys and books which offer experience in particular mathematical concepts and skills. Parents and carers should be encouraged to use existing domestic routines, such as shopping and cooking, for counting, comparisons of quantities, and for using the language of shape and space, and measures (Aubrey *et al.* 2000).

Professional development in mathematics for practitioners

Role of adult

As we saw in Chapter 1, many adults admit to fear and dislike of mathematics and this is often compounded by their lack of real understanding of basic mathematical concepts. As mathematics in the early years forms the building blocks of children's understanding, misconceptions or misunderstanding of language can inhibit a child's future learning and continue the cycle of mathematically disaffected children who become mathematically disaffected adults. Adults therefore need to develop their own confidence in understanding the basic concepts and language, and how these can be developed through both planned and unplanned interventions. In order to encourage such confidence, regular staff development should be built into the planning cycle, so that all adults have opportunity to explore the mathematical opportunities which will be taught in the near future. It may be appropriate to ask one adult in the setting to take responsibility for the development of mathematics. This responsibility would include identifying professional development needs and, with the budget holder, finding ways of meeting such needs. Aspects of mathematics which should be considered on a regular cycle for professional development are:

- *Adult confidence with mathematical concepts.* This will involve working both on attitudes and on understanding the mathematics and how children learn it as described in this book.
- *The planning cycle.* A regular review of the setting's mathematics planning cycle, which covers not just what is included, but how it is explored by the children, will help to

identify the strengths and weaknesses of the planning and lead to a more effective approach. Consideration should also be given to the balance given to each area of mathematics.

■ *Assessment of mathematical concepts and skills.* Reviewing how the assessments are made, the outcomes of these assessments, how they are recorded and what use is made of them, will help to ensure that assessment is made for a purpose and lead into forward planning. Assessment review will also help to identify any aspects of the mathematics curriculum which are less likely to be assessed on a regular basis, and identify ways of addressing such issues.

■ *Resource provision and organisation.* The range of resources on offer to the children and how these are accessed should be reviewed on a regular basis. This review will offer opportunities to ensure that all adults are familiar with the range of resources and their uses, as well as the learning opportunities that can arise from using specific resources.

Glossary

For a fuller account of mathematical terms and their uses see Rogers (2006).

aggregation   addition as bringing together or combining two numbers or sets

array   objects, or numbers, arranged in rows and columns

attribute   a characteristic of an object (thing or person)

augmentation   addition as increasing

bar graph   a graph using bars to donate quantity or numbers (also known as a bar chart)

block graph   a graph using blocks to donate numbers with one block for each item represented

cardinal number   how many there are in a set: the last number in a count is the cardinal value of the set

classification   identification of an object by specific attributes, such as colour, texture, shape, or size

commutative   the order in which numbers are added (or multiplied) makes no difference to the outcome: 3 + 4 = 4 + 3 = 7

conservation   *of length:* that two objects of the same length are still the same length when one is moved. Young children believe that the one that is further forward is longer than the other one as they do not compare both ends of the objects

conservation   *of number:* recognition that, no matter what order, or how displayed, a given set has the same number of items in it. Young children believe that when the objects are spread out there are more than when they were closer together

Both sets contain six objects

cyclic pattern   arrangement in an enclosed, repeating pattern

difference   subtraction as comparison: the difference between 6 and 2 is 4

elements   items in a set: for example, in a drawing of a face, the elements would include eyes, ears, nose, and mouth

enclosure	surrounding, such as the ring drawn for a face
equivalence	similarity or sameness: *of number:* having the same numerical value: 3 + 2 = 2 + 3 = 1 + 4 = 5
	of shape: two shapes are equivalent when they are the same size and shape
iconic recording	marks based on one-to-one counting to represent number e.g. tallies
infinity	where there are no limits of size or number
linear pattern	a pattern that can be continued to infinity, not closed as in a cyclic pattern

nominal number	a number used to name something e.g. 14 bus number
numeral	the written symbol for a number, e.g. 2, 46, 399
order	an arrangement of objects or numbers which shows increases in size or quantity
ordinal number	1. number used to show an order: coming 2nd in a race; 3rd January; counting the cars, making the red one come third; 2. the concept of continuous number as represented by points on a number line
partition	separate a set into two subsets

A set of buttons, partitioned by colour: 4 black and 5 white

pattern	an arrangement of objects or numbers etc. which follows a rule
pictograph	graph using pictures to compare quantities
pictographic recording	children's recording of quantity or number using pictures
proximity	nearby-ness of objects
schema	a repeatable pattern of behaviour which is not tied to specific contexts: so, an enclosing schema might include making enclosures with bricks; making loops with string; drawing circles
separation	identification of an object from others nearby
sequence	an arrangement of objects: when this is repeated it forms a pattern
subitize	instantly recognise a small quantity, usually between one and five, without having to count how many
symbolic recording	recording or quantity or number using numerals and other mathematical symbols e.g. + − = . . .
take away	subtraction by partitioning and removing one part
tessellation	tiling with shapes which fit together leaving no gaps

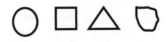

regular tessellating hexagons

topology	study of properties of shapes which remain unchanged when the shape is stretched or bent but not broken; these shapes can be reshaped to form one another

References and further reading

Althouse, R. (1994) *Investigating Mathematics with Young Children*, New York: Teachers College Press.

Anderson, A., Anderson, J. and Shapiro, J. (2004) 'Mathematical discourse in shared storybook reading', *Journal for Research in Mathematics Education*, 35(1): 5–33.

Anghileri, J. (1997) 'Uses of counting in multiplication and division', in I. Thompson (ed.) *Teaching and Learning Early Number*, Buckingham: Open University Press.

Ashcroft, M. H., Kirk, E. P. and Hopko, D. (1998) 'On the cognitive consequences of mathematics anxiety', in C. Donlan (ed.) *The Development of Mathematical Skills*, Hove: Psychology Press.

Askew, M. and Wiliam, D. (1995) *Recent Research in Mathematics Education 5–16: OFSTED Reviews of Research*, London: HMSO.

Askew, M., Brown, M., Rhodes, V., Johnson, D. and Wiliam, D. (1997) *Effective Teachers of Numeracy*, London: Kings College, London.

Assel, M. A, Landry, S. H., Swank, P., Smith, K. E. and Steelman, L. M. (2003) 'Precursor to mathematical skills: examining the roles of visual-spatial skills, executive processing and parenting factors', *Applied Developmental Science*, 7(1): 27–38.

Athey, C. (2007) *Extending Thought in Young Children: A Parent-teacher Partnership*, 2nd edn, London: Paul Chapman.

Atkinson, S. (ed.) (1992) *Mathematics with Reason*, London: Hodder & Stoughton.

Aubrey, C. (1997) *Mathematics Teaching in the Early Years: An Investigation of Teachers' Subject Knowledge*, London: Falmer.

Aubrey, C. and Godfrey, R. (2003) 'The development of children's early numeracy through Key Stage 1', *British Educational Research Journal*, 29(6): 821–840.

Aubrey, C., Godfrey, R. and Godfrey, J. (2000) 'Children's early numeracy experiences in the home', *Primary Practice*, 26: 36–42.

Aunio, P. and Niemivirta, M. (2010) 'Predicating children's mathematical performance in grade one by early numeracy', *Learning and Individual Differences*, 20: 427–435.

Baroody, A. J. (1985) 'Mastery of basic number combinations: internalization of relationships or facts?', *Journal for Research in Mathematics Education*, 16(2): 83–98.

Baroody, A. J. (1987) 'The development of counting strategies for single digit addition', *Journal for Research in Mathematics Education*, 18(2): 141–157.

Baroody, A. J. (1989) 'Kindergarteners' mental addition with single digit combinations', *Journal for Research in Mathematics Education*, 20(2): 159–172.

Baroody, A. J. (2000) 'Does mathematics instruction for three- to five-year-olds really make sense?' *Young Children*, 5(4): 61–67.

Beilock, S. L., Gunderson, E. A., Ramirez, G. and Levine, S. C. (2010) 'Female teachers' math anxiety affects girls' math achievement', *Proceedings of the National Academy of Sciences*, 107(5): 1860–1863, online at http://www.pnas.org/content/107/5/1860.full.pdf (accessed 25 September 2011).

Beneke, S. J., Ostrosky, M. M. and Katz, L .G. (2008) 'Calendar time for young children', *Young Children*, May.

Bergeron, J. C. and Herscovics, N. (1990) 'Kindergartners' knowledge of the preconcepts of number', in L. P. Steffe and T. Wood (eds) *Transforming Children's Mathematics Education. International Perspectives*, Hillsdale, NJ: Lawrence Erlbaum Associates.

Berti, A. E. and Bombi, A. S. (1981) 'The development of the concept of money and its value: a longitudinal study', *Child Development*, 52(4): 1179–1182.

Brannon, E. M. (2002) 'The development of ordinal numerical knowledge in infancy', *Cognition*, 83(3): 223–240.

Brizuela, B. M. (2005) 'Young children's notations for fractions', *Educational Studies in Mathematics*, 62: 281–305.

Broadhead, P., Wood, E. and Howard, J. (2010) 'Understanding playful learning and playful pedagogies – towards a new research agenda', in P. Broadhead, J. Howard and E. Wood (eds) *Play and Learning in the Early Years: From Research to Practice*, London: SAGE.

Bruner, J. S. (1966). *Toward a Theory of Instruction*, Cambridge, MA: Belknap Press.

Bunker, L. K., Johnson, C. E. and Parker, J. E. (1982) *Motivating Kids Through Play*, West Point, NY: Leisure Press.

Buxton, L. (1981) *Do You Panic about Maths?: Coping with Maths Anxiety*, London: Heinemann.

Caddell, D., Crowther, J., O'Hara, P. and Tett, L. (2000) 'Investigating the roles of parents and schools in children's early years education', paper presented at European Conference on Educational Research; Edinburgh, 20–23 September 2000.

Cantlon, J. F., Brannon, E. M., Carter, E. J. and Pelphrey, K. A. (2006) 'Functional imaging of numerical processing in adults and 4-y-old children', *PLoS Biology*, 4(5). Available online: http://www.plosbiology. org/article/info:doi/10.1371/journal.pbio.0040125 (accessed 5 September 2011).

Carpenter, T. P., Franke M. L. and Levi, L. (2003) *Thinking Mathematically: Integrating Arithmetic and Algebra in Elementary School*, Portsmouth, NH: Heinemann.

Carpenter, T. P., Franke M. L., Jacobs, V. R., Fennema, E. and Empson, S. B. (1998) 'A longitudinal study of invention and understanding in children's multidigit addition and subtraction', *Journal for Research in Mathematics Education*, 29(1): 3–20.

Carraher, T. N. and Schliemann, A. D. (1990) 'Knowledge of the numeration system among pre-schoolers', in L. P. Steffe and T. Wood (eds) *Transforming Children's Mathematics Education. International Perspectives*, Hillsdale, NJ: Lawrence Erlbaum Associates.

Carruthers, E. (1997) 'A number line in the nursery classroom: a vehicle for understanding children's number knowledge', *Early Years*, 18(1): 9–15.

Carruthers, E. and Worthington, M. (2004) 'Young children exploring early calculation', *Mathematics Teaching*, 187: 30–34.

Carruthers, E. and Worthington, M. (2009) 'Children's mathematical graphics: understanding the key concept', *Primary Mathematics*, 13(3). Available online: http://nrich.maths.org/6894 (accessed 5 September 2011).

Casey, B., Kersh, J. E. and Young, J. M. (2004) 'Storytelling sagas: an effective medium for teaching early childhood mathematics', *Early Childhood Research Quarterly*, 19(1): 167–172.

Casey, B. M., Andrews, N., Schindler, H., Kersh, J. E., Samper, A. and Copley, J. (2008) 'The development of spatial skills through interventions involving block building activities', *Cognition and Instruction*, 26: 269–309.

Charlesworth, R. and Lind, K. K. (1990) *Math and Science for Young Children*, Albany, NY: Delmar.

Clarke, S. and Atkinson, S. (1996) *Tracking Significant Achievement in Primary Mathematics*, London: Hodder & Stoughton.

Clay, M. (1975) *What Did I Write?*, Auckland: Heinemann Ed.

Clements, D. H. and Sarama, J. (2011) 'Early childhood teacher education: the case of geometry', *Journal of Mathematics Teacher Education*, 14: 133–148.

Clements, D. H., Swaminathan, S., Hannibal, M. A. Z. and Sarama, J. (1999) 'Young children's concepts of shape', *Journal for Research in Mathematics Education*, 30(2): 192–212.

Coltman, P. (2006) 'Talk of a number: self-regulated use of mathematical meta-language by children in the foundation stage', *Early Years: Journal of International Research & Development*, 26(1): 31–48.

Coltman, P., Petyaeva, D. and Anghileri, J. (2002) 'Scaffolding: learning through meaningful tasks and adult interaction', *Early Years: Journal of International Research & Development*, 22(1): 39–49.

Concise Oxford English Dictionary (2002) Oxford: Oxford University Press.

Copeland, R. W. (1979) *How Children Learn Mathematics. Teaching Implications of Piaget's Research*, New York: Macmillan.

Copley, J. V. (2000) *The Young Child and Mathematics*, Washington DC: NAEYC.

Cox, M. V. and Wright, R. (2000) 'Relative heights of males and females in children's drawings', *International Journal of Early Years Education*, 8(3): 217–226.

Cubey, P. (1999) 'Exploring block play: a study of block play in three early childhood centres in England in January 1998', *Early Childhood Practice*, 1(1): 6–27.

Davies, M. (1995) *Helping Children to Learn through a Movement Perspective*, London: Hodder & Stoughton.

DCSF (2008) *Mark Making Matters*, Nottingham: Department for Children, Schools and Families.

DES (Department for Education and Science) (1988) *Mathematics for Ages 5 to 16. Proposals of the Secretary of State for Education and Science and the Secretary of State for Wales*, London: Central Office of Information.

Devlin, K. (2003) *Mathematics: The Science of Patterns*, New York: First Owl Books.

DfEE/QCA (Department for Education and Employment/Qualifications and Curriculum Authority) (1999) *Key Stages 1 and 2 of the National Curriculum*, London: HMSO.

Diaz, R. M. (2008) 'The role of language in early childhood mathematics', *Dissertation Abstracts International Section A: Humanities and Social Sciences*, 69(6-A): 21–33.

Donaldson, M. (1978) *Children's Minds*, London: Fontana.

Dowling, M. (1988) *Education 3 to 5: A Teachers' Handbook*, London: Paul Chapman.

Early Childhood Mathematics Group (1997) *A Desirable Approach to Learning Mathematics*, London: BEAM.

Fischer, F. E. (1990) 'The part-part-whole curriculum for teaching number in the kindergarten', *Journal for Research in Mathematics Education*, 21(3): 207–215.

Fisher, J. (2008) *Starting from the Child: Teaching and Learning in the Foundation Stage*, 3rd edn, Maidenhead: Open University Press.

Fisher, J. (2010) *Moving on to Key Stage 1: Improving Transition from the Early Years Foundation Stage*, Maidenhead: McGraw Hill Open University Press.

Flores, R. L. (2007) 'Effect of poverty on urban preschool children's understanding of conventional time concepts', *Early Child Development and Care*, 177(2): 121–132.

Fox, J. L. and Diezmann, C. M. (2007) 'What counts in research? A survey of early years' mathematical research, 2000–2005', *Contemporary Issues in Early Childhood*, 8(4): 301–312.

Fuson, K. C. (1984) 'More complexities in subtraction', *Journal for Research in Mathematics Education*, 15(3): 214–225.

Fuson, K. C. and Willis, G. B. (1988) 'Subtracting by counting up: more evidence', *Journal for Research in Mathematics Education*, 19: 402–420.

Fuson, K. C., Richards, J. and Briars, D. (1982) 'The acquisition and elaboration of the number word sequence', in C. J. Brainerd (ed.) *Progress in Cognitive Development: Children's Logical and Mathematical Cognition*, New York: Springer-Verlag.

Gallistel, C. R. and Gelman, R. (1992) 'Preverbal and verbal computation', *Cognition*, 44: 43–74.

Garrick, R., Threlfall, J. and Orton, A. (1999) 'Pattern in the nursery', in A. Orton (ed.) *Pattern in the Teaching and Learning of Mathematics*, London: Cassell.

Geist, E. (2001) 'Children are born mathematicians: promoting the construction of early mathematical concepts in children under five', *Young Children*, 56(4): 12–19.

Geist, E. (2010) 'The anti-anxiety curriculum: combating math anxiety in the classroom', *Journal of Instructional Psychology*, 37(1): 24–31.

Gelman, R. (2006) 'Young natural-number arithmeticians', *Current Directions in Psychological Science*, 15(4): 193–197.

Gelman, R. and Gallistel, C. R. (1986) *The Child's Understanding of Number*, Cambridge, MA: Harvard University Press.

Gelman, R. and Meck, E. (1992) 'Early principles aid initial but not later conceptions of number', in J. Bideau, C. Meljic and J. P. Fischer (eds) *Pathways to Number*, Hillsdale NJ: Erlbaum, pp.171–189.

Gifford, S. (1997) 'When should they start doing sums', in I. Thompson (ed.) *Teaching and Learning Early Number*, Buckingham: Open University Press.

Gifford, S. (2005) *Teaching Mathematics 3–5*, Maidenhead: Open University Press.

Gilmore, C. K., McCarthy, S. E. and Spelke, E. S. (2007) 'Symbolic arithmetic knowledge without instruction', *Nature*, 447(7144): 589–591.

Ginsburg, H. P. (2006) 'Mathematical play and playful mathematics: a guide for early education', in D. G. Singer, R. M. Golinkoff and K. Hirsh-Pasek (eds) *Play = Learning: How Play Motivates and Enhances Children's Cognitive and Social-emotional Growth*, New York: Oxford University Press, pp.145–166.

Gopnik, A. and Meltzoff, A. N. (1992) 'Categorization and naming: basic-level sorting in eighteen-month-olds and its relation to language', *Child Development*, 63: 1091–1103.

Greenes, C., Ginsburg, H. P. and Balfanz, R. (2004) 'Big math for little kids', *Early Childhood Research Quarterly*, 19(1): 159.

Griffin, S. and Case, R. (1997) 'Re-thinking the primary school math curriculum: an approach based on cognitive science', *Issues in Education*, 3(1): 1–49.

Gura, P. (ed.) (1992) *Exploring Learning. Young Children and Blockplay*, London: Paul Chapman.

Hachey, A. C. (2009) 'I hate math: what we want young children NOT to learn', *Texas Child Care*, Fall: 2–7.

Hall, N. (1987) *The Emergence of Literacy*, London: Hodder & Stoughton.

Hall, N. (ed.) (1989) *Writing with Reason*, London: Hodder & Stoughton.

Hannula, M. M., Räsänen, P. and Lehtinen, E. (2007) 'Development of counting skills: role of spontaneous focusing on numerosity and subitizing-based enumeration', *Mathematical Thinking and Learning*, 9(1): 51–57.

Haylock, D. (2010) *Mathematics Explained for Primary Teachers*, 4th edn, London: Sage.

Haylock, D. and Cockburn A. (1997) *Understanding Early Years Mathematics*, London: Paul Chapman.

Haylock, D. and Cockburn A. (2008) *Understanding Mathematics for Young Children*, London: Sage.

Hespos, S. J., Begum, D., Rips, L. J. and Christie, S. (2008) 'Infants make quantity discriminations for substances', manuscript under review. Available online: http://groups.psych.northwestern.edu/infantcognitionlab/SandDraft27.pdf (accessed 25 September 2010).

Hewitt, K. (2001) 'Blocks as a tool for learning: historical and contemporary perspectives', *Young Children*, 56(1): 6–13.

Hughes, M. (1986) *Children and Number: Difficulties in Learning Mathematics*, Oxford: Basil Blackwell.

Hunting, R. P. and Sharpley, C. F. (1988) 'Fraction knowledge in pre-school children', *Journal for Research in Mathematics Education*, 19(2): 175–180.

Hutchin, V. (1996) *Tracking Significant Achievement in the Early Years*, London: Hodder & Stoughton.

Inhelder, B. and Piaget, J. (1964) *The Early Growth of Logic in the Child*, London: Routledge & Kegan Paul.

Kamii, C., Miyakawa, Y. and Kato, Y. (2004) 'The development of logico-mathematical knowledge in a block-building activity at ages 1–4', *Journal of Research in Childhood Education*, 19(1): 44–57.

Kemler, D. G. (1982) 'The ability for dimensional analysis in preschool and retarded children: evidence from comparison, conservation, and prediction tasks', *Journal of Experimental Child Psychology*, 34: 469–489.

Lave, J. (1988) *Cognition in Practice: Mind, Mathematics and Culture in Everyday Life*, Cambridge: Cambridge University Press.

Leavy, A. (2008) 'An examination of the role of statistical investigation in supporting the development of young children's statistical reasoning', in O. N. Saracho and B. Spodek (eds) *Contemporary Perspectives on Mathematics in Early Childhood Education*, Charlotte, NC: Information Age Publishing.

Le Corre, M. L. and Carey, S. (2007) 'Why the verbal counting principles are constructed out of representations of small sets of individuals: a reply to Gallistel', *Cognition*, 107: 650–662.

Le Corre, M. L., Van de Walle, G., Brannon, E. M. and Carey, S. (2006) 'Revisiting the competence/performance debate on the acquisition of counting principles', *Cognitive Psychology*, 52: 130–169.

Leder, G. (1992) 'Guest editorial: attitudes to mathematics', *Mathematics Education Research Journal*, 4(3): 1–7.

Lerman, S. (1996) 'Intersubjectivity in mathematics learning', *Journal for Research in Mathematics Education*, 27(2): 133–150.

Lesh, R., Post, T. and Behr, M. (1987) 'Representations and translations among representations in mathematics learning and problem solving', in C. Janvier (ed.) *Problems of Representation in the Teaching and Learning of Mathematics*, Hillsdale, NJ: Erlbaum, 33–40.

Lourenco, S. F and Huttenlocher, J. (2008) 'The representation of geometric cues in infancy', *Infancy*, 13(2): 103–127.

Lovell, K. (1971) *The Growth of Understanding in Mathematics: Kindergarten Through Grade Three*, New York: Holt, Rinehart & Winston.

McCrink, K. and Wynn, K. (2004) 'Large number addition and subtraction by 9-month-old infants', *Psychological Science*, 15(11): 776–781.

McCrink, K. and Wynn, K. (2009) 'Operational momentum in large-number addition', *Journal of Experimental Child Psychology*. Available online: doi:10.1016/j.jecp.2009.01.013 (accessed 5 September 2011).

MacDonald, A. (2010) 'Heavy thinking: young children's theorising about mass', *Australian Primary Mathematics Classroom*, 15(4): 4–8.

Markman, E. and Seibert, J. (1976) 'Classes and collections: internal organization and resulting holistic properties', *Cognitive Psychology*, 8: 561–577.

Mason, J. (1991) 'Questions about geometry', in D. Pimm and E. Love (eds) *Teaching and Learning School Mathematics*, London: Hodder & Stoughton.

Matthews, G. and Matthews, J. (1990) *Early Mathematical Experiences*, London: Longman.

May, P. (2011) *Child Development in Practice: Responsive Teaching and Learning from Birth to Five*, Abingdon: Routledge.

Meadows, S. (2006) *The Child as Thinker*, 2nd edn, Hove: Routledge.

Meints, K., Plunkett, K., Harris, P. L. and Dimmock, D. (2002) 'What is "on" and "under" for 15-, 18- and 24-month-olds? Typicality effects in early comprehension of spatial prepositions', *British Journal of Developmental Psychology*, 20:113–130.

Montague-Smith, A. (2002) *Mathematics in Nursery Education*, 2nd edn, London: David Fulton.

Moyles, J. (2005) *The Excellence of Play*, 2nd edn, Maidenhead: Open University Press.

Muldoon, K. P., Lewis, C. and Berridge, D. (2007) 'Predictors of early numeracy: is there a place for mistakes when learning about number?', *British Journal of Developmental Psychology*, 25: 543–558.

Munn, P. (1997) 'Children's beliefs about counting', in I. Thompson (ed.) *Teaching and Learning Early Number*, Buckingham: Open University Press.

Nunes, T. and Bryant, P. (1996) *Children Doing Mathematics*, Oxford: Blackwell.

Oates, J. (ed.) (1994) *The Foundations of Child Development*, Oxford: Blackwell.

Orton, A. (ed.) (2005) *Pattern in the Teaching and Learning of Mathematics*, London: Continuum.

Pepper, K. L. and Hunting, R. P. (1998) 'Preschoolers' counting and sharing', *Journal for Research in Mathematics Education*, 29(2): 164–183.

Piaget, J. (1952) *The Child's Conception of Number*, London: Routledge & Kegan Paul.

Piaget, J. (1953) 'How children develop mathematical concepts', *Scientific American*, 189(5): 74–79.

Piaget, J. (1966) *Biology and Knowledge*, Edinburgh: Edinburgh University Press.

Piaget, J. (1980) 'The psychogenesis of knowledge and its epistemological significance', in M. Piattelli-Palmarini (ed.) *Language and Learning*, Cambridge, MA: Harvard University Press.

Piaget, J. and Inhelder, B. (1967) *The Child's Conception of Space*, London: Routledge & Kegan Paul.

Piaget, J., Inhelder, B. and Szeminska, A. (1960) *The Child's Conception of Geometry*, London: Routledge & Kegan Paul.

Poirier, C., Lecuyer, R. and Cybula, C. (2000) 'Categorisation of geometric figures composed of three or four elements by 3-month-old infants', *Cahiers de Psychologie Cognitive*, 192: 221–244.

Potter, M. C. and Levy, E. I. (1968) 'Spatial enumeration without counting', *Child Development*, 39: 265–273.

Price, A. J. (1993) *Developing a Concept of Number at Key Stage One: Can the Principles of Developmental Writing Help?*, Open University: unpublished MA dissertation.

Price, A. J. (2000a) 'The role of real world scripts in the teaching and learning of addition', *Zentralblatt für Didaktik der Mathematik*, 2000/5. Available online: http://www.emis.de/journals/ZDM/zdm005a3.pdf (accessed 5 September 2011).

Price, A. J. (2000b) *Communication, Construction and Community: Learning Addition in Primary Classrooms*, unpublished doctoral thesis, Oxford University.

Price, A. J. (2001) 'Atomistic and holistic approaches to the early primary mathematics curriculum for addition', *Proceedings of the 24th International Conference for the Psychology of Mathematics Education*, Utrecht, Netherlands.

Price, A. J. (2003) 'Establishing a mathematical community of practice in the primary classroom', *Proceedings of the Third Conference of the European Society for Research in Mathematics Education*. Available online: http://www.dm.unipi.it/~didattica/CERME3/proceedings/Groups/TG8/TG8_Price_cerme3.pdf (accessed 5 September 2011).

Quinn, P. C., Slater, A. M., Brown, E. and Hayes, R. A. (2001) 'Developmental change in form categorisation in early infancy', *British Journal of Developmental Psychology*, 19: 207–218.

Ricciuti, H. N., Marney, T. and Ricciuti, A. E. (2006) 'Availability and spontaneous use of verbal labels in sorting categorization by 16–23-month-olds', *Early Childhood Research Quarterly*, 21(3): 360–373.

Rogers, K. (2006) *Illustrated Dictionary of Maths*, London: Usborne.

Ross, C. and Browne, N. (1993) *Girls as Constructors in the Early Years*, Stoke-on-Trent: Trentham Books.

Sarama, J. and Clements, D. H. (2009) *Early Childhood Mathematics Educational Research – Learning Trajectories for Young Children*, London: Routledge.

Schiff, W. (1983) 'Conservation of length redux: a perceptual linguistic phenomenon', *Child Development*, 54: 1497–1506.

Schubauer-Leoni, M. L. and Perret-Clermont, A.-N. (1997) 'Social interactions and mathematical learning', in T. Nunes and P. Bryant, *Learning and Teaching Mathematics*, Hove: Psychology Press.

Schwartz, B. N. (1978) *Psychology of Learning & Behaviour*, New York: Norton.

Secada, W., Fuson, K. and Hall, J. (1983) 'The transition from counting-all to counting-on', *Journal for Research in Mathematics Education*, 14: 47–57.

Sharp, C. (1998) *Age of Starting School and the Early Years Curriculum*, paper prepared for the NFER's Annual Conference, London, 6 October 1998. Available online: http://www.nfer.ac.uk/nfer/publications/44417/44417.pdf (accessed 17 September 2011).

Sheridan, M. D. (1977) *Spontaneous Play in Early Childhood*, Windsor: NFER-Nelson.

Siegler, R. S. (1987) 'The perils of averaging data over strategies: an example from children's addition', *Journal of Experimental Psychology*, 116(3): 250–264.

Siraj-Blatchford, I., Sylva, K., Muttock, S., Gilden, R. and Bell, D. (2002) *Researching Effective Pedagogy in the Early Years*, DfES: London.

Skemp, R. R. (1971) *The Psychology of Learning Mathematics*, London: Penguin.

Slaughter, V., Itakura, S., Kutsuki, A. and Siegal, M. (2011) 'Learning to count begins in infancy: evidence from 18 month olds' visual preferences', *Proc. R. Soc. B* doi: 10.1098/rspb.2010.2602. Available online: http://www.psy.uq.edu.au/research/ecdc/media/pub/2011-02-infant-counting.pdf (accessed 16 February 2011).

Sophian, C. (1987) 'Early developments in children's use of counting to solve quantitative problems', *Cognition and Instruction*, 4(2): 61–90.

Sophian, C. (1995) 'Representation and reasoning in early numerical development: counting, conservation and comparisons between sets', *Child Development*, 66: 559–577.

Sophian, C. (1996) *Children's Numbers*, Oxford: Westview.

Sophian, C. (1998) 'A developmental perspective on children's counting', in C. Donlan (ed.) *The Development of Mathematical Skills*, Hove: Psychology Press.

Stephen, C. and Wilkinson, J. E. (1999) 'Rhetoric and reality in developing language and mathematical skill: plans and playroom experiences', *Early Years*, 19(2): 62–72.

Strauss, M. and Curtis, L. (1984) 'Development of numerical concepts in infancy', in C. Sophian (ed.) *The Origins of Cognitive Skills*, Hillsdale, NJ: Erlbaum.

Sugarman, S. (1981) 'The cognitive basis of classification in very young children: an analysis of object-ordering trends', *Child Development*, 52: 1172–1178.

Suriyakham, L. W. (2007) 'Input effects on the development of the cardinality principle: does gesture count?', *Dissertation Abstracts International: Section B: The Sciences and Engineering*, 68(5-B): 3430.

Thatcher, D. (2001) 'Reading in the math class: selecting and using picture books for math investigations', *Young Children*, July: 20–27.

Thompson, I. (1997a) 'The early years number curriculum today', in I. Thompson (ed.) *Teaching and Learning Early Number*, Buckingham: Open University Press.

Thompson, I. (1997b) 'Developing young children's counting skills', in I. Thompson (ed.) *Teaching and Learning Early Number*, Buckingham: Open University Press.

Thompson, I. (1997c) 'The role of counting in derived fact strategies', in I. Thompson (ed.) *Teaching and Learning Early Number*, Buckingham: Open University Press.

Thorpe, P. (1995) 'Spatial concepts and young children', *International Journal of Early Years Education*, 3(2): 63–73.

Threlfall, J. (2005) 'Repeating patterns in the early primary years', in A. Orton (ed.) *Pattern in the Teaching and Learning of Mathematics*, London: Continuum.

Threlfall, J. and Bruce, B. (2005) 'Just counting: young children's oral counting and enumeration', *European Early Childhood Education Research Journal*, 13(2): 63–77.

Tsamir, P., Tirosh, D. and Levenson, E. (2008) 'Intuitive non-examples: the case of triangles', *Educational Studies in Mathematics*, B: 81–95.

Turati, C., Simion, F. and Zanoin, L. (2003) 'Newborns' perceptual categorization for closed and open geometric forms', *Infancy*, 4(3): 309–325.

Van den Heuvel-Panhuizen, M. and Van den Boogaard, S. (2008) 'Picture books as an impetus for kindergartner's mathematical thinking', *Mathematical Thinking and Learning*, 10(4): 341–373.

Vygotsky, L. S. (1978) *Mind In Society*, Cambridge, MA: MIT Press.

Vygotsky, L. S. (1986) *Thought and Language* (rev. edn, ed. A. Kozulin), Cambridge, MA: MIT Press.

Wagner, S. and Walters, J. (1982) 'A longitudinal analysis of early number concepts: from numbers to number', in G. Forman (ed.) *Action and Thought*, New York: Academic Press.

Walden, R. and Walkerdine, W. (1982) *Girls and Mathematics: The Early Years*, Bedford Way Papers 8. London: University of London Institute of Education.

Warren, E. and Miller, J. (2010) 'Exploring four year old Indigenous students' ability to pattern', *International Research in Early Childhood Education*, 1(2): 42–56.

Weiland, L. (2007) 'Experiences to help children learn to count on', *Teaching Children Mathematics*, 71(4): 188.

Williams, P. (2008) *Independent Review of Mathematics Teaching in Early Years Settings and Primary Schools*, London: DCSF.

Wood, D., Bruner, J. and Ross, G. (1976) 'The role of tutoring in problem solving', *Journal of Child Psychology and Psychiatry*, 17: 89–100.

Worthington, M. and Carruthers, E. (2006) *Children's Mathematics: Making Marks, Making Meaning*, 2nd edn, London: Paul Chapman.

Wynn, K. (1990) 'Children's understanding of counting', *Cognition*, 36: 155–193.

Wynn, K. (1992) 'Addition and subtraction by human infants', *Nature*, 358: 749–750.

Wynn, K. (1998) 'Numerical competence in infants', in C. Donlan (ed.) *The Development of Mathematical Skills*, Hove: Psychology Press.

Resources

Bee-Bot: Inclusive Technology Registered Office: Riverside Court, Huddersfield Road, Delph. Oldham. OL3 5FZ. Website: http://www.inclusive.co.uk/bee-bot-p2482.

Numicon: © Oxford University Press. Website: http://www.numicon.com.

Roamer: Valiant Technology, Myrtle House, 69 Salcott Road, London, SW11 6DQ. Tel: 020 7924 2366. Website: http://www.valiant-technology.com/us/pages/roamer_home.php.

Useful websites

Children's Mathematics Network: www.childrens-mathematics.net

A Maths Dictionary for Kids: www.amathsdictionaryforkids.com

Index

abacus 31, **38**; Slavonic abacus 31, **32**

accommodation 8

addition 15, 16, 53–6, 58–60, 61–2, 64–6, **69–71**, **72**, 73–4, 80, **81**, 82, 85, 160, **212–13**; aggregation 55, **223**; augmentation 55, **223**; counting all/ on 59–60, 62, 64–5, 66–7, **70**

adult focused activities 43–4, 73, 75, 98, 133, 164, 188, 198, 201, 203–6

adult initiated activities 15, 43, 47, 79–80, 109, 140, 169, 193, 198, 203, **204**, 207–8

adult intervention in children's play 42–3, 73–5, 98, 127, 133, 164, 206, 221

algebra 4, 5, 11, 83

angle 17, 117, 120, 146, 148–50, 152, 154, **170**, 172

anxiety and negative attitudes to mathematics 3, 4–6, 13, 42, 197, 221

apprenticeship (model of learning) 10–11, 157, 200

approximation 146, **161**, **216**

area 146, 147, 148, 149, 152, 154, 155, **156**, **169**, 171

array **85**, 223

assessment; assessing understanding of key concepts **39–40**, **69–71**, **99–100**, **134–6**, **161–3**, **186–7**, **221–8**; assessment criteria 210–11; observation 48, 80, 111, 140, 170–1, 193–4, 199, 202, 219; parental contributions to; records 220; record keeping 219–20; significant achievement 210–11, 218–19; using assessment criteria 211–18

assimilation 8

attributes 223; in handling data 176, 177, 179–82, **186**, **193**, 194, 217; in measure 152; in pattern 88, 90; in shape 117–18, 120–1, 147

babies 3, 7, **8**, 24, 25–6, 29, 58, 86, 91, 116, 119–20, 146, 149, 177, 185

balance scale (*or* beam balance) 146, 150, 153, 155, 157, **161**, **170**

bar chart **175**, 178–9, 183, 223

Beebot 125, 131, **134–6**, 142, 160, **170**, 172, 215

behaviourism 7

block graph 178, **179**, 183, 223

block play 13, **70**, 72, **81**, 88, 96, **110**, 120, 132–3, 138, **141**, **170**, **193**, 200

calculators 19, 72

calendars 19, **48**, 50, 151, 159, **162**, 169, 173

capacity 146, 147–50, 153–4, 155, 156, **157**, **162**, **170**, 171–3, 201, **216**

cardinal number 23, 24, 27, 30, 41, 48, 52–3, 65–7, 223

cardinal principle *see* principles of counting

characteristics *see* attributes

child initiated activities 47, 80, 109, 140, 169, 193, 197, 199, 207, 219

circle **18**, 116–17, 119–20, 125–7, 132, **135**, 143, 151

commutative 60, **223**

comparison 87, 112, 122, 176; in handling data 182, **183**; in measures 145–6, 149, 151, 153, 154–6, 171, 172; in number 29, 52, 61, **81**, **89**, 204

concept maps 39, 69, 99, 134, 161, 186, 203

connections 15, 23–4, 62

conservation; of measures 147–8, 150, 151, 223; of number 24–5, 223

constructivism 8–9, 10, 116

continuous, of measures 145

counter example **18**

counting; counting on/back 31, 40, **50**, *see also* addition and subtraction; counting out a given quantity 28, 31, 33; development 24, 26, 29–30; errors 49, 55; experience 28, 30–7; planning 38–42, **205**, 209; principles of counting 7, 26–9; reciting number names 7, 11, 26–7, 31, 49